Theories of Nationalism

Theories of Nationalism

A Critical Introduction

Umut Özkırımlı

Foreword by Fred Halliday

St. Martin's Press
New York

147991

THEORIES OF NATIONALISM

St. Martin's Press, Scholarly and Reference Division, 175 Fifth Avenue, New York, N.Y. 10010

First published in the United States of America in 2000

This book is printed on paper suitable for recycling and made from fully managed and sustained forest sources.

Printed in Hong Kong

ISBN 0–312–22941–0 clothbound
ISBN 0–312–22942–9 paperback

Library of Congress Cataloging-in-Publication Data
Özkırımlı, Umut.
Theories of nationalism : a critical introduction / Umut Özkırımlı
; foreword by Fred Halliday.
p.   cm.
Based on author's Ph.D. dissertation.
Includes bibliographical references and index.
ISBN 0–312–22941–0 (cloth). — ISBN 0–312–22942–9 (pbk.)
1. Nationalism.   I. Title.
JC311.O93   1999
320.54—dc21   99–42150
                                                          CIP

To my mother and father

Contents

Foreword

Anyone who sets out to provide a critical survey of theories of nationalism needs to be intrepid. The range of the material is immense, and rapidly developing. The various theories relate to a historical force that itself arouses great passion. At the same time theories of nationalism touch upon broader issues and trends in the social sciences – the sociology of knowledge, the impact of ideologies, the formation of communities and of movements, the role of the state, the very direction, or lack thereof, of modern history.

Umut Özkırımlı, a Turkish scholar, has succeeded in writing such a comparative and critical survey. His book provides a comprehensive, balanced and critical overview of current debates on nationalism: it represents a substantial resource for students and teachers of the subject, and for those who seek to relate debates on nationalism to other issues, analytic and normative, in contemporary intellectual life. In the course of such a survey, and not only in the final prospective chapters, Özkırımlı also suggests reflections on nationalism in general. This he does through the critique of other writings, and through the gentle but astute adjudication of contentious issues. This is at once an informed survey of a field of literature and, in its own right, an intervention in the subject.

The focus of this study is, quite properly, on the theories of nationalism that have emerged since the 1960s. Yet one may ask of theories of nationalism the question that those theories ask of nationalism itself – where they come from. Ernest Gellner asked of nations whether they have navels. Gellner's answer, a more relaxed and agnostic one than his association with a cogent modernism would suggest, is that some nations do have navels, some achieve them, and some have navels thrust upon them. Theories of nationalism clearly have navels. Primordialist theories have navels that relate them not so much to social theory as such, but to broader assumptions about the continuing existence of communities over centuries, something reflected in much history of nations, and in now fashionable writing in political theory on the prevalence of traditions, communities and civilizations. Liberal, Marxist, Durkheimian, and Weberian theories all derive their analytic strength, and their underlying sense of the direction of history, from broader, and anterior, social theories. The more recent trends to which Özkırımlı draws attention – feminism, social psychology and postmodernism – exemplify, once again, this derivation.

If it is one of the strengths of Özkırımlı's book that he allows these underlying assumptions of theory to be assessed, it is equally to be welcomed that, in his concluding chapter, he provides his own independent analysis of how the subject can move forward. Eschewing the aspiration to a general theory of nationalism, one that would encompass both ideology and movement, he focuses instead on what is general, a discourse of nationalism. At the same time, and drawing on the insights of gender and postmodernism, he stresses the lack of finality in nationalism: not only are there multiple definitions of nationalism available at any one time, but in response to social and political change, prevailing definitions of the nation change.

In stressing the constant redefinition of nationalist discourse, Özkırımlı also helps to set nationalism in proportion. He offers a way out of what may, in the eyes of nationalists and theorists of nationalism alike, appear to be an all-inclusive world, whereby all that is social and political in the contemporary world is encompassed by the nation, and the study of nationalism itself is divorced from other dimensions of analysis. Nationalism is one, but by no means the only one, of the forces that has shaped and continues to shape the modern world, and its development, like the theories that seek to explain it, has to be seen in this broader context.

It is one of the several contributions of this impressive book that it enables us, by comprehending the range of theories of nationalism, to see these debates in a wider, intellectual and historical context. We may recall Schiller's injunction in *On the Aesthetic Education of Man*: 'One is just as much a citizen of one's age as a citizen of one's state.' In writing this book and in assessing the different theories under review, Umut Özkırımlı has followed that injunction.

London School of Economics   FRED HALLIDAY

Acknowledgements

This book could not have been written without the help and advice of many people. First, I would like to thank Toktamış Ateş who supervised the PhD dissertation on which this book is based. His constant support has always been a source of great inspiration for me.

I owe special thanks to Fred Halliday for kindly accepting my invitation to write the Foreword and for generously sharing his knowledge and ideas with me. His comments and criticisms were extremely helpful in improving the book. Here, I would also like to add that I have benefited greatly from being his student. I am grateful to Gareth Winrow and Jeff Bowen for polishing up my English and for their helpful comments on various drafts of the manuscript. I would also like to express my warm thanks to my publisher Steven Kennedy and his anonymous reviewer for their perceptive criticisms. The book owes a great deal to them. As always, however, the responsibility for the views expressed herein is all mine.

Many thanks are due to Gülberk for her unrelenting love and support. And last but not least, I want to thank my mother and father who taught me, all throughout the years, the meaning of the word 'sacrifice'. It is to them that this book is dedicated.

İstanbul Bilyi University   UMUT ÖZKIRIMLI

1

Introduction

> Thou knowest not how sweet is the *amor patriae*: if such would
> be expedient for the fatherland's protection or enlargement, it would
> seem neither burdensome and difficult nor a crime to thrust the axe
> into one's father's head, to crush one's brothers, to deliver from the
> womb of one's wife the premature child with the sword.
>
> Coluccio Salutati (quoted in James 1996: 30)

No single political doctrine has played a more prominent role in
shaping the face of the modern world than nationalism. Millions
of people around the world have willingly laid down their lives for
their 'fatherlands' and this almost ritualistic mass self-sacrifice continues unabated. Obviously, not everybody displays extremism on
the level of Salutati. But as Elshtain remarks, that sort of extremism has been 'the norm in many of the great and horrible events
of our century' (1991: 400).

Despite this pervasive influence, however, nationalism was not
taken seriously by the social scientists until relatively recently. For
much of the nineteenth and early twentieth century, it was seen as
a passing phase, by liberals and Marxists alike, hence as 'intellec-
tually unproblematic' (Halliday 1997a: 12). It was only in the 1920s
and 1930s, with the pioneering works of historians like Carleton
Hayes, Hans Kohn, Louis Snyder and E. H. Carr, that nationalism
became a subject of sustained academic inquiry. Unlike their predecessors who were mainly interested in ethical issues, these historians took nationalism as a 'discrete subject of investigation'
and made use of sociological factors in their accounts (Smith 1998:
17; Snyder 1997). The number and diversity of the studies of

nationalism increased in the following decades under the impact of the experience of decolonization and the 'proliferation' of new states in Asia and Africa. Subscribing to some version of the then ascendant 'nation-building' model, most of these studies saw nationalism as a concomitant of the modernization processes. The 1980s, on the other hand, mark a turning point in many respects. With the publication of John Armstrong's *Nations Before Nationalism* (1982), Benedict Anderson's *Imagined Communities* (1983), Ernest Gellner's *Nations and Nationalism* (1983), Eric Hobsbawm and Terence Ranger's *The Invention of Tradition* (1983) and Anthony D. Smith's *The Ethnic Origins of Nations* (1986), among others, the debate on nationalism completed its 'adolescence'. In this period, the theories grew more sophisticated and the 'lines of battle' became clearer. Nationalism, which had to wait until 1974 to have its first academic journal, finally had a stimulating, even polemical, literature.

There are, I think, two reasons for the belated development of a fully-fledged literature on nationalism. The first is the general indifference of social scientists to nationalism as a subject of investigation: nationalism was belittled by mainstream academic thinking until quite recently, and its full potential was not properly understood. Interestingly enough, this condescending attitude still prevails to a certain extent. One can observe its reflections in the studies of nationalism which take great pains to justify their 'right to exist': if we take a quick look at the articles and books written in the last few years, we can see that most of them begin by mentioning how important nationalism has become 'recently', that is after the collapse of communism, and by enumerating cases of ethnic conflict from this or that region of the world to support this argument. Even the examples cited are similar: Rwanda, Bosnia, Somalia, Eritrea and so on. This attitude is partly conditioned by the rigidity and conservatism of the established disciplines. A rigid conception of social science rules that political science should study the state or, say, democracy, party systems, equality, justice and power. International Relations should focus on the relations between states and analyse war or peace. Sociology should examine the society, for example the relations between individuals and various collectivities. According to orthodox conceptions which have dominated the established disciplines for many decades, nations and nationalism do not constitute a problem to be investigated: their existence is taken for granted.

This picture, however, is not an accurate representation of reality. Nationalism plays an important role in the creation of many states. In other cases, states have embraced nationalism later, to justify their right to exist in a world of nation-states. If democracy means 'rule by the people', then the people are almost always conceived as a nation. Equality or justice is usually required for the members of the nation, and elites compete for power in order to rule the 'nation'. On the other hand, both war and peace take place among 'nations', or more properly for the 'nations'. Finally, the society of the sociologist is more often than not a 'nation' whose members share a particular culture and live within definite borders. The culture that s/he explores is a 'national' or ethnic culture. In short, there is no area in the social sciences which has not felt, directly or indirectly, the spell of nationalism. Under these circumstances, it is quite surprising to encounter such indifference *vis-à-vis* nationalism. To understand this, we should consider the second reason.

The second reason that deferred scholarly intrusions into national phenomena was the tendency to equate nationalism with its extreme manifestations, that is with separatist movements that threatened the stability of existing states or with aggressive right-wing politics. Such a view confines nationalism to the periphery, treating it as the property of others, not of 'us' (Billig 1995: 5; Calhoun 1997). As Billig contends, ' "our" nationalism is not presented as nationalism, which is dangerously irrational, surplus and alien'; it is presented as 'patriotism', which is good and beneficial (1995: 55). In fact, this view is accepted consciously or unconsciously by all sides, namely by both those who do not take nationalism seriously as a subject of academic inquiry, and those who study it. Nothing illustrates this better than the 'standard introductions' I have alluded to earlier, which mention only protracted ethnic conflicts or wars as examples of nationalism. The same conviction lies behind the depictions of nationalism as a 'tide-like' phenomenon, that is emerging under crisis situations, then suddenly disappearing once normal conditions are restored. One particular manifestation of this is the 'return of the repressed' perspective which impels many commentators to suggest that we are faced with a new wave of nationalism after the collapse of Soviet type communism in 1989 (for example Ignatieff 1993: 2). Brubaker notes that there is a 'quasi-Freudian' flavour in these depictions:

> Lacking the rationally regulative ego of self-regulating civil society, the communist regimes repressed the primordial national id through a harshly punitive communist superego. With the collapse of the communist superego, the repressed eth-nonational id returns in full force, wreaking vengeance, uncontrolled by the regulative ego. (1998: 285–6)

Brubaker argues convincingly that the policies pursued by communist regimes were anything but 'anti-national': 'The regime repressed *nationalism*, of course; but at the same time, it went further than any other state before or since in institutionalising territorial *nationhood* and ethnic *nationality* as fundamental social categories' (*ibid.*: 286). More generally, 'the claim that nationalism is returning implies that it has been away' (Billig 1995: 47). As Billig observes, the wars waged by democratic states are not labelled nationalist by those who subscribe to this view. Ignatieff, for instance, 'hardly mentions the Vietnam or Falklands Wars, let alone the various US sorties into Korea, Panama or Grenada', all of which occur 'during nationalism's so-called quiescent period' (*ibid.*).

This book will diverge from these more conventional accounts which take 'our' nationalism for granted, and will instead endorse an analytical framework developed by a number of scholars in recent years (Balibar 1990; Billig 1995; Brubaker 1996, 1998; Calhoun 1993, 1995, 1997). At the heart of this approach lies the belief that nationalism is not a latent force that manifests itself only under extraordinary conditions, a kind of natural disaster which strikes spontaneously and unpredictably. Nationalism is a discourse that constantly shapes our consciousness and the way we constitute the meaning of the world. It determines our collective identity by producing and reproducing us as 'nationals' (Billig 1995: 6). It is a form of seeing and interpreting that conditions our daily speech, behaviours and attitudes.

Obviously, this is a very general definition, one that might be criticized on the grounds that it does not explain too much or that it overlooks the differences between various types of nationalism. However, I will argue that this 'umbrella definition' is more useful than depictions based on a distinction between 'good' and 'bad' nationalisms or nationalism and patriotism. These definitions not only cause a 'terminological chaos' (Connor 1994: chapter 4), but also present us with the different versions of the same phenomenon as if they are separate phenomena – holding, for instance, that 'patriotism and nationalism represent two very different states of mind' (Billig 1995: 55). It is true that the Serbian militia in Kosovo or the ETA militants have different motives than ordinary French or American citizens, yet all these motives, despite their varying forms and intensity, belong to the same family. What unites them is the nationalist discourse: both the ETA militants who commit acts of terrorism and the French citizens who sing *La Marseillese* in football stadiums use the nationalist discourse to explain, justify, and hence legitimize their actions. The motives and the actions might take different forms, but they are all of the same kind. The definition I have offered above spots this commonality and shows that seemingly disparate emotions, beliefs and actions are all manifestations of the same phenomenon. The problem of overgeneralization, on the other hand, might be resolved by using additional sub-definitions or typologies.

To recapitulate, then, the tendency to equate nationalism with its extreme manifestations was the second reason that delayed the development of a diversified literature, because nationalism was the problem of those in the periphery, not 'ours': when they settled their territorial disputes and completed their nation-building processes, they would likewise reach the stage of 'good', harmless nationalism. This detached stance was accompanied by a certain dose of Eurocentrism. In the words of Löfgren:

> The old nations have images of operetta states and banana republics, and in these caricatures we see clearly the institutionalized patterns for what a proper nation is supposed to look like. Successfully accomplished national projects, such as that of the Swedish or the French, are quickly taken for granted. Unsuccessful examples, on the other hand, serve as examples of unrealistic ambitions or airy-fairy dreams, or merely comic attempts to imitate the old national giants. (1993: 166)

Needless to say, history did not unfold as expected by 'evolutionary determinists' who saw 'the rise of nations as part of the "movement of history", and a stage that was necessary . . . in the development of human history' (Smith 1991b: 353). Not only did the existing problems remain unresolved, but new ones cropped up incessantly. Moreover, the 'good', 'democratic' nationalisms of the developed countries could not thwart the emergence of ethnic discontent or separatist movements within their borders, as was the case in Québec, Northern Ireland or the Basque country.

Today, we witness that both reasons that delayed the development of a fully-fledged literature on nationalism are gradually disappearing. Despite the continuing intransigence of established disciplines who insist in seeing nationalism as an 'academic vogue' like postmodernism, destined to pass away as soon as another 'pastime' is found, nationalism is now one of the most explored subjects in social sciences. Almost every week, new books join the library shelves allotted to the burgeoning literature on nationalism. As Smith rightly observes, 'it has indeed become quite impossible to keep abreast of the tide of publications in the field' (1998: xi). *Canadian Review of Studies in Nationalism* is no longer the only academic journal in the field, and is accompanied by such journals as *Ethnic and Racial Studies, Nationalism and Ethnic Politics* and *Nations and Nationalism.*

As a result of these developments, specialization in the field has increased; new topics like identity, migration, diasporas, multiculturalism and genocide have been discovered; and nationalism has entered the curricula of many universities. A parallel interest can be observed in the media. Newspapers and television news are replete with the details of ethnic conflicts from various regions. Moreover, since the media plays an important role in shaping public opinion, people are on the whole more aware of the conflicts that involve their own countries.

On the other hand, it can also be asserted that the debate on nationalism has reached a more mature stage in recent years. Today, the questions and problems that bedevil the study of nationalism are well-known. The answers provided to these questions or the solution proposals are no longer uniform. In sum, we are faced with a much more diversified literature than 20 years ago: time, now, is ripe for a critical review of the theoretical debate on nationalism and for an assessment of the recent developments in the field.

Objectives

This book has three main objectives: first, to provide a systematic overview of some of the key theories of nationalism and to consider the main criticisms raised against them in a comparative perspective; secondly, to diagnose the deficiencies of the classical debate and to specify the theoretical problems we are still facing; and finally, to propose, in the light of these considerations and criticisms, an analytical framework that can be used in the study of nationalism. Before proceeding, however, certain points relating to the scope of the study should be clarified.

The first of these concerns my choice of period. Most of the theories/approaches reviewed in this study are formulated in the second half of the twentieth century, more specifically since the 1960s. In a way, this was inevitable: it is only in the last three or four decades that a fully-developed 'theoretical' debate on nationalism has emerged. Historians began to write the histories of particular nations or comparative studies of nationalism relatively early, but sociologists and political scientists remained silent on the subject until quite recently (Halliday 1997a, 1997b; Smith 1983). Ironically, however, there are not many studies reviewing the theories and approaches of this period in a systematic way – a notable exception being Smith's recent book *Nationalism and Modernism* (1998). My decision to write this book is also motivated by this astonishing lacuna.

The second point that needs to be clarified relates to my focus on a particular literature, namely the Anglo-Saxon literature. The reason for this is quite simple: most of the studies on nationalism are produced in the Anglo-Saxon world. Books and articles written elsewhere are translated into English, usually, though not always, in a short period of time. Under these circumstances, it is very difficult to talk about a 'meaningful' choice. A student of nationalism who wants to study the theories of nationalism has no alternative but to focus almost exclusively on the Western, particularly the Anglo-Saxon, literature. This is even valid in the case of the studies which criticize the Eurocentric nature of the mainstream literature on nationalism. The works of the Subaltern Studies Group are a good case in point. Scholars like Partha Chatterjee and Ranajit Guha attempted to reinterpret the history of South Asia from the vantage point of the subordinated (Eley and Suny 1996a), but, ironically enough, they have done this in the language of the colonizer, namely English. In short, whether we like it or not, and whether we call it 'cultural imperialism' or 'globalization', English has become a kind of *lingua franca* in most areas of social sciences.

One last point that needs clarification concerns the choice of theories and writers to be included in the study. The first thing to be said is that such a choice cannot be totally objective. Hence, even though I took great pains to include all major theories and approaches, I cannot assert that my selection is perfect or impartial. Many scholars who have made important contributions to our understanding of nationalism are left out because of time and space limitations. Among these, Anthony Giddens (1985), Michael Mann (1995, 1996), Charles Tilly (1975, 1990), Partha Chatterjee (1986, 1990), Liah Greenfeld (1992) are the first that come to mind. The works of some of these scholars will be discussed briefly in Chapter 2 where I will provide an historical overview of the debate and Chapter 6 where I will focus on recent approaches. Suffice it to say at this point that all key sides of the theoretical debate on nationalism will be represented in this book with usually more than one theorist.

Structure of the Book

As I stated earlier, one of the objectives of this book is to offer a critical and comparative review of the main theories of nationalism, focusing mostly on the post-1960s literature. This does not mean, however, that the debates of earlier periods are irrelevant. Contemporary theorists of nationalism are heavily influenced by the assumptions and convictions of their predecessors. With this in mind, I will begin my survey by situating the contemporary debate historically and theoretically. I will identify four stages in the study of nationalism:

• The eighteenth and nineteenth centuries, when the idea of nationalism was born. Here, the contributions of thinkers like Kant, Herder, Fichte, Rousseau, Mill, Marx, Engels, Bauer and Renner, and historians like Michelet, Renan, von Treitschke and Lord Acton will be briefly discussed.

- 1918–45, when nationalism became a subject of academic inquiry. The works of Carleton Hayes, Hans Kohn and Louis Snyder will be considered in this context.
- 1945 to the late 1980s, when the sociologists and political scientists joined the debate and when, partly as a result of this, the debate became much more diversified. Here, the contributions of modernization theorists, for example Daniel Lerner, Karl W. Deutsch and early modernists will be discussed.
- From the late 1980s to the present, when attempts to transcend the classical debate (characteristic of the third stage) have been made.

In Chapter 2, I will also try to locate the main questions around which the debate on nationalism revolves.

The following four chapters will be devoted to the discussion of the main theoretical positions with regard to nationalism. In accordance with the chronological order and the general tendency in the field, I will start my discussion with the primordialist approach. After describing the different versions of primordialism, namely the 'naturalist', 'sociobiological' and 'culturalist' explanations, I will consider the main criticisms levelled against scholars who have subscribed to primordialism. This scheme of presentation will be largely preserved in the subsequent chapters.

Chapter 4 will be reserved for the modernists. In contrast to conventional accounts which treat the modernists as a unitary category, I will divide them into three groups in terms of the key factors they have identified in their accounts of nationalism. Hence, neo-Marxists like Tom Nairn and Michael Hechter who have stressed the importance of economic factors will be discussed under the heading 'economic transformation'; scholars like John Breuilly, Paul Brass and Eric Hobsbawm who have emphasized the role of politics and power struggles between contending elites will be considered under the heading 'political transformation'; finally, scholars like Ernest Gellner, Benedict Anderson and Miroslav Hroch who have given priority to cultural factors will be reviewed under the heading 'cultural transformation'. Needless to say, these are not mutually exclusive categories. As Breuilly has said, 'classifications are simply sets of interrelated definitions. Empirically, they are not right or wrong; rather they are either helpful or unhelpful' (1993a: 9). I will argue that the classification I am introducing here to present the modernist explanations is helpful, at least more helpful than accounts that treat the modernists as a monolithic category.

Chapter 5 will explore the ethno-symbolist position. I will first present the arguments of the two leading figures of this approach, John Armstrong and Anthony D. Smith, then consider the major criticisms raised against ethno-symbolist explanations.

Chapter 6 will be devoted to recent approaches. In this chapter, I will first try to substantiate the claim that we have entered a new stage in the debate on nationalism since the end of the 1980s. Briefly, I will argue that the Eurocentric, gender-blind character of the 'classical' debate on nationalism has been transcended by studies which have drawn our attention to such issues as the differential participation of women in nationalist projects, the daily reproduction of nationhood, the experience of nationalism in postcolonial societies, the specific contributions of the people on the national margins, that is the 'hybrids', to the construction of national identities and the like. Then I will discuss in some detail two well-received analyses of this type, namely Michael Billig's analysis of the daily reproduction of nationhood and Nira Yuval-Davis' study of the gendered dimension of nationalist projects.

In Chapter 7, I will first embark on a critical evaluation of the main theoretical positions. Then, in the light of these considerations, I will propose an analytical framework that might be used in the study of nationalism. This framework, based on a synthesis of ideas put forward by various scholars, will consist of five simple propositions:

Proposition 1.   There can be no 'general' theory of nationalism.
Proposition 2.   There is no 'one' nationalism; not only are there different types of nationalism, but different members of the national or ethnic collectivities promote different constructions of nationhood.
Proposition 3.   The common denominator of all these different movements, ideas, policies and projects is the nationalist discourse. In other words, what unites different nationalisms is the discourse and rhetoric of nationhood.
Proposition 4.   The nationalist discourse can only be effective if it is reproduced on a daily basis.

Proposition 5. Any study of national identity should acknowledge differences of ethnicity, gender, sexuality, class or place in the life-cycle that affect the construction and reconstruction of individual identities.

Further Reading

Despite the renewal of interest in the study of nations and nationalism, there have been very few attempts to provide a theoretical survey of the field. Two important exceptions are Smith (1983) [1971] and (1998). Smith's earlier book is the standard work of reference for the theories of the 1950s and 1960s, especially the model of 'nation-building'. His recent *Nationalism and Modernism*, on the other hand, constitutes a sequel to his first book and focuses on the theories and approaches of the last three decades. Though they do not provide a systematic overview of explanatory accounts of nationalism, the general studies by Calhoun (1997) and McCrone (1998) are very useful as guides in the field since they address many of the issues and debates around the subject.

The last ten years have also witnessed an outpouring of readers which contain articles or extracts from key texts on nationalism. Among these, the following are particularly helpful: Hutchinson and Smith (1994), Dahbour and Ishay (1995), Balakrishnan (1996b), Eley and Suny (1996b) and Woolf (1996).

Apart from these, the reader should also consult *The ASEN Bulletin*, issued by the Association of Ethnicity and Nationalism (based at the London School of Economics) for current publications.

2

Discourses and Debates on Nationalism

All fixed, fast-frozen relations, with their train of ancient and venerable prejudices and opinions, are swept away, all new ones become antiquated before they can ossify. All that is solid melts into air, all that is holy is profaned, and man is at last compelled to face with sober senses, his real conditions of life, and his relations with his kind . . .

Karl Marx–Friedrich Engels, *The Communist Manifesto*

Historical Overview

Nationalism, as an ideology and a social movement, has been very much in evidence since the end of the eighteenth century. In fact, it would not be an exaggeration to say that 'the history of Europe from 1789 to 1945 is synonymous with the history of the growth and development of modern nations' (Baycroft 1998: 3). Yet, as I stated in the introduction, nationalism did not become a subject of academic investigation until well into the first half of the twentieth century. Up to the First World War, interest in nationalism was largely ethical and philosophical. The scholars of this period, predominantly historians and social philosophers, were more concerned with 'the merits and defects' of the doctrine than with the origins and spread of national phenomena (Smith 1983: 257). The nation-state was treated as an alternative to the 'idiocy of rural life and precapitalist parochialism', hence as a progressive stage in the historical evolution of human societies (MacLaughlin 1987: 1). The corollary of this evolutionist view, shared by both the liberals

12

and the Marxists, was that nationalism would gradually wither away with the establishment of a peaceful international order (Halliday 1997d). In this context, the existence of nations was taken for granted. The social and political realities of the period did not leave room for alternative viewpoints: nationalism was the compelling norm and no one could remain indifferent to its emotional appeal. Not surprisingly, then, the scholars of this period were mostly guided by political concerns. In these early commentaries, Smith notes, there was 'no attempt to fashion a general theory applicable to all cases, or to resolve the antinomies of each issue in a coherent and systematic manner' (1998: 10).

This explains why the early works of Carleton Hayes and Hans Kohn are generally regarded as a turning point in the study of nationalism. Hayes and Kohn, 'the twin founding fathers' of the academic scholarship on nationalism in the words of Kemiläinen (1964), never questioned the fundamental assumptions of their predecessors. Yet, their analyses bequeathed important theoretical insights to succeeding generations. The next stage of the study of nationalism, which can be broadly dated from the end of the Second World War, was heavily influenced by the process of decolonization and the establishment of new states in the Third World (Snyder 1997: 233). From the 1960s onwards, the debate was no longer confined to historians. With the participation of sociologists and political scientists, the theoretical literature on nationalism became much more diversified. The debate shows no signs of abating to this day.

In the light of these considerations, a historical overview of the period after the First World War might seem more relevant for the purposes of this book. However, we need a wider historical perspective to make sense of the contemporary theoretical debate. There are mainly two reasons for this. First, despite its belated recognition as an object of study, nationalism as a political doctrine or ideology, that is 'a set of political principles that movements and individuals espouse', has a longer past (Halliday 1997d: 361; cf. Halliday 1997b). It is possible to trace the origins of the idea of nationalism back to German Romantics (eighteenth century), or even to the Enlightenment. Some scholars have indeed explained nationalism primarily as a political doctrine emanating from the musings of dislocated German intellectuals (most notably Kedourie 1994). Others, in a Durkheimian vein, have tended to see nationalism as a modern and secular surrogate for religion, emerging mostly in the painful period of transition to modernity (Smith 1998: Chapter 5). To make sense of these approaches, we need to explore the evolution of the idea of nationalism.

Secondly, and perhaps more importantly, starting the overview from the 1960s would obscure the degree to which contemporary theories are influenced by earlier reflection on nationalism. As I have stated earlier, the post-1960 debates were not born in a vacuum, and in that sense they have to be understood within the framework of the debates and discourses that preceded them, or as Anderson would probably say, out of which – as well as against which – they came into being (1991: 12). Examples that spring to mind include the influence of Gramsci on Tom Nairn, of Lenin on Michael Hechter, of Durkheim on Ernest Gellner and of Weber on Anthony D. Smith – among others. These examples clearly reveal that we need a broader historical perspective if we are to assess the current debates properly.

Taking these points into consideration, I will begin my overview with a discussion of the eighteenth and nineteenth centuries, when the doctrine of nationalism was first framed. My selection of thinkers and scholars will be necessarily incomplete since it is very difficult to determine exactly who – or in that respect which ideas – contributed to the genesis of the nationalist doctrine. This can also explain why scholars who explore the origins of the idea of nationalism highlight different thinkers in their accounts. In what follows, I will try to consider those thinkers whose role in the formation of the idea of nationalism is commonly acknowledged – by most, if not all, scholars. Needless to say, this does not mean that these are the only thinkers who have contributed to the idea of nationalism.

The study of nationalism is generally divided into three stages: before the First World War, 1918–45, and 1945 to the present (Snyder 1997: 231). In what follows I will largely conform to this classification, but with a minor qualification: I will argue that the period after 1945 should not be treated as a single stage. What lies behind this argument is the belief that some of the studies produced in the last decade signal a new stage in the study of nationalism, as they question – and refute – the fundamental premises upon which the 'classical' debate is based. Taking these attempts into account, I will treat the last decade as a separate stage in my historical overview. Obviously, it can be argued that it is too early to speak of a new stage or that most of these analyses are in fact partial and fragmentary (for such an argument see Smith 1998: 219). Against this view, I will stress the importance of these approaches and contend that the issues to which they draw our attention will gradually assert themselves within the academic community. The decision of *Nations and Nationalism*, one of the leading academic journals in the field, to publish a special issue on 'gender and nation' is a clear illustration of this trend.

I will thus identify four stages in the study – although the term 'study' may not be appropriate for the period before 1918 – of nationalism:

- The eighteenth and nineteenth centuries when the idea of nationalism was born;
- 1918–45 when nationalism became a subject of academic inquiry;
- 1945 to the late 1980s when the debate became more diversified with the participation of sociologists and political scientists;
- From the late 1980s to the present when attempts to transcend the 'classical' debate were made.

The Eighteenth and Nineteenth Centuries

The question of whether nationalism had its own 'grand thinkers' has always been a source of great controversy. Gellner's answer to this question is quite clear: 'these thinkers did not really make much difference. If one of them had fallen, others would have stepped into his place. No one was indispensable'. He concludes: 'we shall not learn too much about nationalism from the study of its own prophets' since they all suffered from a pervasive false consciousness (1983: 124–5). In a similar vein, Anderson argues that 'unlike most other isms, nationalism has never produced its own grand thinkers: no Hobbeses, Tocquevilles, Marxes or Webers' (1991: 5). Others, notably O'Leary, disagree with this view: 'It is strange not to classify Weber as a nationalist grand thinker, stranger still that Rousseau, Burke, John Stuart Mill and Friedrich

List are not seen as nationalist grand thinkers . . .' (1998: 87; *cf.* Minogue 1996). This discussion clearly shows that the problem lies in determining who can be considered as a 'nationalist thinker', and not in deciding whether those thinkers who have contributed to the nationalist doctrine are 'grand'.

Whatever the answer given to this question, the origins of the nationalist doctrine are generally traced back to German Romantic thought. But the thinkers of the period were heavily influenced by the ideas of their predecessors. Among these, the ideas of Immanuel Kant, considered by many as the epitome of cosmopolitan thought, were the most important. In fact, according to Kedourie, who explains nationalism in terms of a revolution in European philosophy, it all started with Kant (1994: chapter 2).

Immanuel Kant (1724–1804) was not of course a nationalist. Moreover, he cannot be held responsible for the ways in which his ideas were used. But the political consequences of the ethical and epistemological dualism he developed were far-reaching (Smith 1983: 31–2). At the heart of this dualism lies a separation between the external, that is phenomenal, world and man's inner world. According to Kant, the source of knowledge was the phenomenal world: our knowledge was based on sensations emanating from things-in-themselves. But the phenomenal world was a world of 'inexplicable contingencies' and 'iron necessities', and if our morality were also derived from this kind of knowledge 'then we could never be free but always the slave either of contingency or of blind personal laws' (Kedourie 1994: 14). Morality, then, had to be separated from knowledge, hence the phenomenal world: instead, it should be 'the outcome of obedience to a universal law which is to be found within ourselves'.

Kant held that man could only be free when he obeys the laws of morality which he finds within himself, and not in the external world. This was, according to Kedourie, a revolutionary definition of freedom. Kant equated virtue with free will. On the other hand, neither freedom nor virtue depended on God's commands. Hence the new formula: 'the good will, which is the free will, is also the autonomous will' (Kedourie 1994: 16). This was revolutionary because the formula made the individual the centre and the sovereign of the universe: self-determination was now the supreme good. Smith concludes that this makes republicanism the sole possible form of government, 'for only in a republic can the laws express the autonomous will of the citizens' (1983: 32).

Kant's new formula was not immune from philosophical difficulties. It was Kant's disciple Johann Gottlieb Fichte (1762–1814) who first attempted to solve the problems raised by his doctrine. As opposed to Kant who maintained that the external world is beyond our sensations and that things-in-themselves exist prior to – and independent of – the perceiving self, Fichte held that they are both the product of a universal consciousness and an Ego which embraces everything within itself. Such a theory eliminated Kant's 'inexplicable contingencies' or 'iron necessities' and made the external world – and hence knowledge which emanated from it – comprehensible. According to this view, the world is a coherent whole since it is a manifestation of the Ego (Smith 1983: 32): 'A world takes on reality and coherence because it is the product of a single consciousness, and its parts can exist at all and share in reality only by taking their place within this world' (Kedourie 1994: 29). This view was particularly relevant to politics because it implied that the whole is prior to, and more important than, all its parts: 'knowledge of the parts is illusory; no parts can be known by themselves, since they cannot exist on their own, outside a coherent and ordered whole' (*ibid.*). This was the origin of the famous – infamous? – 'organic theory of the state'. Kedourie sums this up succinctly:

> individuals, as such, are phantoms; they gain reality in so far as they have a place in a whole. Consequently, the freedom of the individual, which is his self-realization, lies in identifying himself with the whole . . . Complete freedom means total absorption in the whole . . . From this metaphysics the post-Kantians deduced a theory of the state . . . The state therefore is not a collection of individuals who have come together in order to protect their own particular interests; the state is higher than the individual and comes before him. It is only when he and the state are one that the individual realizes his freedom. (*Ibid.*: 30)

Another contribution to the doctrine of nationalism comes from 'historicism'. A brief review of the German thinker Johann Gottfried Herder (1744–1803) can help us understand the main arguments of this school of thought (Breuilly 1993a: 56–64). Herder's point of departure is quite simple: only language makes man human. The concept of 'pre-linguistic' man is meaningless for Herder since man is defined by his language capacity. Moreover, 'language can only be learnt in a community. It is synonymous with thought'. And 'every language is different from every other'. The implications of these views are not hard to guess: if language is thought and if it can only be learnt in a community, 'it follows that each community has its own mode of thought' (*ibid.*: 57). In fact, if each language is a different way of expressing universal values, then it is also the manifestation of unique values and ideas. Obviously, the same logic applies to customs, traditions, ceremonies and the like each of which can be considered as another sort of language. 'Community', then, is the sum total of these modes of expression. However, it is more than the mere collection of all these parts but has a unity of its own. Here, once again we encounter the 'organicist' thought. In order to understand a society, it is necessary to learn all the ways of the society in question. Understanding a society is like learning a language. According to the historicist, history is the major form such understanding took: it is the only way of apprehending the spirit of a community (*ibid.*).

In extolling the diversity of cultures, Herder's aim was to oppose the universalism of the Enlightenment. But according to Barnard, 'he had no wish to sacrifice diversity even if this meant a certain degree of tension or conflict, or some disorder and inefficiency, in the conduct of public affairs' (1983: 246). The political order he envisaged was inspired by the example of ancient Hebrews who were conscious of themselves as 'one people' despite their institutional and tribal fragmentation. In such a 'quasi-pluralist' order, individuals would be free to pursue their diverse interests and form a variety of autonomous institutions to serve these interests (*ibid.*: 246–7).

Historicist arguments were carried to the political arena with the help of other ideas. Breuilly contends that the most important of these is the idea of 'authenticity' (1993a: 59). What lies behind this idea is the need to determine what is 'natural' in a particular community and, by implication, what is 'unnatural'. Drawing on this idea, Herder objects to the conquest of one society by another, which he sees as a 'wild mixing together of different human species and nations under one spectre' (cited in Breuilly 1993a: 59). For him, societies are created by nature and nothing is more 'unnatural' than the disruption of the development of a particular society. Fichte joins Herder in the quest for authenticity, arguing that language mirrors the national soul, 'and to purge the language of alien impurities was to defend the national soul against subversion by foreign values'. He also applies these views to a concrete example and argues for the need to protect the German language from the impact of Latin, which he sees as a 'dead language'. As Breuilly notes, these views were taken up by the racist currents of the nineteenth century and linked to 'human nature' (*ibid.*: 60).

The political implications of all these ideas are not hard to guess: national communities are unique, *sui generis* formations. They might have forgotten their true natures or entered a period of recess, but this does not mean that they will not recover and reclaim their true, that is 'authentic', selves. The members of national collectivities should be able to determine their own future – self-determination is the supreme political good – and each nation, which is more than the sum total of all citizens, should establish its own state: 'the fatal equation of language, state and nation, which is the cornerstone of the German version of nationalism' was thus formulated (Smith 1983: 33).

Herder and Fichte were not the only representatives of German Romantic thought. The Lutheran theologian Friedrich Schleiermacher (1768–1834) who developed Kant's doctrines, his friend Friedrich Schlegel (1772–1829), Fichte's disciple F. W. Schelling (1775–1854), the publicist Adam Müller (1779–1805), the dramatist Friedrich Schiller (1759–1805), the publicist Ernst Moritz Arndt (1769–1860) and nationalist agitator Friedrich Jahn (1778–1852) were other important figures of this school of thought (for details see Kedourie 1994; Kohn 1950). However, the contributions of these thinkers are not generally considered to be as important as those of Herder and Fichte.

On the other hand, other ideas have also contributed to the formation of the nationalist doctrine. Chief among these was the principle of self-determination, that is 'the idea that a group of people have a certain set of shared interests and should be allowed to express their wishes on how these interests should best be promoted' (Halliday 1997d: 362), mostly associated with the French political thinker Jean-Jacques Rousseau (1712–78). Actually,

Kedourie does not consider Rousseau's contribution to be important, noting that he did not have a systematic theory of the state
(1994: 32–3). Many scholars, however, disagree with Kedourie and
maintain that Rousseau's writings played a crucial role in shaping
the German Romantic thought (Dahbour and Ishay 1995; O'Leary
1996; Halliday 1997d).

For Rousseau, the biggest danger man faces when living in
society is 'the possible tyranny of will by his fellowmen' (Barnard
1984: 245). To guard against this danger, men need to exchange
their selfish will for the 'general will'. This can only be achieved if
they cease to be natural men and become citizens instead. Natural
men live for themselves, whereas men as citizens depend on the
community of which they are a part. By becoming a citizen, man
exchanges independence for dependence and autarky for participation and '[t]he best social institutions are those which make
individuals most intensely conscious of their mutual interdependence' (*ibid.*: 245). In short, a political association makes sense
only if it can protect men from the capriciousness of others: 'this
it can solely bring about if it substitutes law for the individual, if it
can generate a public will and arm it with a strength that is beyond
the power of any individual will' (*ibid.*: 246).

While Rousseau emphasizes the distinction between man and
citizen, he does not envisage conflictual relations between citizenship and patriotism. For Rousseau, Barnard argues, both 'citizen'
and 'patriot' are conceivable only within the context of the nation-
state: '[n]either citizen nor patriot could qualify as a cosmopolitan' (*ibid.*: 249). On the other hand, it is not easy to engender a
simultaneous consciousness of patriotism and citizenship. It is only
in the canton that 'citizenship is suffused with the passionate zeal
animating the patriot'. A state that is as large as Poland, for
example, cannot bring about this coincidence of citizenship and
patriotism unless, perhaps, it is organized as a confederation of
autonomous states (*ibid.*: 250).

At this stage, it needs to be pointed out that the sources of citizenship and patriotism are different for Rousseau. He defined
patriotism as that 'fine and lively feeling which gives the force of
self-love all the beauty of virtue, and lends it an energy which,
without disfiguring it, makes it the most heroic of all passions'
(cited in *ibid.*). Love of one's own country, Rousseau writes, is 'a

hundred times more ardent and delightful than that of a mistress' (cited in Barnard 1983: 236). Unlike patriotism which is the work of spontaneous will, citizenship is the work of rational will. Rousseau claims that men do not unite simply because they resemble each other. In other words, cultural similarities are not sufficient to become a nation: individuals must see a point in sharing that culture. It follows that,

> what constitutes citizenship is not sentiments of affinity or love but reasoned agreement on what is and what is not in the common interest, and the will to abide by such an agreement. Citizenship, therefore, does not derive from patriotism; while patriotism is a spontaneous and unmediated given, citizenship is an artificial and mediated creation. (Barnard 1984: 252–3)

Rousseau believed that without some degree of political freedom, men have no way of knowing how to give expression to their own will. 'We cannot know what people might do or not do or say if they are enslaved'. (*ibid.*: 260) This stance was particularly clear in the case of the Jews. According to him, the Jews were destined to remain unable to escape the tyranny exercised against them until they had a free and just homeland to live in: 'not until they have "a free state of their own, with schools and universities, where they can speak and debate without risk", shall we be able to know what they have to say or wish to bring about' (*ibid.*).

This brings us to another, very important, source of influence on the development of the idea of nationalism, which was, of course, the French Revolution of 1789. It was, in fact, within the context of the French Revolution that the notion of the nation was put into practice in legal and political terms. For the revolutionaries of 1789, the nation was the only legitimate source of political power (Baycroft 1998: 5). Here the concept 'nation' expressed 'the idea of a shared, common, equal citizenship, the unity of the people': hence the motto of the French Revolution, *liberté, égalité, fraternité* (Halliday 1997d: 362). In this, the revolutionaries were inspired by a book by the abbé Emmanuel Joseph Sieyès entitled *What is the Third Estate?* In the ancien régime, the French parliament, the Estates-General, consisted of three parts: the First Estate, comprising the nobility; the Second Estate, embracing the clergy;

and the Third Estate, representing everyone else. Sieyès argued in his book that all members of the nation were citizens, hence equal before the law. He rejected 'the principle of class and special upper-class feudal privileges, and claimed that the first two estates did not even qualify as parts of the nation' (Baycroft 1998: 6). Halliday notes that this evolution in France was paralleled in the Americas, in the revolt against British rule in the North (1776–83) and in the uprising against Spanish rule in the South (1820–28). In both cases, the basis for the revolt was political, that is the rejection of rule from imperial centres in Europe (1997d: 362).

The translation of these various ideas into a fully-fledged ideology took some time. But the political doctrine we recognize today as nationalism was already in place by the early nineteenth century. On the other hand, scholarly interest in it was still largely ethical. We find two sorts of responses to nationalism in the nineteenth century. The first one, which I will call the 'partisan' for want of a better term, was the approach of scholars and thinkers who were sympathetic to nationalism and who used their works to justify or enhance particular nationalisms. The second was the 'critical' approach of those who have been sceptical of nationalism and who saw it as a temporary stage in the historical evolution of human societies (*cf.* Snyder 1997; Smith 1996a). This critical attitude was not confined to Marxists; some liberals too, notably Lord Acton, were wary of nationalism and its implications. The pioneering figures of the nascent fields of sociology and political science, such as Weber, Durkheim, Tönnies, Mosca and Pareto, did not disturb the pattern set by their predecessors and took their places within one of these two camps.

Before proceeding, however, two caveats must be added to this picture. First, this binary classification does not imply a complete separation between the two categories. There were a number of similarities between those who were sympathetic to nationalism and those who opposed it. Of these, perhaps the most important was that the scholars and thinkers of both camps took the existence of nations and nationalism for granted. None of them questioned the 'naturalness' of nationhood. Second, the labels I attached to these categories do not denote 'eternal' – or absolute – attributes. The attitudes *vis-à-vis* nationalism not only changed from one thinker to the next, but were also subject to fluctuations over time. Hence, the labels in question should be taken at their face value,

that is as rough indicators of the main difference between the attitudes of these two groups of thinkers.

The 'partisan' camp was predominantly populated by historians.
The role of historians in promoting particular national movements
is widely recognized (Smith 1996a). Nationalist historians have
often 'unearthed' (in most cases 'created') the evidence which will
testify to their nation's perennial existence, or 'rediscovered' (in
most cases 'invented') the customs, myths, symbols and rituals
which will form the national culture (Hobsbawm and Ranger
1983). Here, I will briefly discuss the contributions of three such
historians, namely Renan, Michelet and von Treitschke. Renan's
views will be considered at the end of this section since he offered
the most sophisticated analysis of his time and thus had a quite
substantial impact on the thinking of succeeding generations.

The German historian Heinrich von Treitschke's (1834–96)
nationalism was tinged with militarism and anti-semitism (Smith
1996a; James 1996; Guibernau 1996). According to him, the state
is the supreme power: there is no authority above it. Rather, it is
the state which formulates the laws and these are binding over all
individuals that make up its population. The state exerts its power
through war: 'The grandeur of history lies in the perpetual conflict of nations, and it is simply foolish to desire the suppression of
their rivalry'. Thus, for him, war is political science *par excellence*
(von Treitschke 1916, cited in Guibernau 1996: 8). Von Treitschke
argued that the unity of the state should be based on nationality.
However, nationality should not be understood in a restricted
sense, that is as a legal bond. It should be complemented by blood-
relationship – either real or imagined. Guibernau notes that von
Treitschke rarely referred to nationalism in his writings (1996: 41).
But he offers a definition of patriotism: 'genuine patriotism is the
consciousness of co-operating with the body-politic, of being
rooted in ancestral achievements and of transmitting them to
descendants' (cited in Guibernau 1996: 10). These views led him
to support the unification of Germany under Prussian leadership.
He believed that there are two motor forces in history: 'the tendency of every state to amalgamate its population, in speech and
manners, into one single unity, and the impulse of every vigorous
nationality to construct a state of its own' (*ibid.*: 11). Given that
only the large and powerful states counted for him as 'vigorous'
nationalities, it is quite easy to understand why he saw Prussia as

the 'unifying agent' of the German people. The best way to achieve a 'Greater Germany', then, was the incorporation of smaller states into Prussian territories.

The French historian Jules Michelet (1798–1874) on the other hand, saw the nation as the ultimate guarantee of individual freedom (Smith 1996a: 177–8). The Revolution of 1789 had signalled a new era, an era of fraternity, and in this new era there were neither poor nor rich, nobles nor plebeians. The disputes in the society had been solved; enemies had made peace. The new religion was that of patriotism and this religion was 'the worship of man, and the motive force of modern French and European history' (*ibid.*: 178). Michelet supported the nationalist movements in Italy, Poland and Ireland, all part of the Young Europe movement of Mazzini and saw them as 'fraternal sympathizers of France'.

The partisan camp did not consist of historians alone. The renowned English political theorist John Stuart Mill (1806–73) is a good case in point. Like his liberal nationalist predecessors, Mill fused the concept of republican citizenship with the principle of nationality which he defined in the following way:

> a portion of mankind may be said to constitute a Nationality if they are united among themselves by common sympathies which do not exist between them and any others – which make them cooperate with each other more willingly than with other people, desire to be under the same government, and desire that it should be government by themselves or a portion of themselves exclusively. (1996: 40)

Where the sentiment of nationality exists, Mill argued, 'there is a *prima facie* case for uniting all the members of the nationality under the same government, and a government to themselves apart. This is merely saying that the question of government ought to be decided by the governed' (*ibid.*: 41). Here we find, once again, the principle of self-determination to which Mill added the idea of representative government (Halliday 1997d: 362). For him, free institutions were next to impossible in a country made up of different nationalities: 'Among a people without fellow-feeling, especially if they read and speak different languages, the united public opinion, necessary to the working of representative government, cannot exist' (Mill 1996: 41–2). In short, the boundaries of governments should coincide in the main with those of nationalities if we are to have free institutions.

These views enable us to move on to the 'critical' camp. The English historian and philosopher Lord Acton (1834–1902) who published an almost contemporaneous essay on the same theme (1862, reproduced in Balakrishnan 1996b) is a good starting point. Criticizing Mill, Lord Acton suggested that individual freedom was better maintained in a multinational state:

> If we take the establishment of liberty for the realization of moral duties to be the end of civil society, we must conclude that those states are substantially the most perfect which, like the British and Austrian Empires, include various nationalities without oppressing them. (1996: 36)

For Acton, to insist on national unity was to lead to revolution and despotism. The states in which 'no mixture of races has occurred are imperfect' and 'those in which its effects have disappeared are decrepit' (*ibid.*). It follows that 'a State which is incompetent to satisfy different races condemns itself; a State which labours to neutralize, to absorb or to expel them, destroys its own vitality'. Therefore, 'the theory of nationality . . . is a retrograde step in history' (*ibid.*).

The Marxists were indubitably the most important group within the critical camp. That nationalism has always created difficulties for the Marxist school is well-known, and these difficulties have been both political and theoretical (Kitching 1985; Munck 1986; Calhoun 1997). Is nationalism a form of 'false consciousness' which diverts the proletariat from the goal of international revolution? Or should we see the struggle of the proletariat with the bourgeoisie first as a national struggle? If so, then how do such national class struggles relate to the construction of international socialism (Kitching 1985: 99)? Besides these theoretical problems, Marxists were also faced with political exigencies. Communist parties had to change their positions *vis-à-vis* nationalism for tactical and strategic reasons. Sometimes nationalism was condemned (as in the case of nationalist movements against the Austro-Hungarian Empire), sometimes it was ardently supported (as in the case of anti-colonial nationalist movements).

Scholars offer different explanations for this ambivalent attitude and the ensuing lack of a Marxist theory of nationalism. For instance, Kitching argues that the Marxists, having their roots in Enlightenment rationalism, could not satisfactorily explain to themselves, let alone to others, 'how loyalty to a nation and particularly the placing of national identity above a class identity can be a rational thing to do'. For this reason, he contends, they have offered psychological explanations and saw nationalism as a manifestation of ideologically motivated 'irrational emotions' (Kitching 1985: 99). Calhoun notes that 'none of the other great social and political analysts has been as widely castigated for failure to grasp the importance of nationalism as Marx and Engels', and points to their overconfident internationalism for this failure (1997: 26). According to Calhoun, their greatest error was their assumption that people would respond to the material challenges of global economic integration simply as workers. However, 'workers suffered economic privations as heads of households, as members of communities, as religious people, as citizens – not just as workers' (*ibid.*: 27). Moreover, even when they thought of themselves as members of the working class, most workers continued to think of themselves first as members of particular occupations – as silk weavers, clockmakers and so on. In short, their responses to economic inequalities were shaped by their other identities as well, not only by their class loyalties. Guibernau, on the other hand, tries to account for Marx and Engels' failure to deal adequately with nationalism by pointing to their quest for a 'grand theory' capable of explaining all stages of societal evolution. For Marx, the central attribute of all social systems from Ancient Greece to present times was 'class struggle'. Accordingly, he explained the social, political and ideological aspects of societies by reference to economy, that is the mode and relations of production. In this context, Guibernau maintains, nationalism was a marginal phenomenon: 'Marx's emphasis upon the political sphere as "superstructure" led him to downplay both the nation-state and nationalism as major influences upon historical change' (1996: 42).

This 'classical' problem of Marxism has triggered a lively debate among the Marxists of the twentieth century. According to Poulantzas, for instance, the failure to theorize nationalism reveals all the impasses of traditional Marxism (Poulantzas 1980, cited in James 1996: 49). Poulantzas rejects the claim that the Marxists have underestimated nationalism by calling attention to the various debates that have taken place within the workers' movement. For him, the fact that no theory of nationalism could be formulated despite all these passionate debates shows clearly that there is no Marxist theory of the nation (James 1996: 49). Others disagree with him. One group of writers maintains that 'it is more important to recognize the strength of the [Marxist] theory of nationalism than worry about its imperfections (Blaut 1982, cited in James 1996: 50). Another group directly targets on the claim that there is no Marxist theory of the nation. Nimni (1991) for example rejects the idea that Marx and Engels' position *vis-à-vis* nationalism is conditioned by political exigencies, arguing that, despite their fragmentary nature, their writings on the nation have an underpinning coherence. Similarly, Munck criticizes attempts to deride the socialists who did try to come to grips with nationalism – namely Bauer, Ber Borochov, Connolly and Gramsci – and claims that they provide important insights into the nature of nationalism: 'It is now necessary to forge some kind of coherent Marxist approach to nationalism on the basis of these writers' (1986: 168). Neo-Marxists have also tried to overcome 'Marxism's great historical failure' by formulating a theory of their own (for example Hechter 1975; Nairn 1981; Hroch 1985). Some of these attempts will be discussed in Chapter 4.

For Marx (1818–83) and Engels (1820–95), who lived and worked through the age of nationalism, 'the modern nation was the direct result of a process whereby the capitalist mode of production superseded feudalism' (Nimni 1991: 18). It was the transition to a capitalist economy that forced the existing social formations in Western Europe to become more homogeneous and politically centralized. According to Nimni, this conceptualization of national formation was conditioned by their tendency to explain every significant social phenomenon in terms of an overall developmental logic, which led them to see nationalism as a necessary but temporary stage in the evolution of history (*ibid.*: 3–4).

It was in the context of this evolutionary logic that Marx and Engels revived the Hegelian distinction between 'historic' and 'non-historic' nations (Munck 1986: 9). Nimni notes that in their writings, the term nation was reserved for the permanent population of a nation-state, whereas an ethno-cultural community that had not achieved full national status, that is lacked a state of its own, was referred to as a nationality (1991: 23). They believed that nationalities will either become nations by acquiring a state of their own or remain as 'historyless peoples' (*Geschichtslosen Völker*). These non-historical nationalities were inherently reactionary, because they were unable to adapt to the capitalist mode of production. As their existence depended on the survival of the old order, they were necessarily regressive (*ibid.*).

In line with this general attitude, Marx and Engels supported the unification processes of what they considered to be historic nations, for example Germany and Italy, while rejecting those of small, non-historical nationalities – as in the case of the movements against the Austro-Hungarian and Russian empires. More generally, Marx and Engels thought that a common language and traditions, or geographical and historical homogeneity, were not sufficient to constitute a nation. 'Rather, a certain level of economic and social development was required, with a priority given to larger units' (Munck 1986: 11). According to Munck, this explains why they have objected to the ceding of Schleswig and Holstein to Denmark in 1848. For them, Germany was more revolutionary and progressive than the Scandinavian nations because of its higher level of capitalist development.

Marx and Engels did not change this stance during the revolutions of 1848. For them, only the great, historic nations of Germany, Poland, Hungary and Italy fulfilled the criteria for viable national states. Other, less dynamic nationalities, 'these residual fragments of peoples', were not worthy of working class support. Engels was particularly harsh towards Southern Slavs whom he described as 'peoples which have never had a history of their own ... [who] are not viable and will never be able to achieve any kind of independence' (Marx and Engels 1976, cited in Munck 1986: 12).

Some commentators claim that Marx and Engels revised their attitudes on the nationality problem during the 1860s (Munck 1986; Guibernau 1996). Munck points to the Crimean War of 1853–56, where they supported the independence of the Slav peoples from the Ottoman Empire, to illustrate this change of attitude. The Irish case, he contends, is even a better example (1986: 15). Marx and Engels thought that England could not embark on a revolutionary path until the Irish question had been solved to the latter's advantage: 'The separation and independence of Ireland from England was not only a vital step for Irish development but was also essential for the British people since "A nation that oppresses another forges its own chains"' (Nimni 1991: 33).

At this stage, it is important to stress that there is no universal agreement on the relevance of the Irish case. Munck considers it as a turning point in Marx and Engels' treatment of the national question and devotes a whole section to it in his book (1986: 15–20). Nimni, on the other hand, explains their support for Irish independence in terms of their general sympathy for the cause of historic nations. However, this support never extends to non-historical nations. In that sense, there is no contradiction or incoherence in their analytical logic. The Irish and Polish national movements deserved to be supported, because they were advancing the course of progress by establishing national states 'capable of developing a healthy contradiction between the proletariat and the bourgeoisie' (Nimni 1991: 33). The non-historical nations, on the other hand,

> either cannot develop a bourgeoisie, because they are peasant nations, or they cannot develop a state of their own, because they either live in a mixed area of residence or they are too small to create an internal market. Thus these nations must seek alliances with the defenders of the old order: the irresistible flow of progress requires either the voluntary assimilation or the annihilation of these national communities. (*Ibid.*)

A final point that needs to be underlined concerns Marx and Engels' commitment to internationalism. According to Munck, the founding fathers of Marxism never betrayed the internationalism of the *Communist Manifesto* where they wrote:

> National differences and antagonism between peoples are daily more and more vanishing, owing to the development of the bourgeoisie, to freedom of commerce, to the world market, to uniformity in the mode of communication and in the conditions of life corresponding thereto. (1976: 507)

Similarly, in his article on Friedrich List's *Das nationale System der politischen Ökonomie*, Marx commented:

The nationality of the worker is neither French, nor English, nor German, it is labour, free slavery, self-huckstering. His government is neither French, nor English, nor German, it is capital. His native air is neither French, nor English, nor German, it is factory air. The land belonging to him is neither French, nor English, nor German, it lies a few feet below the ground. (Marx and Engels 1975, cited in Guibernau 1996: 16)

Engels expressed similar views. He argued that the proletariat should only think in international terms because: 'the International recognises no country; it desires to unite, not dissolve. It is opposed to the cry for Nationality, because it tends to separate people from people, and is used by tyrants to create prejudices and antagonism' (cited in Guibernau 1996: 16).

On the other hand, certain sections in the *Communist Manifesto*, particularly those on the nature of the struggle of the proletariat, demonstrate a more complicated perspective:

Though not in substance, yet in form, the struggle of the proletariat with the bourgeoisie is at first a national struggle. The proletariat of each country must, of course, settle matters with its own bourgeoisie. (1976: 495)

or:

Since the proletariat must first of all acquire political supremacy, must rise to be the leading class of the nation, must constitute itself *the* nation, it is, so far, itself national, though not in the bourgeois sense of the word. (*Ibid.*: 502–3)

Some commentators claim that these phrases reflect their ambivalence on the national question. On the one hand, the workers are called upon to embark on a national struggle, that is against their own bourgeoisies; on the other hand, they are expected to remain loyal to the cause of international revolution. The question of how these two seemingly paradoxical objectives can be reconciled is left unanswered. According to other scholars however, notably Munck, the meaning of these phrases is far from being ambiguous. The workers should first become the leading class ('national class' in the first German edition) in their nation: only then can they work to diminish national antagonisms. In saying this, Munck concludes, Marx and Engels do not betray their internationalism (1986: 24; *cf.* Guibernau 1996: 18).

The most sophisticated account of nationalism within the Marxist tradition comes from Otto Bauer (1881–1938). Bauer's outstanding *Die Nationalitätenfrage und die Sozialdemokratie* (1907) has been variously described as 'the first substantial Marxist analysis of nation-states and nationalism' (Bottomore 1983, cited in James 1996: 48), 'the most important and convincing attempt among Marxists of the period to understand nationalism' (Breuilly 1993a: 40) and 'the first full-length study of nationalism from a historical standpoint' (Smith 1996a: 182). A brief overview of the historical and political context in which Bauer wrote his book will enable us to better evaluate his ideas, since they were primarily designed to meet the immediate needs of the Austrian Social Democrats who were trying to solve the problems their party – and in general the Austro-Hungarian empire – confronted (Smith 1996a: 181).

What dominated Austrian politics from 1897 onwards was the so-called 'nationalities question' (Breuilly 1993a: 40–1; Stargardt 1995). This problem took the form of ethnic antagonism between Czechs and Germans living in Bohemia. This antagonistic situation eventually led to the establishment of 'national socialist' political parties which tried to draw upon ethnic working class support. Other parties, notably the Austrian Social Democratic Party, were organized at a national level. The Austrian Social Democrats had explicitly recognized differences of nationality within their own ranks. According to Breuilly, this was particularly interesting in a party which claimed to subscribe to Marxism (1993a: 40). However, the attitude of the party changed when ethnic conflicts increased and began to threaten the labour movement. First, it recognized nationality differences on a territorial basis: a Czech worker could remain in the Czech sections of the party only if he was living in Czech-dominated areas. Later, recognition of nationality became more personal: now, the Czech worker could remain in Czech sections even when living in German areas as long as he so wished. This change of attitude shows clearly that the importance of national identity in the party's internal organization was gradually increasing. The same tendency could be observed in the party's political programme. The party first advocated the idea of realizing socialism under a unitary state; then moved to the defence of some form of federalism; finally, espoused 'a complex notion of political organisation and national autonomy' (Breuilly 1993a: 40). This shift in the party's programme reflected the fluctuations in the views of the leading figures of the movement, namely Karl Renner (1870–1950) and Otto Bauer.

Renner's solution to the problems emanating from differences of nationality was to separate the state and the nation (Stargardt 1995). He argued that economic and social issues as well as defence, justice and foreign policy should be delegated to the state. National functions, on the other hand, should be restricted to education and culture. The state should adopt federalism in its internal organization. Finally, national autonomy should be organized on the basis of the so-called 'personality principle', that is the sum total of individuals claiming a particular nationality. This principle became the hallmark of Austrian Social Democracy in the 1900s (*ibid.*: 90).

Bauer began his theoretical analysis by asking Renan's famous question: *Qu'est-ce qu'une nation?* The nation for him is 'a community of character that grows out of a community of destiny rather than from a mere similarity of destiny' (Bauer 1996: 52). Each nation has a character which, in turn, is defined as 'the totality of physical and mental characteristics that are peculiar to a nation'. The nations are far more contingent entities than nationalists' communities of language and shared culture. Moreover, 'the national character is changeable; in no way is the nation of our time linked with its ancestors of two or three millennia ago' (*ibid.*: 40–1). How did, then, this community of character come into being? For Bauer, the emergence of this community, the Herderian community of language, depended on various modernizing processes, including the breakdown of peasant subsistence farming and the following uprooting of the rural population by capitalism, the drawing of isolated rural areas into regional economic relationships so that dialects could become more homogeneous (*ibid.*: 43–5; Stargardt 1995: 97–8). There was also a second stage in which a 'cultural community' bridging the gap between the linguistic and national communities was created. Here, the focus was on the development of a 'high culture' and with it, a 'high language' above all spoken dialects. On the other hand, the most important factor in the transition from a cultural community to a nation was 'sentiment', a sense of the community's own shared destiny. For Bauer, commonality of destiny was at least as important as commonality of past, hence his definition of the nation as, above all, a 'community of fate'.

Bauer also found a way of bringing nation and class together. He argued that the national culture is shaped by the contribution of various classes. In a socialist society, conflicts among different nationalities would cease, because antagonistic relations were based upon class divisions. Once class divisions were removed, national distinctions would give rise to cooperation and coexistence. In other words, as long as national identity is not distorted by class divisions, the members of the nation would be able to participate in the national experience in a more intense manner. Bauer drew this conclusion by observing Czech–German relations in Austria–Hungary. 'It was essential to separate national (cultural and non-antagonistic) from class (economic and antagonistic) issues'. (Breuilly 1993a: 40) This could only be achieved by giving each nation a satisfying degree of autonomy, leaving conflict to focus around class divisions.

Before moving on to Renan, the last thinker I will review in this section, a few words on the contributions of the twin founding fathers of sociology, Émile Durkheim (1858–1917) and Max Weber (1864–1920), will be helpful. At the turn of the century, it was quite clear that the nation was not going to fade away in the foreseeable future. But, one generation after Marx and Engels, there were still no systematic studies of nationalism – or, in the words of James, 'anything approaching what we might call a theory of the nation' (1996: 83). Social theorists of the period did explore many of the issues neglected by earlier generations, including religion, but nationalism was generally ignored – with the partial exceptions of Georg Simmel who tried to make sense of the process of national integration, arguing that the French owe their national unity to their fight with Britain, and Gaetano Mosca who claimed that nationalism was replacing religion and becoming the chief factor of moral cohesion in Europe (James 1996: 86–7). Neither Durkheim nor Weber attempted to disturb this general 'reticence' on nationalism. Imbued with the geopolitics of their age, they were content to ally themselves with one of two camps (both writers were sympathetic to their respective nationalisms). However, their writings contained a number of themes that were to become central to the theories of the succeeding generations (Smith 1998: 13).

Durkheim's views on nationalism can be distilled from his writings on religion and the *conscience collective* (McCrone 1998: 18). Influenced by the events of the Third Republic (1870–1914), notably by the defeat by Prussia in 1870, the Paris Commune and the Dreyfus Affair, 'he did not approve of nationalism, denouncing it as an extreme and morbid form of patriotism' (*ibid.*). Smith argues that two aspects of Durkheim's work have been influential on contemporary theories of nationalism, more specifically, the modernist paradigm. The first was 'his analysis of religion as the core of moral community and his consequent belief that "there is something eternal in religion"... because all societies feel the need to reaffirm and renew themselves periodically through collective rites and ceremonies' (Smith 1998: 15). The second aspect was 'his analysis of the transition from "mechanical" to "organic" solidarity' (*ibid.*). Basically, Durkheim argued that traditions and the influence of the *conscience collective* decline, along with impulsive forces, such as affinity of blood, attachment to the same soil, ancestral worship and community of habits. Their place is taken by the division of labour and its complementarity of roles (*ibid.*). This aspect of his work was particularly influential on some modernist theories of nationalism, notably that of Ernest Gellner.

Weber, on the other hand, was 'both a cosmopolite and a contradictorily dispassionate nationalist' (James 1996: 89). According to Smith, the aspects of his work that proved most influential for subsequent theories included

> the importance of political memories, the role of intellectuals in preserving the 'irreplaceable culture values' of a nation, and the importance of nation-states in the rise of the special character of the modern West. (1998: 13)

Of these, the third aspect was the most important. For Weber, the nation was in essence a political concept. He defined it as 'a community of sentiment which would adequately manifest itself in a state of its own' (1948, cited in Smith 1998: 14). In other words, what distinguished nations from other communities was the quest for statehood. This particular conception of nationhood, Smith argues, 'has inspired a number of latterday theorists of nation-states to emphasise the political dimensions of nationalism and especially the role of the modern Western state' (*ibid.*).

The last scholar whose contribution will be discussed in this section is the French historian Ernest Renan (1823–92), who offered perhaps the most insightful analysis of this period. Some of the ideas contained in the famous lecture he delivered at Sorbonne in 1882, entitled *Qu'est-ce qu'une nation?* (1990), had a substantial impact on the theories of the succeeding generations and made him a figure of almost compulsory citation. Renan's formulations will therefore be a perfect stepping-stone to the studies of the twentieth century.

In this lecture, Renan rejected the popular conceptions that defined nations in terms of objective characteristics such as race, language or religion. He asked:

> How is it that Switzerland, which has three languages, two religions, and three or four races, is a nation, when Tuscany, which is so homogeneous, is not one? Why is Austria a state and not a nation? In what ways does the principle of nationality differ from that of races? (1990: 12)

For him, nations were not eternal entities. They had their beginnings and they will have an end. The nation is 'a soul, a spiritual principle';

> A nation is . . . a large-scale solidarity, constituted by the feeling of the sacrifices that one has made in the past and of those that one is prepared to make in the future. It presupposes a past; it is summarized, however, in the present by a tangible fact, namely, consent, the clearly expressed desire to continue a common life. A nation's existence is, if you will pardon the metaphor, a daily plebiscite, just as an individual's existence is a perpetual affirmation of life. (*Ibid.*: 19)

In short, race, language, material interest, religious affinities, geography and military necessity were not among the ingredients which constituted a nation; a common heroic past, great leaders and true glory were. Another, very important, ingredient was 'collective forgetting': 'forgetting, I would even go so far as to say historical error, is a crucial factor in the creation of a nation . . . No French citizen knows whether he is a Burgundian, an Alan, a Taifale, or a Visigoth, yet every French citizen has to have forgotten the massacre of Saint-Bartholomew' (*ibid.*: 11). What Renan wanted, then, was to affirm 'the primacy of politics and shared history in the genesis and character of nations' (Smith 1996a: 178).

These ideas take us to the twentieth century. The analyses of Renan and Bauer reflect the growing importance of nationalism as a political ideology and movement, and as a subject of academic investigation in its own right (*ibid.*: 182). The political repercussions of the doctrine of nationalism and the difficulties it gave birth to required more neutral analyses. In other words, nationalism had to be understood, not defended or criticized. The experiences of the First World War and its aftermath made this need all the more acute.

1918–45

The need for dispassionate analyses of nationalism was satisfied to a certain extent by 'the labours of sociologically inclined historians from the 1920s' (Smith 1998: 16). Snyder argues that the early writings of Carleton Hayes and Hans Kohn surpassed their predecessors in five distinct ways:

> They defined nationalism as a discrete subject of investigation, they treated nationalism as a positive fact rather than a compelling norm, they recognised that nationalism was in some sense a historical development, they used comparative analysis and they generally avoided biological analogies. (1997: 233)

On the other hand, there was also an important similarity between the studies of this period and that of the earlier generations. Historians like Carleton Hayes, Hans Kohn, Alfred Cobban, E. H. Carr and Louis Snyder were still taking the nation for granted, that is as a 'given'. This tacit presupposition inevitably limited the analytical effectiveness of their studies. Nevertheless, their writings opened a new era in the study of nationalism and acted as a constant source of inspiration for modern theorists.

We encounter two kinds of studies in the period between 1918–45. First, there were the histories of particular nationalisms. As Breuilly observes, these 'stories' tend to become absorbed into their subject: 'the very restriction to a "national" framework implies agreement with the nationalist argument that there is a nation' (1985: 65). Questions starting with 'why' are usually bypassed. A typical story of this kind begins with the traditional, pre-national state of affairs. The historian highlights the weaknesses of the pre-national institutions and criticizes the lack of political centralization. The story continues with the crumbling of traditional institutions in the face of modernizing forces. In the *dénouement*, the nationalists come and save the nation from vanishing by restoring the national unity (Breuilly 1996: 156–7). Breuilly argues that the narrative form explains nothing, as it is built on highly dubious assumptions. Moreover, narratives do not bring out the contingency of outcomes. These stories tend not to state the plain fact that things could have been otherwise (*ibid.*: 157–8). Smith also criticizes the narrative and chronological format of these studies and adds their European bias to the list of criticisms (1983: 257).

Secondly, there were the typologies. Most scholars of the period tried to construct classificatory schemes to order the varieties of nationalism into recurring types (Smith 1996a: 182). According to James, this reflected the urge to avoid the notorious problem of definition and the difficulty of formulating a theory of the nation (1996: 127).

Smith considers Hayes to be the first scholar to adopt a more neutral stance towards nationalism, one that seeks to distinguish the various types of nationalist ideology (1996a: 182). For Hayes,

> nationalism, the paramount devotion of human beings to fairly large nationalities and the conscious founding of a political 'nation' on linguistic and cultural nationality, was not widely preached and acted upon until the eighteenth century. (1955: 6)

Individuals had been patriotic about their city, locality, ruler or empire, but not about their nationality. The idea that 'nationalities are the fundamental units of human society and the most natural agencies for undertaking needful reforms and for promoting human progress' began to receive emphatic endorsement in Europe only in the eighteenth century (*ibid.*: 10). According to Hayes, modern nationalism manifested itself in six different forms (1955; for a concise summary see Snyder 1968: 48–53):

Humanitarian Nationalism

This was the earliest and for some time the only kind of formal nationalism. Expounded in the eighteenth century, the first doctrines of nationalism were infused with the spirit of the Enlightenment. They were based on natural law and presented as inevitable, therefore desirable steps in human progress. In object, they were all strictly humanitarian. Hayes holds that humanitarian nationalism had three main advocates: the Tory politician John Bolingbroke who espoused an aristocratic form of nationalism, Jean-Jacques Rousseau who promoted a democratic nationalism and finally, Johann Gottfried von Herder who was mainly interested in culture, not politics. As the eighteenth century neared its end, humanitarian nationalism underwent an important transformation. Democratic nationalism became 'Jacobin'; aristocratic nationalism became 'traditional'; and nationalism which was neither democratic, nor aristocratic became 'liberal'.

Jacobin Nationalism

This form of nationalism was based in theory on the humanitarian democratic nationalism of Rousseau, and was developed by revolutionary leaders for the purpose of safeguarding and extending the principles of the French revolution. Developing in the midst of foreign war and domestic rebellion, Jacobin nationalism acquired four characteristics: it became suspicious and quite intolerant of internal dissent; it eventually relied on force and militarism to attain its ends; it became fanatically religious; and it was characterized by missionary zeal. The Jacobins rendered their nationalism much more exclusive than that of their predecessors. Their tragedy was that 'they were idealists, fanatically so, in a wicked world' (Hayes 1955: 80). Hence, the more they fought, the more nationalist they grew. They bequeathed to the succeeding generations the idea of 'the nation in arms' and 'the nation in public schools'. Jacobin nationalism also set the pattern for twentieth-century nationalisms, in particular Italian fascism and German national socialism.

Traditional Nationalism

Certain intellectuals who opposed the French Revolution and Napoleon embraced a different form of nationalism. Their frame of reference was not 'reason' or 'revolution', but history and tradition. They detested everything that Jacobinism was supposed to stand for. Hence, while the latter was democratic and revolutionary, traditional nationalism was aristocratic and evolutionary. For the traditionalists, nationality and the state had just evolved. It was not necessary to discuss their origins. In that sense, the state was not a mere partnership to be made or dissolved at will. It was a combination between the living, the dead and those yet to be born. Its most illustrious exponents were Edmund Burke, Vicomte de Bonald and Friedrich von Schlegel. Traditional nationalism was the powerful motivating force of the revolts within France and in back of the growing popular resistance on the Continent, as exemplified in the nationalist awakenings in Germany, Holland, Portugal, Spain and even Russia.

Liberal Nationalism

Midway between Jacobin and traditional nationalism was liberal nationalism. It originated in England, 'that country of perpetual compromise and of acute national self-consciousness' (*ibid.*: 120), in the eighteenth century. Its leading spokesman was Jeremy Bentham who was intent on limiting the scope and functions of government in all spheres of life. For him, nationality was the proper basis for state and government. War, in this context, was peculiarly bad and should be eliminated. Bentham's liberal nationalism quickly spread from England to the Continent. His teachings were appropriated in Germany (Wilhelm von Humboldt, Baron vom Stein, Karl Theodor Welcker), France (François Guizot, Victor Hugo, Casimir-Périer) and in Italy (Guiseppe Mazzini). There were many differences in detail among these apostles with regard to the scope and implications of liberal nationalism. But they all assumed that each nationality should be a political unit under an independent constitutional government which would put an end to despotism, aristocracy and ecclesiastical influence and assure to every citizen the broadest practicable exercise of personal liberty. Liberal nationalism managed to survive the First World War. Yet it also suffered a transformation. 'Its liberalism waned as its nationalism waxed' because it had to compete now with a new form of nationalism (*ibid.*: 163).

Integral Nationalism

In the journal *L'Action Française*, Charles Maurras – the chief protagonist of this type of nationalism – defined integral nationalism as 'the exclusive pursuit of national policies, the absolute maintenance of national integrity and the steady increase of national power – for a nation declines when it loses its might' (cited in Hayes 1955: 165). Integral nationalism was hostile to the internationalism of humanitarians and liberals. It made the nation not a means to humanity, but an end in itself. It put national interests above those of the individual and those of humanity, refusing cooperation with other nations. On the other hand, in domestic affairs, integral nationalism was highly illiberal and tyrannical. It required all citizens to conform to a common standard of manners and morals, and to share the same unreasoning enthusiasm for it. It would subordinate all personal liberties to its own purpose and if the people should complain, it would abridge democracy in the name of 'national interest'. The philosophy of integral nationalism was derived from the writings of a varied and numerous group of theorists in the nineteenth and twentieth centuries, such as Auguste Comte, Hippolyte Adolpe Taine, Maurice Barrès and Charles Maurras. Integral nationalism flourished in the first half of the twentieth century, especially in countries like Italy and Germany. Its impact was also felt in countries like Hungary, Poland, Turkey and Yugoslavia.

Economic Nationalism

Superimposed upon these developing forms was continuing economic nationalism. Initially, political considerations lay behind this nationalism, but then a tendency developed to regard the state as an economic as well as a political unit. Tariffs were erected, economic self-sufficiency was praised. The resultant struggle for markets and raw materials came during the rise of integral nationalism. Economic nationalism merged with imperialism and became one of the driving forces of contemporary history.

Such is, in summary form, Hayes' typology. Snyder maintains that this classification is distinguished by two characteristics: 'it stresses a chronological, or vertical, approach, treating nationalism from its origins in modern form in the French Revolution; and its area is limited mainly to the European continent' (1968: 64). Smith criticizes this strong regional, that is Franco–English, bias. He also notes a more basic problem, namely the formulation of a typology based on purely ideological distinctions. He argues that such a typology is not 'easily amenable to sociological analysis, for different strands of the ideology may be found within a single movement, e.g. Traditional, Jacobin and Integral elements in Syrian Ba'athism' (1983: 196).

A much more influential typology was that of Hans Kohn. For him, nationalism was the fruit of a long historical process. He argues that 'modern nationalism originated in the seventeenth and eighteenth centuries in northwestern Europe and its American settlements. It became a general European movement in the nineteenth century' (1957: 3). The age of nationalism, he continues, brought a sense of conscious and growing differentiation: it has made 'the divisions of mankind more pronounced and has spread the consciousness of antagonistic aspirations to wider multitudes of men than ever before' (*ibid.*: 4). Kohn distinguished between two types of nationalism, namely 'Western' and 'Eastern' nationalisms, in terms of their origins and main characteristics (Kohn 1967: 329–31; Snyder 1968: 53–7; Smith 1983: 196; Smith 1996a: 182). In the Western world, for instance in England, France, the Netherlands, Switzerland, the United States and the British dominions, nationalism was the product of political and social factors. It was preceded by the formation of the national state or coincided with it. In Central and Eastern Europe and in Asia, on the other hand, nationalism arose later and at a more backward stage of social and political development. In conflict with the existing state pattern, it found its first expression in the cultural field and sought for its justification in the 'natural' fact of a community held together by traditional ties of kinship and status. The frontiers of the existing polity rarely coincided with that of the rising nationality.

Western nationalism was born out of the spirit of the Enlightenment. It was closely connected in its origin with the concepts of individual liberty and rational cosmopolitanism: thus, it was optimistic, pluralistic and rationalist. It was largely the expression of the political aspirations of the rising middle classes. Moreover, 'nationalism in the West stressed the political reality' (Snyder 1968: 55). The nation was regarded as a vital, existing, real thing. Political integration was sought around a rational goal.

Nationalism in the non-Western world rejected or belittled the spirit of the Enlightenment: instead, the authoritarian uniformity of state and faith was praised. Nationalism meant collective power and national unity, independence from foreign domination (rather than liberty at home) or the necessity for expansion by the superior nation. It reflected the aspirations of the lower aristocracy and the masses. Since it was not rooted in a political and social reality, it lacked self-assurance and this inferiority complex was often compensated by overconfidence. The dependence on the West, which remained for a long time the model, coupled with social backwardness, produced a much more emotional and authoritarian nationalism. The non-Western world was also detached from political reality. It became absorbed in a search for the ideal fatherland. Its nationalism was mostly concerned with myths and dreams of the future, without immediate connection with the present.

The two nationalisms had different conceptions of nation. The Western idea was that nations emerged as voluntary unions of citizens. Individuals expressed their will in contracts, covenants and plebiscites. Integration was achieved around a political idea and special emphasis was laid upon the universal similarities of nations. In the non-Western world, the nation was regarded as a political unit centering around the irrational, pre-civilized folk concept. Nationalism found its rallying point in the folk community, elevating it to the dignity of an ideal or a mystery. Here, emphasis was put on the diversity and self-sufficiency of nations.

As this brief summary reveals, Kohn was much more interested in the moral worth of different types of nationalism than in providing a descriptive classification of these types. Nevertheless,

Snyder maintains that Kohn's typology 'clarifies many inconsistencies and contradictions surrounding the meaning of nationalism'. It shows 'how the idea of nationalism could be communicated by cultural diffusion, while at the same time its meaning and form could take on characteristics directed by the aims and aspirations of the peoples concerned' (Snyder 1968: 56–7). On the other hand, the moralistic overtones of the classification leave Kohn vulnerable to the charge of Eurocentrism. Critics contend that 'the typology is far too favourable to the Western world, that he cleanses Western nationalism of tribal impurities, and that he disregards any manifestations of anti-democratic or non-Western nationalism in the West' (Snyder 1968: 57). Snyder holds that this criticism is unjust. For him, Kohn does not overlook the deleterious effects of nationalism in the West as well as in non-Western nations. His formula, Snyder argues, takes into account gradations of light and shadow: 'the open, pluralistic society is never perfect' (*ibid.*).

However, this was not the only criticism levelled against Kohn's typology. Smith raises a range of objections to this scheme: it is silent about Latin American and African experiences; its spatial distinction between 'East' and 'West' is not adequate since Spain, Belgium and Ireland, being at the time socially backward, belong to the 'Eastern' camp; some nationalisms like that of Turkish or Tanzanian elites blend 'voluntarist' and 'organic' elements in a single movement; too many levels of development, types of structure and cultural situations are included within each category (1983: 197). Nevertheless, Kohn's classification proved to be very long-lived and cast its shadow on the typologies of later periods.

Another contribution to the typologies of the period comes from Snyder himself. In his earlier work, Snyder opted for a chronological classification of nationalisms (1954; see also 1968: 48):

- *Integrative nationalism* (1815–71). In this period, nationalism was a unifying force. It helped consolidate states that had outgrown their feudal divisions and united others that had been split into various factions. The unifications of Germany and Italy were the products of this phase.
- *Disruptive nationalism* (1871–90). The success of nationalism in moulding the unification of Germany and Italy aroused the enthusiasm of subject nationalities in other countries. The

minorities in the Ottoman Empire, Austria–Hungary and other conglomerate states sought to break out of oppression.

- *Aggressive nationalism* (1900–45). The first half of the twentieth century witnessed the collision of opposing national interests and the explosive impact of two world wars. During this period, nationalism became identical with imperialism.
- *Contemporary nationalism* (1945–). This most recent form of nationalism asserted itself partly in colonial revolts against European imperialism. This period of colonial emancipation and nation-building saw the extension of nationalism into a global framework.

The historical taxonomy developed by Snyder is not immune from criticisms. Smith argues that it is unhistorical: for example, the Serbian, Greek and Belgian movements are early (in the 'integrative' phase) and of major importance: all three were 'disruptive' of the existing political systems. Conversely, the Japanese and Indian cases were 'integrative' although they appeared in the 'disruptive' period. Moreover, the dates chosen are arbitrary, being based largely on the German model (Smith 1983: 194; Smith 1996a: 184).

Noting that chronological conceptualization has little meaning for the 'new' nationalisms of the period since 1945, Snyder developed a continental or regional classification in his later work. This classification, he contended, is based on general area characteristics and should not be confused with such movements as Pan-Africanism, Pan-Arabism or Pan-Americanism (1968: 64–8):

- *Europe: Fissiparous nationalism.* In Europe, the new nationalism recapitulates the experience of the old and tends to remain fragmented, split and particularistic. It reflects the ideology of the small nations as the ultimate politico-economic units. Despite talks about a United States of Europe or about Europe being a 'third force', nationalism remains strong and unbending.
- *Africa: Black nationalism.* African nationalism emerged with an explosive impact and one state after another gained its independence. An important element in this process was the appearance of a dominant ethnic motif. This was the predictable response of peoples who have been subject to white imperialism for many decades. In form, African nationalism was

imitative of Western models, but deep inside, there was a racial core of hostility to white domination.

- *The Middle East: Politico-religious nationalism.* The experience of liberation, independence and nation-building in the Middle East was similar to that of Africa. Here, nationalism was affected by the area's close proximity to Western civilisations. The religious element always played a crucial role in it. The rise of Arab nationalism, the reconstruction of Israel and the appearance of state nationalism in Turkey and Egypt were conditioned by many factors, but in all these cases religious nationalism, tinged with political overtones, was a common denominator.

- *Asia: Anticolonial nationalism.* The developmental pattern of nationalism in Asia was mercurial and unpredictable. While varying from country to country, it is distinguished generally by an anti-Western tone. It is quite sensitive to domination from the outside. In Asian nationalism, the psychological motivations of anti-imperialism and anti-colonialism are more stronger than economic drives.

- *Latin America: Populist nationalism.* In Latin America, nationalism had a revolutionary tinge, 'reflecting generations of political change affected by rebellion against established but "temporary" authority' (Snyder 1968: 67). Democracy was utilized only in form: its spirit or deeper meaning did not prevail. Power was reserved for the strongest group, usually the military junta. This process, removed from that of British parliamentary rationalism, was a combination of 'Spanish pride, fickleness and fierce sense of independence'. The party in power often claimed exclusive monopoly of the national image. And the many variants of nationalism had in common the idea of opposing the 'Yankee domination'.

- *The United States: Melting-pot nationalism.* The United States was composed of people who were driven out of their homelands and came to a strange land, becoming in a relatively short period of time more alike than they were different. 'Their nationalism was an amalgam of spiritual idealism (libertarianism and egalitarianism) and materialism (business and industry)' (*ibid.*). Under the influence of the Puritan heritage, American nationalism took on a moralistic tone, a desire to convince the rest of the world that the American form of government was the best on earth and that all other peoples should imitate American virtues and ideals. When the United States took on the leadership role, the core of this nationalism was retained, while added to them were such characteristics as transition from provincialism to nationalism, retreat from autarchic isolationism and anti-communism.

* *The Soviet Union: Messianic nationalism.* The aim of communism in the Soviet Union was to destroy the archaic Czarist society cursed by capitalistic, bourgeois nationalism. Ironically, however, Soviet Russia revived Czarist messianic nationalism in another form. Earlier Czarist nationalism had confined itself to Russification of contiguous areas. The new Soviet nationalism, on the other hand, sought expansion not only in neighbouring countries, but in any weak area of the capitalist world. The Soviet urge for expansion took on the fervour of the Islamic *jihad* against unbelievers.

According to Smith, these general, necessarily overlapping, regional types only serve to point up the global diffusion of nationalism. Nevertheless, they act as a corrective to the Eurocentrism of earlier typologies (1996a: 184).

Another typology, largely forgotten in recent discussions of nationalism (Gellner 1995a: 20), was that of the renowned British historian E. H. Carr. Carr was more interested in delineating the various stages of European nationalism than the ethical value of it. For him, 'the nation is not a "natural" or "biological" group – in the sense, for example, of the family'. It is not a definable and clearly recognizable entity: 'It is confined to certain periods of history and to certain parts of the world' (Carr 1945: 39). Carr concedes that the modern nation has a place and function in the wider society. But, he continues, the claim of nationalism to make the nation 'the sole rightful sovereign repository of political power and the ultimate constituent unit of world organization' has to be challenged and rejected (*ibid.*).

According to Carr, 'the modern history of international relations divides into three partly overlapping periods, marked by widely differing views of the nation as a political entity' (*ibid.*: 1; see also Smith 1996a: 183). The first period began with the gradual dissolution of the medieval unity of empire and church and the establishment of the national state. It was terminated by the French Revolution and the Napoleonic wars. In this period, the nation was identified with the person of the sovereign. International relations were simply relations between kings and princes. Equally characteristic of the period was 'mercantilism', whose aim was not to promote the welfare of the community and its members, but to augment the power of the state – of which the sovereign was the embodiment.

The second period, Carr argues, 'was essentially the product of the French Revolution and, though its foundations were heavily undermined from 1870 onwards, lasted on till the catastrophe of 1914' (1945: 2). This was the most orderly and enviable period of international relations. Its success depended on balancing nationalism and internationalism, and on striking a compromise between political and economic power so that each can develop on its own lines. The diffusion of the idea of popular-democratic nationalism, first formulated by Rousseau, also played a role in this.

The third period, on the other hand, began to take shape at the end of the nineteenth century (after 1870) and reached its culmination between 1914 and 1939. This period was characterized by the catastrophic growth of nationalism and the bankruptcy of internationalism. The reestablishment of national political authority over the economic system – 'a necessary corollary of the socialization of the nation', in the words of Carr (*ibid.*: 27) – was crucial in bringing about this state of affairs.

Carr is not pessimistic about the future of international relations. He believes that the modern nation-state is under attack from within and from without, 'from the standpoint of idealism and from the standpoint of power':

> On the plane of morality, it is under attack from those who denounce its inherently totalitarian implications and proclaim that any international authority worth the name must interest itself in the rights and well-being not of nations but of men and women. On the plane of power, it is being sapped by modern technological developments which have made the nation obsolescent as the unit of military and economic organization and are rapidly concentrating effective decision and control in the hands of great multi-national units. (*Ibid.*: 38)

The future, Carr concludes, depends on the strength of each of these forces and on the nature of the balance that may be struck between them.

In passing, let us note that Carr's typology has been criticized by Smith for failing to allow for the possibility of a wave of anti-colonial nationalisms or renewed European and Third World secession nationalisms. This, according to Smith, reflects the moral and teleological basis of his analysis, as well as its Eurocentrism (1996a: 183). This brings us to the third stage of the theoretical debate on nationalism, heralded by the end of the Second World War.

1945 to the Late 1980s

The experience of decolonization, that is the dissolution of colonial empires and the establishment of new states in Asia and Africa, coupled with general developments in the social sciences, inaugurated the most intensive and prolific period of research on nationalism. The earlier studies of this period were produced under the sway of the modernization school, then ascendant within American social science. This was mainly caused by the incursion of American political scientists into the debate. Actually, political scientists like Apter, Coleman, Binder, Halpern, Pye and Emerson were more interested in the general problems of development than nationalism *per se*. However, the processes of nation-building were central to political and economic development, and it was not possible to study these processes without taking nationalism into account. Smith argues that the contributions of modernization theorists were crucial in that they helped to shift the study of the causes and consequences of nationalism away from its European setting on to a broader, global plane (1983: 258).

The point of departure of modernization theories was the classical sociological distinction between 'traditional' and 'modern' societies. Drawing on this distinction, scholars of the period posited three different stages in the modernization process: tradition, transition and modernity. In these accounts, modernization signified a breakdown of the traditional order and the establishment of a new type of society with new values and new relationships. Smith summarizes this line of argument aptly:

> To survive painful dislocation, societies must institutionalise new
> modes of fulfilling the principles and performing the functions

with which earlier structures can no longer cope. To merit the title, a new 'society' must reconstitute itself in the image of the old . . . Mechanisms of reintegration and stabilisation can ease and facilitate the transition; among them are collective ideologies like nationalism which spring up naturally in periods of social crisis, and appear meaningful and effective for the participants of the situation. (1983: 49–50)

Nationalism, then, has a clear 'function' in these accounts. It can provide identity in a time of rapid change; it can motivate people to work for further change; it can provide guidelines in such fields as the creation of a modern educational system and of a standard 'national' culture (Breuilly 1993a: 418–19). The archetype of such functionalist accounts was Daniel Lerner's *The Passing of a Traditional Society* (1958).

Lerner's book was based on the story of three characters from Balgat, a little village in Turkey, near the capital Ankara (Smith 1983: 89–95). These characters represented the different stages of the modernization process: the village Chief, contented, paternal, fatalistic was the epitome of traditional Turkish values; the Grocer, restless, unsatisfied, was the man of transition; and Tosun, Lerner's informant from the capital city was the man of modernity. The underlying logic was simple: 'all societies must pass from a face-to-face, traditional stage through an ambivalent, uncertain "transition" to reach finally the plateau of the modern, "participant" and national society and culture' (Smith 1983: 90). That there will be a transition to the Western model of society was undisputed: the only thing that mattered was 'pace'. Where did nationalism stand in this picture? Although nationalism only received a passing mention in Lerner's story, it was implicitly there as the ideology of 'Transitionals', to use Smith's term (*ibid.*: 94). It was a natural part of the transition process, an inevitable consequence.

Lerner's account was a typical example of a whole range of theories inspired by the modernization paradigm. All these accounts shared the basic assumption that nationalism was a concomitant of the period of transition, helping to alleviate the sufferings caused by that process. Predictably, functionalist theories of nationalism have been subject to many criticisms. The main objections to such accounts can be summarized as follows:

- Functionalist theories derive explanations from end-states. In these accounts, consequences precede causes and events are treated as wholly beyond the understanding of human agents (O'Leary 1996: 86). This inevitably limits the range of choices initially open to individuals who might respond rationally to their situation, hence redefine and modify it (Minogue 1996: 117; Smith 1983: 51). Smith argues that there are a large number of cases of traditional communities which failed to develop any form of protest when subjected to modernization. Most functionalist accounts, he continues, cannot cope with these exceptions (1983: 51). Moreover, Smith notes that most of the goals that are thought to be served by nationalism are logically and historically posterior to the emergence of a nationalist conceptual framework: thus, they cannot be invoked to explain it.

- Functionalist explanations are too holistic. The functions of nationalism, that is solidarity or modernization, are such large terms that one can hardly connect something as specific as nationalism to them. In the light of this observation, Breuilly asks the following question: 'Is one suggesting that without nationalism these things could not be achieved' (1993a: 419)?

- Functionalist theories cannot explain the variety of historical responses to modernization. Smith asks: 'Why was Pakistan's type of nationalism of the so-called neo-traditional kind, whereas Turkey's was secularist? Why the Bolshevik response in Russia, the Fascist in Italy, the socialist in Yugoslavia and Israel?' (1983: 53).

- There are a multitude of functions which it is suggested nationalism can serve. For some, Breuilly observes, it helps modernization; for others, it helps maintain traditional identities. There is no agreed interpretation: nationalism is associated with different functions in different contexts (1993a: 419).

- Functionalists tend to simplify and reify the ideal-types of 'tradition' and 'modernity'. The reality, however, is much more complex. Moreover, these types are modelled on Western valuations (Smith 1983: 50).

Another variant of the modernization theories is the so-called 'communications approach', generally associated with the idea of 'nation-building'. The most illustrious exponent of this approach was the American political scientist Karl W. Deutsch (1966). Deutsch begins by defining a 'people' as a large group of persons linked by complementary habits and facilities of communication. For Deutsch, '[m]embership in a people essentially consists in wide complementarity of social communication. It consists in the ability to communicate more effectively, and over a wider range of subjects, with members of one large group than with outsiders' (1966: 97). Drawing on these preliminary conceptual clarifications, he proposes a functional definition of nationality:

> In the political and social struggles of the modern age, *nationality*, then, means an alignment of large numbers of individuals from the middle and lower classes linked to regional centers and leading social groups by channels of social communication and economic intercourse, both indirectly from link to link and directly with the center. (*Ibid.*: 101)

In the age of nationalism, nationalities press to acquire a measure of effective control over the behaviour of their members. They strive to equip themselves with power, with some machinery of compulsion strong enough to make the enforcement of commands possible: 'Once a nationality has added this power to compel to its earlier cohesiveness and attachment to group symbols, it often considers itself a *nation* and is so considered by others' (*ibid.*: 104–5). This process is underpinned by a variety of functionally equivalent arrangements. More specifically, what set nation-building in motion were socio-demographic processes like urbanization, mobility, literacy and so on. The communications mechanisms had an important role to play in this scenario. They had to provide new roles, new horizons, strange experiences and imaginings to keep the process going smoothly (Smith 1983: 99).

The communications approach in general and Deutsch's model in particular had their share of criticisms:

*   The crucial defect of this approach, Smith argues, is its omission of the particular context of beliefs, interpretations and interests within which the mass media operate. The mechanisms of communications were always those developed in the West and their effects outside the West were held to be identical to the Western results (1983: 99, 101).

- The conception of mass communication in these theories is uni-dimensional. Communication systems do not convey one single ideology, that is 'modernization', and the messages conveyed are not perceived in the same manner by the individuals that make up a community. In fact, Smith notes, 'exposure to mass communications systems does not automatically carry with it the desire for "modernity" and its benefits' (1983: 101).
- Breuilly remarks that intensified communications between individuals and groups can as often lead to an increase in internal conflict as to an increase in solidarity. Moreover, such conflict or solidarity may be expressed in terms other than nationalist ones. The structures of communication do not indicate what types of conflict and solidarity exist within a particular community and therefore cannot in itself predict what kinds of nationalism will develop (1993a: 406–7).

Deutsch's work gave a fresh impetus to the debate on nationalism. The 1960s saw the burgeoning of interdisciplinary interest in national phenomena, a sudden increase in the number of studies which treated nationalism as a subject in itself and, partly as a result of this, a diversification of theoretical perspectives. It was in this context that the pioneering works of the modernist approach, namely Kedourie's *Nationalism* and Ernest Gellner's *Thought and Change*, were published. Modernist explanations became the dominant orthodoxy in the field until the early 1980s.

Kedourie's conservative attack on nationalism was a milestone in the evolution of the theoretical debate. For him,

> nationalism is a doctrine invented in Europe at the beginning of the nineteenth century ... Briefly, the doctrine holds that humanity is naturally divided into nations, that nations are known by certain characteristics which can be ascertained, and that the only legitimate type of government is national self-government. ([1960] 1994: 1)

As we have seen earlier, Kedourie traces the origins of this doctrine back to German Romantic thought. He explains it in terms of a revolution in European philosophy, showing how this revolution took place and which thinkers have contributed to it. He attaches a great weight in his account to the role played by Kant's epistemological dualism, the organic analogy developed by Fichte and his disciples, and historicism. But the story does not end here. The revolution in ideas, Kedourie holds, was accompanied by an upheaval in social life: 'at the time when the doctrine was being elaborated, Europe was in turmoil . . . Things which had not been thought possible were now seen to be indeed possible and feasible' (1994: 87). At this point, Kedourie draws our attention to the low social status of German romantics whose upward mobility was blocked at the time (Smith 1983: 33). The younger generation was spiritually restless, dissatisfied with things as they were, eager for change. This restlessness was partly caused by the legend of the French Revolution. But what really caused it was 'a breakdown in the transmission of political habits and religious beliefs from one generation to the next' (Kedourie 1994: 94). Kedourie's depiction of this situation is quite vivid:

> The sons rejected the fathers and their ways; but the rejection extended also to the very practices, traditions, and beliefs which had over the centuries moulded and fashioned these societies which suddenly seemed to the young so confining, so graceless, so devoid of spiritual comfort, and so unable to minister to the dignity and fulfilment of the individual. (*Ibid.*: 95)

According to Kedourie, this revolt against old ways can also explain the violent nature of many nationalist movements, because the latter, ostensibly directed against foreigners, were also the manifestation of a clash of generations: 'nationalist movements are children's crusades; their very names are manifestoes against old age: Young Italy, Young Egypt, the Young Turks' (*ibid.*: 96). Such movements satisfied an important need,

> [the need] to belong together in a coherent and stable community. Such a need is normally satisfied by the family, the neighbourhood, the religious community. In the last century and a half such institutions all over the world have had to bear the brunt of violent social and intellectual change, and it is no accident that nationalism was at its most intense where and when such institutions had little resilience and were ill-prepared to withstand the powerful attacks to which they became exposed. (*Ibid.*)

These frustrated, but passionate, young men turned to literature and philosophy which seemed to give way to a nobler world, 'a world more real and more exciting than the real world', failing to notice that philosophical speculation was incompatible with the civil order. However, there was no effective means to control the 'musings' of young men since they were not the fruit of conspiracy: 'They were inherent in the nature of things; they have emanated from the very spirit of the age' (*ibid.*: 100).

'This is a powerful and original thesis', Smith comments (1983: 34). But this originality did not make it immune to criticism. The major objections to Kedourie's account can be summarized as follows:

- Gellner disagrees with Kedourie on the question of Kant's contribution to the doctrine of nationalism. For him, 'Kant is the very last person whose vision could be credited with having contributed to nationalism'. In fact, 'if a connection exists between Kant and nationalism at all, then nationalism is a reaction against him, and not his offspring' (1983: 132, 134). Smith joins Gellner here and argues that even if Kedourie's interpretation of Kant is right, he forgets Kant's debt to Rousseau (1983: 35).

- As noted at the beginning of this section, Gellner argues, *contra* Kedourie, that we shall not learn too much about nationalism by the study of its own prophets (1983: 125). Similarly, Smith accuses Kedourie of 'intellectual determinism'. The social and political factors in Kedourie's account, for example the blocked mobility of the German intelligentsia, the breakdown of traditional ways, are overshadowed by the developments in the intellectual arena: social factors become contributory or intervening variables in what amounts to a single-factor explanation (1983: 37–8).

- Smith objects to Kedourie's use of the 'need to belong', arguing that this factor does not provide an answer to the following questions: 'why only at certain times and places it was the nation which replaced the family, the religious community, the village'; 'why does this need appear to affect some and not others in a given population'; 'how can we measure it in relation to other factors'? Without these answers, Smith concludes, the argument is 'a piece of circular psychologism' (1983: 35). A similar point is made by Breuilly who argues that 'identity needs' cover much more than nationalism. He notes that some of those who have suffered from an identity crisis turned to other ideologies – of class, of religion; some accepted the changes that have taken place and sought simply to advance their interests as much as possible under the new conditions; some turned to drink; and about most we know nothing. He also remarks that nationalism has not received its strongest support from those groups which one would imagine to have been most damaged from an identity crisis (1993a: 417).

- Finally, Smith maintains, Kedourie's model does not explain how ideas have contributed to the breakdown of existing structures. He notes that rapid social change has occurred before the eighteenth century as well. Traditional institutions were always criticized, most of the time by the younger generations. Why, then, did nationalism appear so sporadically in earlier eras? What was unique about the recent onslaught on tradition (1983: 39–40)?

The 1970s have witnessed a new wave of interest in nationalism. The input of neo-Marxist scholars who emphasized the role of economic factors in their accounts was particularly important in that context. Significant contributions of the period include Michael Hechter's *Internal Colonialism: The Celtic Fringe in British National Development, 1536–1966* (1975) and Tom Nairn's *The Break-up of Britain* ([1977] 1981) amongst many others. The debate received a new twist in the 1980s. The works of John Armstrong (1982) and Anthony D. Smith (1986) laid the groundwork for an 'ethno-symbolist' critique of modernist theories. Ironically, the great classics of the modernist approach were also published in this period. Ernest Gellner's *Nations and Nationalism*, Benedict Anderson's *Imagined Communities* and Eric Hobsbawm and Terence Ranger's *The Invention of Tradition*, all published in 1983, set the scene for the ardent – sometimes even polemical – discussions of the last decade (all these theories will be discussed at length in Chapters 4 and 5). With these studies, the debate on nationalism reached its most mature stage.

From the Late 1980s to the Present

I have argued before that we have entered a new stage in the debate on nationalism since the end of the 1980s. This argument will be substantiated at length in Chapter 6 which is devoted to recent approaches. Here, I will briefly consider the following question: what separated the studies of the last decade from those of earlier periods?

The answer is quite simple: some of the studies produced in this period tried to transcend the 'classical' debate – which covered most of the twentieth century and reached its heyday in the last three decades – by questioning the fundamental tenets upon which it is based and by adding new dimensions to the analysis of national phenomena. What underlay these attempts was the belief that the classical debate has become unnecessarily polarized around certain issues, such as the modernity of nations, and failed to address many problems the analysis of which might greatly enhance our understanding of nationalism. For example, mainstream scholars did not attempt to understand why nationhood is still so basic to modern politics and culture. They did offer various explanations of the 'origins' of nations, but they took 'our' nationhood – or, one might say, 'nationhood-in-the-present' – for granted. Not satisfied with such simplistic accounts, a number of recent studies tried to identify 'the factors that lead to the continual production and reproduction of nationalism as a central discursive formation in the modern world' (Calhoun 1997: 123; Billig 1995).

Moreover, the classical debate ignored the experiences of the so-called 'marginal' groups. Ethnic minorities, blacks, women, postcolonial societies could hardly find themselves a place in the mainstream literature. Again, a range of studies produced in the last decade tried to compensate for this decades-long neglect (see for example Chatterjee 1986; Bhabha 1990b; Yuval-Davis 1997).

Finally, the interaction between the studies of nationalism and research conducted in other fields, like diasporas, multiculturalism, identity, migration, citizenship, racism, increased. To this were added the insights gained from alternative epistemological approaches like feminism or postmodernism. These allowed for a richer understanding of the dialectic of national self-identification. In the light of these observations, I think, it can be fairly concluded that we have reached a new stage in the study of nationalism, in fact a stage which promises to be more prolific than the previous ones.

Main Questions, Fundamental Problems

The preceding discussion has suggested that the 'academic' debate
on nationalism reached its most mature stage in the second
half of the twentieth century. Many of the issues discussed in the
literature took shape in that period. In this section, I will try to
identify the main questions around which the contemporary
theoretical debate revolves. These are:

- What is the nation? What is nationalism?
- What are the origins of nations and nationalisms? To what
  extent are they modern phenomena?
- What are the different types of nationalism?

It is important to note at the outset that these are not the only
questions addressed by the scholars of nationalism. However, even
a cursory glance at their writings will reveal that most of the other
issues they explored derive from these three questions. In that
sense, they can be regarded as 'primary' questions, that is questions that most – if not all – theorists address, as opposed to 'secondary', or derivative, questions that appear in particular studies.
Some of these secondary questions will also be mentioned in the
discussion that follows. It should also be stressed that the number
of primary questions and the priority attached to any one of them
varies. While some scholars argue that it is not possible to understand nationalism without first agreeing on basic definitions,
others contend that the most important problem is the relationship of nationalism to the processes of modernization. Still others,
on the other hand, set out to develop typologies, holding that a
theory that will explain various forms of nationalism cannot be
devised. These different viewpoints will also be explored below.

What is the Nation? What is Nationalism?

In a recent essay, Tilley argues that 'most arguments in the academia could be resolved if people would first take the time to define
their terms' (1997: 497). Nowhere is this principle better demon-
strated, she continues, than in the proliferating literature on ethnicity. The same could easily be argued in the case of nationalism.

In fact, this is probably the only point on which there is a general consensus among the scholars of national phenomena. How, then, can we account for this lack of agreement or, to put it differently, for the existence of a plethora of definitions, each stressing a different aspect of their subject-matter?

Walker Connor, an eminent scholar of nationalism who has written extensively on the problems of definition, answers this question by pointing to the widespread misuse of the key terms, in particular the 'interutilization' of the words 'state' and 'nation' (1994: 92). Actually, the origins of this confusion go back to the 1780s, when Jeremy Bentham invented the term 'international' for what we would now call 'interstate relations' (I owe special thanks to Fred Halliday for reminding me of this point). As Connor notes, the tendency to equate nation with state is not restricted to the academia. We can observe its reflections on the political scene, as the misnomers the 'League of Nations' or the 'United Nations' demonstrate (*ibid.*: 97).

What underlies this confusion is the ambiguity of the relationship between 'nation' and other, 'kindred', concepts such as ethnicity, ethnic group and so on. That nationhood is different from other objective criteria forming the basis of individual or collective identities such as class, region, gender, race or religious belief is commonly accepted. But the degree to which each of these elements contributes to the construction of national identities, hence to the definition of the nation, is a source of great controversy. The differences of opinion that exist on this subject are echoed in the competing definitions circulating in the literature. While some scholars emphasize 'objective' criteria like religion, language or race, others stress the importance of 'subjective' criteria such as self-awareness or solidarity in the definition of a nation. Most scholars employ a combination of the two. A similar disagreement exists between those who see the nation as a 'self-defined' (that is self-awareness) entity and those who see it as 'other-defined' (that is recognition by the international community).

The case of nationalism is no more promising. As Breuilly notes, nationalism can refer to ideas, to sentiments and to actions (1993a: 404). Each definition will have different implications for the study of nationalism: those who define it as an idea will focus on the writings and speeches of nationalist intellectuals or activists; those who see it as a sentiment will concentrate on the development of language or other shared ways of life and try to see how these 'folk ways' are taken up by the intelligentsia or the politicians; finally, those who treat nationalism as a movement will focus on political action and conflict (*ibid.*).

On the other hand, Kellas contends that nationalism is both an 'idea' and a 'form of behaviour' (1991: 3). Nationalism is a 'doctrine' for Kedourie (1994: 1), an 'ideological movement' for Smith (1991a: 51), a 'political principle' for Gellner (1983: 1) and a 'discursive formation' for Calhoun (1997: 3).

So far, I have argued that the study of nationalism has been severely impaired by the misuse of the key terms, which is in turn caused by the ambiguous relationship of the concepts of nation and nationalism to kindred concepts – such as ethnicity, ethnic group and so on. However, there are two more factors that exacerbate this situation.

The first is the 'idealist' thinking about nations and nationalism. Mainly advocated by nationalist ideologues, but also taken up by mainstream scholarship until the second half of the twentieth century, this way of thinking saw nations as natural and/or primordial entities. Those who espoused this view mostly shied away from defining the nation – which they took for granted – and embarked on devising typologies (Symmons-Symonolewicz 1985: 215). This approach has been subject to growing criticisms from the 1960s onwards and largely discredited by recent studies of ethnicity and nationalism.

The second factor is the close relationship between the concept of nation and politics. As Calhoun remarks, 'the notion of nation is so deeply imbricated in modern politics as to be "essentially contested", because any definition will legitimate some claims and delegitimate others' (1993: 215). Scientific knowledge, methodologies, definitions do not evolve in a socio-historical vacuum (MacLaughlin 1987). Scholars are inevitably affected by the political context in which they develop their ideas, hence the definitions they formulate reflect an intricate complex of interests and relationships. Breuilly sums this up brilliantly: 'the sheer universality and apparent power of nationalism has created a vast range of cases and vested interests which make it difficult to agree upon basic approaches to the subject' (1985: 65).

This brief discussion shows clearly that 'imprecise vocabulary' continues to sabotage our efforts to understand nationalism. Given the abundance of definitions and the lack of general agreement on any one of them, I have refrained from prioritizing any one definition in the course of this discussion. I have also tried to keep the number of examples at a minimum since many competing definitions of the concepts of nation and nationalism will be provided in the following chapters.

What are the Origins of Nations and Nationalisms? To what Extent are they Modern Phenomena?

The second key question addressed by the scholars concerns the origins and the nature of national phenomena. This question is the forebear of a large number of secondary questions: What is the relationship between nationalism and the processes of modernization? In other words, to what extent are nations and nationalisms the products of modern conditions such as capitalism, industrialization, urbanization and secularism? How did the rise of the modern state affect the emergence of nationalism? How do modern nations relate to pre-modern ethnic communities? Are nations just the lineal descendants of their medieval counterparts? Or are they the recent creations of a nationalist intelligentsia frustrated by the vagaries of the *ancien régime*? Is nationalism a kind of 'myth' invented and propagated by elites who then use it to mobilize the masses in support of their struggle to get or maintain power? Is it a kind of 'opium' diverting the masses from fulfilling their true selves?

One can multiply these questions. But the point is that all these secondary questions derive from the same basic dilemma: to what extent are nations and nationalisms modern phenomena? The attempts to resolve this dilemma have laid the foundations of arguably the most fundamental divide of the theoretical debate on nationalism, namely that between the 'primordialists' and the 'modernists'. Broadly speaking, those who think that nations are 'perennial' entities fall within the former category and those who believe in the modernity of nations and nationalism fall within the latter. This classification is widely accepted in today's literature. The labels attached to the categories may vary: some prefer the term 'essentialist' in place of 'primordialist'; others opt for the epithet 'instrumentalist' or 'constructivist' instead of 'modernist'.

But the description of the categories and the logic of classification remain the same. It should be pointed out that a third category has been added to this classification in recent years. This category consists of 'ethno-symbolists' who portray their position as a middle way between these two polar opposites. Very briefly, ethno-symbolists stress the durability of pre-modern ethnic ties and show how ethnic cultures set limits to elite attempts to forge the nation.

It is important to stress that not all scholars are content with the conventional classification. For example, Conversi (1995) introduces a five-tiered classification with the addition of 'homeostatic' and 'transactionalist' approaches to the categories I have mentioned above. On the other hand, there are also scholars who insist in keeping the twofold classification by merging the ethno-symbolists into the primordialists (see for example Breuilly 1996: 150). In the remainder of the book, I will follow the conventional threefold classification, mainly to represent the general tendency in the field. However, I will also review the criticisms levelled against this classification and introduce my own categorization in the concluding chapter.

What are the Different Types of Nationalism (if any)?

The final question concerns the varieties of nationalism. As we have seen earlier in this chapter, this was in fact the only question addressed by a whole generation of scholars, and the classificatory schemes developed by Kohn, Hayes and Snyder were discussed in that context. However, typologies are not peculiar to first-generation studies. Arguing that no single, universal theory of nationalism is possible, some scholars continue to espouse the view that the best way to deal with nationalism is to develop typologies (for example Hall 1993). In their view, nationalism is a chameleon-like phenomenon, capable of assuming a variety of ideological forms. It is not possible to account for all these variations in a single, 'grand' theory. However, this should not condemn us to complete particularism: 'to the contrary, middle ground can be cultivated by delineating various ideal types of nationalism' (Hall 1993: 1).

Predictably, typologies abound in the literature, even if we leave the earlier ones aside. Here, I will just enumerate a few examples: Smith follows Kohn's lead and draws a distinction between a

'Western' civic-territorial model of the nation which produces 'territorial' nationalisms and an 'Eastern' ethnic-genealogical model which produces 'ethnic' nationalisms (1991a: 79–84). Breuilly identifies three categories on the basis of the relationship between the nationalist movement and the state to which it either opposes or controls: 'separation', 'reform' and 'unification'. He then divides each of these categories into two sub-categories according to the nature of the political entity that is opposed, that is 'opposed to non-nation-states' and 'opposed to nation-states' (1993a: 9); Hall introduces a classification that consists of five categories on the basis of the characteristic logic and social underpinning of various forms of nationalism. The titles he chooses for his categories are rather singular: 'the logic of the asocial society', 'revolution from above', 'desire and fear blessed by opportunity', 'risorgimento nationalism', 'integral nationalism' (1993). Alter identifies three varieties, namely 'risorgimento', 'reform' and 'integral' nationalisms (1989). Finally, Sugar distinguishes four types of nationalism in Eastern Europe: 'bourgeois', 'aristocratic', 'popular' and 'bureaucratic' nationalisms.

This list can be doubled or even tripled. But such an exhaustive list would not be helpful at this stage. More examples will be given when discussing the particular theories. Suffice it to say that almost all scholars recognize the multifarious nature of nationalism, while some go one step further and argue that sorting the different types according to their intrinsic features is all that can be achieved theoretically.

Further Reading

There is a vast literature on nationalist ideology. The best source on the genesis of the idea of nationalism, however, is still Kedourie (1994), originally published in 1960. Kedourie's book suffers from an overemphasis on the role of intellectuals, especially the German Romantics, but is very useful for all that. For Rousseau's ideas on patriotism and citizenship see Barnard (1984); for a comparison of Rousseau and Herder see Barnard (1983). Historians' responses to nationalism are the subject of an insightful article by Smith (1996a) [1992]. For Mill's reflections on nationality see the short extract in Woolf (1996) [1861].

The relationship between Marxism and nationalism has been the subject of a heated debate for the last three or four decades. A survey of the controversy can be found in Munck (1986) and Nimni (1991). On Austrian Social Democrats see Stargardt (1995), who not only provides a review of their main ideas, but also presents a vivid description of the social and political context which shaped these ideas. The reader should also consult Bauer (1996) [1924], the first chapter of his classic *Die Nationalitätenfrage und die Sozialdemokratie*, for one of the earliest attempts to theorize nationalism within the Marxist camp.

The famous lecture Renan delivered in 1882 can now be found in English: see Bhabha (1990b). For Durkheim and Weber see Guibernau (1996), chapter 1 and James (1996), chapter 4. A concise summary of the relevance of their ideas for the studies of subsequent periods is given in Smith (1998): 13–16.

As we have seen earlier, the first half of the twentieth century witnessed the rise of a number of general historical studies on nationalism. Of these, the following are still relevant: Hayes (1955) [1931], Kohn (1967) [1944] and Carr (1945).

For the modernization theories of the 1950s and 1960s, the work to consult is Smith (1983), originally published in 1971. Smith offers a comprehensive overview of the main theories of nation-building, together with a balanced criticism of them. Among primary sources, Deutsch (1966) [1953], regarded by many as the classic example of the communications approach, and Kedourie (1994) [1960], one of the pioneering works of the modernist paradigm, should be mentioned.

3

Primordialism

Our nationality is like our relations to women: too implicated in our moral nature to be changed honourably, and too accidental to be worth changing.

George Santayana (quoted in Gellner 1983)

What is Primordialism?

The earliest paradigm of nations and nationalism is the primordialist. To begin with, primordialism is an approach, not a theory. It is an 'umbrella' term used to describe scholars who hold that nationality is a 'natural' part of human beings, as natural as speech, sight or smell, and that nations have existed since time immemorial. In that respect, it is not different from the terms 'modernist' or 'ethno-symbolist', which are all used to classify various theories with regard to their common characteristics, thereby enabling researchers to compare them systematically.

The common denominator of the modernists is their conviction in the modernity of nations and nationalism; that of the ethno-symbolists is the stress they lay in their explanations on ethnic pasts and cultures; finally, that of the primordialists is their belief in the antiquity and naturalness of nations. Beyond these common denominators, the theories developed by the scholars of each category exhibit a bewildering diversity. Nevertheless, when we take a quick glance at the literature on nationalism, we notice that the primordialists are treated as a more homogeneous category than, say, the modernists. The shallowness of this view has been

64

revealed by recent debates on ethnicity. The primordialists are not unlike the modernists or any other category in terms of the diversity they harbour. I will turn to these differences in a while, but let us first focus on the term 'primordialism' itself.

The term comes from the adjective 'primordial' which is defined in three ways: 'first in order of time, original, elemental'; 'first in order of appearance in the growth or development of an organism (biological meaning)'; and 'an elementary principle, first, primeval, transcending' (*The New International Webster's Comprehensive Dictionary of the English Language*, 1996 edn). It is generally thought that Edward Shils is the first one to have employed this term. In his famous 1957 article, Shils uses the term 'in reference to relationships within the family' (Eller and Coughlan 1993: 184). He argues that the strength of the attachments one feels for her/his family members does not stem from interaction, but from 'a certain ineffable significance . . . attributed to the tie of blood' (Shils 1957: 142). For Shils, these attachments could only be described as 'primordial'. Shils states that his conceptualization of primordial relations was influenced by several books on the sociology of religion, notably by A. D. Nock's *Conversion* and Martin P. Nilsson's *Greek Popular Religion*. Eller and Coughlan argue that this might also explain the mystical and spiritual language he uses to describe the attachments to family and kin (1993: 184). Clifford Geertz, another name identified with primordialism, uses a similar definition:

> By a primordial attachment is meant one that stems from the 'givens' – or, more precisely, as culture is inevitably involved in such matters, the assumed 'givens' – of social existence: immediate contiguity and kin connection mainly, but beyond them the givenness that stems from being born into a particular religious community, speaking a particular language, or even a dialect of a language, and following particular social practices. These congruities of blood, speech, custom, and so on, are seen to have an ineffable, and at times overpowering, coerciveness in and of themselves. (Geertz 1993: 259)

It needs to be stressed at the outset that we cannot consider primordialist accounts of nationalism independently from the debate on ethnicity. Primordialist arguments are first formulated to explain the origins and strength of ethnic identities. Thus, both Shils and Geertz use the term 'primordial' to describe the nature of ethnic attachments. This led some writers to suggest that there are in fact two separate debates, one over the antiquity of nations between the 'perennialists' and the 'modernists' and another over the nature of ethnic ties between the 'primordialists' and the 'instrumentalists' (Smith 1994: 376). This confusion inevitably reflects on the discussions of primordialism. In what follows, I will try to separate these debates as much as possible and try to show how, that is in which meanings, the term is imported from the literature on ethnicity.

I have already noted that the primordialists do not form a monolithic category. Thus, it is possible to identify three different versions of primordialism. For the sake of a more systematic presentation, I will call them the 'naturalist', 'sociobiological' and 'culturalist' approaches. The classification I will use here is inspired by Smith's recent works (1994: 376–7; 1995: 31–3; 1998: chapter 7). Another classification is developed by Tilley (1997). She divides the primordialist approaches again into three categories and calls them the 'biological', 'psychological' and 'cultural' approaches. However, Tilley's classification is designed for ethnic identities and based on different definitions than the ones adopted here.

The Naturalist Approach

This approach, which can be considered as the most extreme version of primordialism, asserts that national identities are a 'natural' part of all human beings, just like speech or sight: a man has a nationality as he has a nose and two ears (Gellner 1983: 6). The nation to which one belongs is predetermined, 'naturally fixed': in other words, one is born into a nation in the same way s/he is born into a family (Smith 1995: 31). The division of humanity into different groups with different cultural characteristics is part of the natural order and these groups will tend to exclude others (Lieven 1997: 12). Those who subscribe to this view hold that nations have 'natural frontiers', hence, 'a specific origin and place in nature, as well as a peculiar character, mission and destiny' (Smith 1995: 32). As Smith notes, the naturalists do not make a distinction between nations and ethnic groups. Nationalism is an attribute of humanity in all ages (*ibid.*).

Not surprisingly, this is the view endorsed by most, if not all, nationalists. Since the nineteenth century, this 'ideological view of the past', to use Hutchinson's words (1994), has continued to shape the works of nationalist historians and the rhetoric of elites who were struggling to get or maintain state power. Thus, historians like Frantisek Palacky, Eoin MacNeill and Nicolae Iorga, all influential figures in their respective national movements, claimed that nations were primordial entities that 'were objectively identifiable through their distinctive way of life, their attachment to a territorial homeland, and their striving for political autonomy' (Hutchinson 1994: 3). According to them, the past was the story of the nation's perpetual struggle for self-realization.

There are a number of recurrent themes in every nationalist narrative. Let me briefly illustrate some of these themes with the help of an essay by the Turkish patriot Tekin Alp [Moise Cohen], taken from Kedourie's *Nationalism in Asia and Africa* (1971). First, there is the theme of the antiquity of the ('particular') nation:

> . . . it was high time to make the whole world, and to begin with the Turks themselves, understand that Turkish history does not begin with Osman's tribe, but in fact twelve thousand years before Jesus Christ . . . The exploits of the Osmanlı Turks constitute merely one episode in the history of the Turkish nation which has founded several other empires. (*Ibid.*: 210)

Second, there is the theme of golden age:

> Whilst the rest of humanity was living in caves, leading a most primitive life, the Turk had already in his motherland become civilized enough to know the use of wood and metal . . . At a time when the Turks had reached a high level of culture in their own motherland, the peoples of Europe were still in a savage state and lived in complete ignorance. (*Ibid.*: 216, 219)

Third, there is the theme of the superiority of the national culture:

> '[i]f the Turks had not entered Muslim society, the civilization which we call Islamic would not have existed . . . It is because the

Turks who created this movement were superior to the other Muslim peoples from the point of view of culture and civilization. (*Ibid.*: 221)

Fourth, there is the theme of periods of recess, or in Gellner's words 'periods of somnolence' (1997: 93):

> ... the Turks were agents of culture and progress, and ... they have never ceased to be such except when subjugated by foreign cultures and moral forces. The civilized nations must not take into account this short period of decadence, when the Turkish people were acting out of character' (Kedourie 1971: 210).

Finally, there is the theme of the national hero, who comes and awakens the nation, ending this 'accidental' period of decadence:

> He [Kemal Atatürk] could not tolerate therefore this false conception of Turkish history which was current among some of the Turkish intellectuals ... He has therefore taken it into his head to eliminate it by means of a revolutionary outburst which would subject it to the same fate as the other misconceptions from which the Turkish people have suffered for centuries. (*Ibid.*: 211)

As I have alluded to above, Smith distinguishes two separable claims within the naturalist version of primordialism. Some writers suggest that nations have existed since time immemorial without subscribing to the view that they result from any kind of 'primordial' ties (Smith 1984). Smith introduces the term 'perennialism' to cover this less radical version of primordialism. The term comes from the adjective 'perennial', which means 'continuing or enduring through the year or through many years' and 'growing continuously, surviving' (*The New International Webster's Comprehensive Dictionary of the English Language*, 1996 edn): hence the name 'perennialist' for those who see nations as historic entities which have developed over the centuries, with their intrinsic characteristics largely unchanged (Halliday 1997a; Smith 1984, 1995). Smith maintains that perennialists need not be primordialists since it is possible to concede the antiquity of ethnic and national ties without holding that they are 'natural'.

One of the core ideas of perennialism is that 'modern nations are the lineal descendants of their medieval counterparts' (Smith 1995: 53). According to this view, we might come across nations in the Middle Ages, even in the antiquity. Modernity, 'for all its technological or economic progress, has not affected the basic structures of human association'; on the contrary, it is the nation and nationalism which engenders modernity (*ibid.*). The perennialists concede that nations may experience periods of recess or decadence in the course of their historical journey: but 'bad fortune' cannot destroy the national 'essence'. All that is necessary is to 'rekindle the fires of nationalism', to reawaken the nation. Minogue uses the metaphor of the Sleeping Beauty to depict this view: the nation is the Sleeping Beauty who awaits a kiss to be revived, and the nationalists are the prince who will provide this 'magical' kiss (Smith 1995: 168).

Smith's distinction between primordialism and perennialism seems to be a useful one. There are, indeed, very few students of nationalism who continue to endorse the 'bedrock' primordialist position. In the words of Brubaker, 'no serious scholar today holds the view that is routinely attributed to primordialists in straw-man setups, namely that nations or ethnic groups are primordial, unchanging entities' (1996: 15). On the other hand, it is always possible to find scholars who believe in the antiquity of nations and nationalism.

The question of 'who can be considered as a perennialist in the literature on nationalism' has been the subject of much controversy. For example, Smith treats John Armstrong as a perennialist (Smith 1984), whereas Armstrong is regarded by many scholars as the pioneer of ethno-symbolism. This controversy stems partly from definitional problems, whose resolution depends on how we classify scholars who maintain that the formation of nations should be examined in *la longue durée*. If we decide that the latter approach is ethno-symbolism, then we should place scholars like Armstrong and Llobera in the same category as Smith. If, on the other hand, we conclude that such a perspective is perennialist, then we should consider Smith as a perennialist as well. There are in fact scholars who adopt this latter position (Breuilly 1996). Let me conclude this sub-section with the views of two scholars from the perennialist camp, Josep R. Llobera (1994) and Adrian Hastings (1997).

Perennialists do not identify a specific date of birth for nationalism. Thus, while Llobera traces the origins of nations back to the Middle Ages (1994: 219–21), Hastings argues that national consciousness has been shaped in England – the first nation according to him – between the fourteenth and sixteenth centuries (1997: 5). More specifically, Llobera holds that only if we adopt a very restricted definition of nationalism can we conclude that it is a recent phenomenon and claims that a rudimentary sense of national identity existed already in the medieval period (1994: 220). Hastings, on the other hand, argues that it is possible to identify English nationalism of a sort in the fourteenth century, especially in the long wars with France and contends that this nationalism has completed its development in the sixteenth and seventeenth centuries (1997: 5). These examples reveal clearly that for perennialist writers the origins of both nations and nationalism stretch back to the medieval period – that is, well beyond the modern ages. The 'essence' which differentiates any particular nation from others manages to remain intact despite all vicissitudes of history. To focus exclusively on the modern period, that is on the last two centuries, in order to understand the processes of nation formation is in this context 'a recipe for sociological disaster' (Llobera 1994: 3).

The Sociobiological Approach

The sociobiological approach to nationalism has gained new momentum in recent years with the works of a range of scholars who have applied the findings of the new field of sociobiology to the study of ethnic ties. The basic question asked by sociobiology is: 'why are animals social, that is, why do they cooperate?' (van den Berghe 1978: 402). According to Pierre van den Berghe, the leading exponent of this approach in the literature on nationalism, the answer to this question was long intuitively known: 'animals are social to the extent that cooperation is mutually beneficial'. What sociobiology does, van den Berghe argues, is to supply the main genetic mechanism for animal sociality, namely kin selection to increase inclusive fitness:

> an animal can duplicate its genes directly through its own reproduction, or indirectly through the reproduction of relatives with

which it shares specific proportions of genes. Animals, therefore, can be expected to behave cooperatively, and thereby enhance each other's fitness to the extent that they are genetically related. This is what is meant by kin selection. (*Ibid.*: 402)

Van den Berghe claims that kin selection, or mating with relatives, is a powerful cement of sociality in humans too. In fact, both ethnicity and race are extensions of the idiom of kinship: 'therefore, ethnic and race sentiments are to be understood as an extended and attenuated form of kin selection' (*ibid.*: 403). That the extended kinship is sometimes putative rather than real is not important. Just as in the smaller kin units, the kinship is often real enough 'to become the basis of these powerful sentiments we call nationalism, tribalism, racism, and ethnocentrism' (*ibid.*: 404). If that is the case, then how do we recognize our 'kin'? According to van den Berghe, 'only a few of the world's societies use primarily morphological phenotypes to define themselves'. It follows that cultural criteria of group membership are more salient than physical ones, if the latter is used at all. In a way, this is inevitable because neighbouring populations resemble each other in terms of their genetic composition. Eye color in Europe, van den Berghe notes, is a good case in point. The further north one goes, the higher the proportion of lightly pigmented eyes. 'Yet, at no point in the journey is there a noticeable discontinuity'. The criteria for identifying kinsmen, on the other hand, should discriminate more reliably between groups than within groups. In other words, 'the criterion chosen must show more *inter*group than *intra*-group variance'. Cultural criteria, like differences of accent, body adornment and the like, meet this requirement far more reliably than physical ones (*ibid.*: 406–7).

Noting that kin selection does not explain all of human sociality, van den Berghe identifies two additional mechanisms: reciprocity and coercion. 'Reciprocity is cooperation for mutual benefit, and with expectation of return, and it can operate between kin or between non-kin. Coercion is the use of force for one-sided benefit'. All human societies continue to be organized on the basis of all three principles of sociality. But, van den Berghe adds, 'the larger and the more complex a society becomes, the greater the importance of reciprocity'. (*ibid.*: 403) Moreover, while kin selection – real or putative – is more dominant in intra-group relations, coercion becomes the rule in inter-ethnic (or inter-racial) relationships. Ethnic groups may occasionally enter into a symbiotic, mutually beneficial relationship (reciprocity) but this is usually short-lived: relations between different groups are more often than not antagonistic (*ibid.*: 409).

The Culturalist Approach

This approach, which might also be called 'cultural primordialism', is generally associated with the works of Edward Shils and Clifford Geertz. Eller and Coughlan argue that the concept of primordialism used in the works of these writers contains three main ideas:

1. Primordial identities or attachments are 'given', *a priori*, underived, prior to all experience and interaction – in fact, all interaction is carried out *within* primordial realities. Primordial attachments are 'natural', even 'spiritual', rather than sociological . . . [T]hey have no social source. Accordingly, those things called primordial presumably have long histories.
2. Primordial sentiments are 'ineffable', overpowering, and coercive . . . If an individual is a member of a group, he or she *necessarily* feels certain attachments to that group and its practices (especially language and culture).
3. Primordialism is essentially a question of emotion and affect (1993: 187).

These arguments have revealed a misinterpretation – caused by a careless reading of Geertz and Shils – which went largely unnoticed for many years and led to a highly polemical discussion (see for example Grosby 1994; Tilley 1997). As might be recalled, Geertz cites the congruities of blood, language, religion and particular social practices among the objects of ethnic attachments. Contrary to Eller and Coughlan's formulations, however, Geertz never suggests that these objects are themselves 'given' or primordial: rather, they are 'assumed' to be given by individuals. What attributes the quality of being 'natural' or mystical to the 'givens of social existence' are the perceptions of those who believe in them. In the words of Smith,

Geertz is underlining the power of what we might term a 'participants' primordialism'; he is not saying that the world is constituted by an objective primordial reality, only that many of us believe in primordial objects and feel their power. (1998: 158)

As Tilley forcefully argues, Geertz's approach to culture can in fact be considered as 'constructivist'. Nothing illustrates this better than these words she takes from *The Interpretation of Cultures*:

Believing with Max Weber, that man is an animal suspended in webs of significance he himself has spun, I take culture to be those webs, and the analysis of it to be therefore not an experimental science in search of law but an interpretative one in search of meaning. (1993: 5)

The same goes for Shils. Eller and Coughlan infer from Shils' 1957 essay that he believes in the sacredness of primordial attachments. The evidence, they contend, is provided by his following assertion: 'the primordial property . . . could have had sacredness attributed to it' (Shils 1957: 142). But, like Geertz, Shils did not attribute sacredness to these attachments (Tilley 1997). Instead, he noted that the attachment derives his strength from 'a certain ineffable significance . . . *attributed* to the tie of blood' (Shils 1957: 142, emphasis added). Ironically enough, Eller and Coughlan refer to these words as well, before reaching their final verdict on Shils. Here, it should be noted that Eller and Coughlan are not the only ones who have fallen prey to this misconception; many scholars have taken their share of the confusion (see for example Brass 1991).

Cultural primordialism in a Geertzian way, then, may be defined as an approach which focuses on the webs of meaning spun by the individuals themselves. As Tilley explains convincingly, Geertz is in fact 'making use of the term "primordial" more in its sense of "first in a series" . . . in order to highlight the ways in which foundation concepts provide the basis for other ideas, values, customs or ideologies held by the individual' (1997: 502).

Such a definition enables me to advance a somewhat controversial claim, namely that some scholars who advance a 'subjective' definition of the nation might also be considered as cultural primordialists. One example might be Walker Connor who defines the nation as 'a group of people who *feel* that they are ancestrally related.' Connor continues: 'It is the largest group that can command a person's loyalty because of *felt* kinship ties; it is, from this perspective, the fully extended family' (Connor 1994: 202, emphases added). Now, Connor is seen by many scholars as a modernist (for example Hutchinson 1994). In a way this is true, since he explicitly rejects the claim that nations have existed in the Middle Ages (Connor 1994: 210–27), but this does not contradict with the definition of 'cultural primordialism' I have proposed above. Such a definition does not specify any date for the emergence of nations and/or nationalism – neither did Geertz. It only states that individuals do feel attached to certain elements of their culture, assuming that they are 'given', 'sacred' and 'underived'. The approach, then, deals with perceptions and beliefs. This is also what Connor chooses to stress as the above quotation demonstrates. In the same essay, he suggests that what influences attitudes and behaviour is not 'what is' but 'what people perceive as is' (1994: 197). This, I think, makes him a cultural primordialist in the sense I have specified above.

Let me briefly recapitulate what I have said so far before moving on to the criticisms raised against primordialist explanations. Apart from the *naturalist approach* characterizing the writings of nationalists, primordialism appears in three different forms in the literature on nationalism. *Perennialists* argue that nations have always existed and that modern nations are nothing but the extensions of their medieval counterparts. *Sociobiologists* seek the origins of ethnic and national ties in genetic mechanisms and instincts, treating the nation as an extension of the idiom of kinship, or a kind of superfamily. Finally, *cultural primordialists* focus on the perceptions and beliefs of the individuals. What generates the strong attachments people feel for the 'givens of social existence', the culturalists contend, is a belief in their 'sacredness'.

A Critique of Primordialism

Several objections have been raised against the primordialist approach. For the sake of clarity, I will mainly focus on the general criticisms, only mentioning the particular charges brought against the different versions of primordialism when necessary. This will also enable me to avoid the risk of ending up with an exhausting list. The criticisms I will discuss relate to five aspects of primordialist explanations: the nature of ethnic and national ties, the origins of ethnic and national ties, the relationship of ethnic and national bonds with other types of personal attachments, the question of emotion and affect, the date of the emergence of nations.

The Nature of Ethnic and National Ties

One common denominator of the primordialists – with the exception of culturalists – is their belief in the 'givenness' of ethnic and national ties. If the strong attachments generated by language, religion, kinship and the like are given by nature, then they are also fixed, or static. They are transmitted from one generation to the next with their 'essential' characteristics unchanged. In other words, what we witness today is merely a reassertion of the national essence. This view is challenged in recent years by an ever-growing number of studies on ethnicity. These studies stress the role of individual choice in the construction of ethnic identities, claiming that 'far from being self-perpetuating, they require creative effort and investment' (Hoben and Hefner 1990, cited in Eller and Coughlan 1993: 188). They are redefined and reconstructed in each generation as groups react to changing conditions. It follows that the content and boundaries of ethnic identities are fluid, not fixed. Eller and Coughlan, following Nagel, suggest that the recent studies provide a compelling case for seeing ethnicity as 'a socially constructed, variable definition of self and other, whose existence and meaning is continuously negotiated, revised and revitalized' (Nagel 1991, cited in Eller and Coughlan 1993: 188).

A similar argument comes from Brass, who espouses an 'instrumental' approach to ethnicity (1991: 70–2). For him, some primordial attachments are clearly variable. To begin with, Brass contends, many people speak more than one language, dialect or code in multilingual developing societies. Many illiterate people in these countries, far from being attached to their mother tongues, will not even know its name when asked. In some cases, members of different ethnic groups will choose to change their language in order to provide better opportunities for their children or to differentiate themselves further from other ethnic groups. Finally, Brass argues, many people never think about their language anyway, nor do they attach to it any emotional significance.

The situation is not different for other sources of ethnic and national attachments. Religions too have been subject to many changes over the centuries. Brass holds that 'shifts in religious practices brought about under the influence of religious reformers are common occurrences in pre-modern, modernizing, and even in postindustrial societies' (*ibid.*: 71). Moreover, some people in cosmopolitan settings have engaged themselves in alternative spiritual quests. As for the place of birth, it can be conceded that one's homeland is still important for some people; but, Brass remarks, many people have migrated by choice from their native places and a considerable proportion of them have chosen to assimilate to their new society and have lost any sense of identification with their homelands. More importantly, a person's attachment to her/his region or homeland rarely becomes politically significant unless there is some degree of perceived discrimination against the region or its people in the larger society. Besides, even the fact of one's place of birth is subject to variation since a region may be defined in many ways. When it comes to kinship connections, Brass claims that 'the range of genuine kin relationships is usually too small to be of political significance' (*ibid.*). 'Fictive' kin relationships may extend the range of ethnic groups but the fact that they are fictive presumes their variability by definition. Moreover, the meaning of such fictive relationships will naturally vary from person to person since the 'imagined' character of the attachment will be dominant in these relationships.

On the other hand, Smith argues that 'ethnic ties like other social bonds are subject to economic, social and political forces, and therefore fluctuate and change according to circumstances' (1995: 33). Intermarriages, migrations, external conquests and the importation of labour have made it very unlikely for many ethnic groups to preserve 'the cultural homogeneity and pure "essence" posited by most primordialists' (*ibid.*).

Some primordialists concede that the boundaries and content of ethnic identities may change in time. But they insist that the 'essence' of the ethnic culture, for example its origin myths and symbols, persists through time. According to Brass, even this bedrock position poses a number of problems. He claims that except for certain ethnic groups which have rich cultural heritages like the Jews, many movements create their cultures 'after-the-fact'. These movements were not any less successful in generating cohesion and solidarity than those of the groups with a richer cultural heritage. He cites the 'mushroom growth' of ethnic political movements in the United States to illustrate this point (1991: 72–3). Eller and Coughlan argue the same for the new ethnic groups appearing under colonial rule. They note that in many parts of the world, especially in Africa, 'new ethnic identities and groups are being created which claim, and receive from some researchers, primordial status. These new primordials (a shocking contradiction in terms) are "made", not "given"' (1993: 188). In most of these cases, the appropriate cultural givens were lacking, so they were often constructed (Kasfir 1979, cited in Eller and Coughlan 1993: 188).

In short, then, the assumption that primordial attachments and the cultural sources that generate them are 'given' does not square with facts. It should be stressed that this criticism is not the preserve of instrumentalist scholars: as we have seen, ethnosymbolists, notably Smith, express similar concerns.

The Origins of Ethnic and National Ties

Another fundamental claim of the primordialists (with the exception of cultural primordialists) is that ethnic and national attachments are 'underived', hence prior to all social interaction. This automatically creates a mystical aura around them: primordial sentiments are ineffable, that is 'incapable of being expressed in words', thus unanalysable. Eller and Coughlan claim that 'primordialism has tended to treat the identification of "primordial" attachments as the successful and inevitable end of analysis' (1993: 189).

Brass disagrees with this primordialist assertion. He argues that the knowledge of ethnic cultures does not enable us to predict either which ethnic groups will develop a successful political movement or the form this movement will assume. He cites the creations of Israel and Pakistan as examples. According to Brass, a knowledge of orthodox Judaism or traditional Islam in India would have suggested that the least likely possibilities would have been the rise of a Zionist movement or the movement for the creation of Pakistan since the traditional religious authorities in both cases were opposed to a secular state (1991: 73). A similar point is raised by Breuilly who argues that the use of ethnic cultures in a nationalist manner will transform their meanings. He suggests that 'it is the way in which nationalism constructs identities anew, even if that construction involves appeals to history and culture and sees itself as discovery rather than construction, to which one must pay attention' (1993a: 406).

Zubaida joins Brass and Breuilly by arguing that there is no systematic way of designating a nation (1978: 53). He raises the question 'why does India constitute a "nation" while the old Ottoman Empire, arguably with greater homogeneity than modern India, did not?'. The answer, he maintains, lies in historical conjunctures: 'There is no systematic way in which any social theoretical discourse can justify the state of nationhood in the one case and deny it in the other' (*ibid.*).

Gellner approaches this problem in his own remarkable way (1996b; 1997: chapter 15). For him, the crucial question is: 'do nations have navels?' The analogy here is with the philosophical argument about the creation of mankind (McCrone 1998: 15). If Adam was created by God at a certain date, then he did not have a navel, because he did not go through the process by which people acquire navels. The same goes with nations, says Gellner. The ethnic, the cultural national community is rather like the navel. 'Some nations have it and some don't and in any case it's inessential' (1996b: 367). If modernism tells half the story, that for him is good enough, because 'the additional bits of the story in the other half are redundant' (*ibid.*: 370). He refers to the Estonians to illustrate his argument. The Estonians, he argues, are a clear example of highly successful navel-free nationalism (1997: 96–7):

> At the beginning of the nineteenth century they didn't even have a name for themselves. They were just referred to as people who lived on the land as opposed to German or Swedish burghers and aristocrats and Russian administrators. They had no ethnonym. They were just a category without any ethnic self-consciousness. Since then they've been brilliantly successful in creating a vibrant culture . . . It's a very vital and vibrant culture, but it was created by the kind of modernist process which I then generalise for nationalism and nations in general. (1996b: 367–8)

Let us note in passing that this criticism is valid in the case of socio-biological explanations as well. These accounts, based on such presumably 'universal' factors as blood ties, kinship relationships, are not able to explain why only a small proportion of ethnic groups become aware of their common identity, while others disappear in the mists of history. If we accept that ethnic groups are extensions of the idiom of kinship, that is superfamilies, then this has to be valid in the case of all ethnic groups. But as some scholars have underlined, for every successful nationalist movement there are *n* unsuccessful ones (Gellner 1983: 44–5; Halliday 1997a: 16). Why do some groups effectively establish their own political roof, while others fail? Sociobiological explanations are silent on this issue. Moreover, Smith notes, the mechanisms proposed by sociobiologists do not explain 'why the quest for individual reproductive success should move beyond the extended family to much wider cultural units like *ethnies*' (1995: 33).

The Relationship of Ethnic and National Bonds with Other Types of Personal Attachments

Another objection raised against the primordialists concerns their tendency to give priority to ethnic and national identities among other forms of identity. Smith argues that 'human beings live in a multiplicity of social groups, some of which are more significant and salient than others at various times' (1995: 33). Individuals have multiple identities and roles – familial, territorial, class, religious, ethnic and gender (Smith 1991a: 4). These categories sometimes overlap and/or complement each other; at other times, they clash. It is not possible to predict which identity will be dominant at a particular point in time. The salience of each category changes according to circumstances.

The Question of Emotion and Affect

Primordialism is about emotions and affect. Even the terminology used reflects this: attachment, bond, tie, sentiment. The affect dimension makes primordial identities qualitatively different from other kinds of identities, such as those of class (Eller and Coughlan 1993: 187).

Eller and Coughlan, while recognizing the important role emotions play in human social life, object to their mystification. They argue that the mystification of the primordial has led to a fallacy, namely the desocializing of the phenomenon. It is suggested that these emotional ties are not born in social interaction, but are just there, 'implicit in the relationship (kin or ethnic) itself' (1993: 192). According to Eller and Coughlan, the source of this fallacy 'is the failure of sociology and anthropology to deal intelligibly with emotion' (*ibid.*). To illustrate this, they refer to Durkheim's observations on religion. The crucial question, they contend, is 'how are sentiments (religious or ethnic) induced in people?' The answer is the same for both: in rituals. Rituals

> magically work their effect on participants, making some sensations stronger, producing others at that very moment. There is little or no awareness of the day-to-day activities which might produce or reproduce sentiment or knowledge, religious or otherwise. (*Ibid.*: 193)

It seems difficult to disagree with Eller and Coughlan's assertions. However, it must be stressed once again that Geertz, who is their main target, does not deserve these criticisms. On the contrary, the way out of this impasse is hidden in Geertz's writings. As Tilley forcefully argues:

> the 'primordial' elements of culture are not affect but the cognitive framework which shapes and informs affect . . . Certain assumptions or knowledge systems set the stage for affect, and to the extent that such knowledge systems form a kind of cognitive substratum not only for affect but for most conscious thought, they might be said to be 'primordial'. (1997: 503)

The Date of the Emergence of Nations

A final criticism concerns the perennialists' belief in the antiquity of nations and nationalism. Zubaida (1978) refutes this claim from a modernist viewpoint in an article written more than 20 years ago. According to Zubaida, the most serious problem the nationalists face is the historical novelty of both the concept of nation and the forms of political units now called nation-states. Many of the states and empires in history ruled over diverse populations. Neither the state personnel, nor the subject population were ethnically homogeneous. The rulers more often than not had a different ethnicity than the population they ruled over. Moreover, 'shared ethnicity between ruler and ruled did not always constitute grounds for favour or mutual support' (1978: 54). In other words, ethnicity was not as important as it is today (see also Breuilly 1993a: 406).

Zubaida turns to the Ottoman Empire to illustrate his arguments. He notes that the state and military apparatus of the Ottoman Empire was not exclusively Turkish – it included various Caucasian ethnicities, Albanians and Kurds, and the Turkish-speaking populations were not favoured over others. In short, 'within this form of political organisation, the units of identity and solidarity were by no means always those of ethnicity, common language, culture, etc., but varied and overlapped in different times and places' (*ibid.*). Even wars and conflicts were different from the ones we witness today. The contending sides were not ethnically homogeneous; members of the same ethnic groups were fighting each other in the service of different lords. According to Zubaida, nationalists, for the sake of establishing historical continuity, 'evade these obstacles, or explain them away as manifestations of past national oppressions and dispersions' (*ibid.*: 55). Breuilly makes the same point by arguing that being a German in eighteenth-century Germany did not have the same meaning as to be a German today. Two centuries ago Germanness was only *an* identity among others – social estate, confession and so on. (1993a: 406).

Another attempt to counter the arguments put forward by perennialists comes from Smith (1991a: 45–51). The fact that Smith is an ethno-symbolist, hence more sensitive to ethnic pasts and cultures than the modernists, makes this attempt even more interesting. He begins his critique by asking the following question: 'Were there nations and nationalism in antiquity?'

Smith tries to answer this question by observing some premodern civilizations. Ancient Egypt is his first stop. Smith argues that while ancient Egyptians constituted what he calls an *ethnie*, that is ethnic community, with a corresponding ethnocentrism, they were far from being a nation in the contemporary sense of the word (1991a: 45). Its economy was divided into regions and districts; the production was directed to self-subsistence, not interregional trade. Legally, there was no idea of citizenship, hence no conception of rights and duties. Education was class-divided and far from being centralized. Finally, while there were common myths and memories that differentiated the Egyptians from other peoples, these operated largely through religious institutions and 'were unable to compensate for the regionalism that so often undermined the unity of the Egyptian state'. (*ibid*.: 46) In sum, it is more correct to call ancient Egypt an ethnic state than a nation. Smith also argues that it is not possible to speak of an Egyptian nationalism since nationalism can be defined as an ideology – and a movement – which presupposes 'a world of nations, each with its own character, and a primary allegiance to the nation as the sole source of political power and the basis of world order' (*ibid*.: 46–7). It was difficult to find such movements even in the medieval world, let alone in ancient Egypt.

Smith then turns to ancient Greeks and Jews. In the case of ancient Greece, Smith points to the fact that unity was more cultural than political. In fact, even in the cultural sphere the picture was more complex as religious rituals and artistic forms varied from one city-state to the next. So again, Smith claims, it is more appropriate to speak of a Greek ethnocentrism. As for the Jews, it can be suggested that they were displaying more unity than the two previous examples. But here, religion made things more difficult since there was 'near-identity in Jewish thought and practice of what we consider to be separate [phenomena], namely the religious community and the nation with religious messianism and nationalism' (*ibid*.: 48).

What complicates matters further in all these cases and in general for any attempt to see whether there were nations and nationalism in antiquity is lack of evidence, even from the small ruling strata (Smith 1991a: 47). In the words of Connor,

> Such vast disagreement among eminent authorities [on the question of when nations have emerged] has been made possible by the near absence of conclusive evidence. Nationalism is a mass phenomenon. The fact that members of the ruling elite or intelligentsia manifest national sentiment is not sufficient to establish that national consciousness has permeated the value

systems of the masses. And the masses, until recent times totally or semi-illiterate, furnished few hints concerning their view of group-self. (1994: 212)

These and other criticisms led to a marginalization of the extreme versions of primordialism in the literature on nationalism. Some scholars even suggested that the sociological usage of primordialism should be abandoned altogether 'because of its lack of empirical support and its inherent social passivity and anti-intellectualism' (Eller and Coughlan 1993: 200). Obviously, these views are not shared by everybody. Brass, for instance, while sharply criticizing some of the arguments advanced by primordialists, concedes that the primordialist perspective is relevant to our understanding of ethnic groups with long and rich cultural heritages (1991: 74). He admits that such heritages provide an effective means of political mobilization. Similarly, Smith defends the concept by arguing that it enables us to understand the enduring power and hold of ethnic ties (1995: 34).

I would suggest that the real importance of the concept lies elsewhere. Primordialism, as defined by Geertz and elaborated by Tilley, that is in the sense of webs of meaning spun by individuals and the strong emotions these meanings generate, enables us to explore how these meanings are produced and reproduced, and how these 'knowledge systems suggest themselves as "givens", prior to individual thought and action' (Tilley 1997: 503). The concept underlines the importance of perceptions and beliefs in guiding human action. In this context, it seems quite unreasonable to follow Eller and Coughlan's suggestion and remove the term from the sociological lexicon.

Further Reading

Any bookshop will contain a plethora of nationalist histories stressing the primordial roots of particular nations. A useful introduction in this respect is a collection of essays edited by Kedourie (1971). Compiled from the writings of various nationalists, the book illustrates many of the themes that recur in nationalist narratives. For a sociobiological account of nationalism see van den Berghe (1978). For cultural primordialism see the famous articles by Shils (1957) and Geertz (1993)

[1973], chapter 10. For a critique of primordialism from an instrumentalist standpoint see Brass (1991). A comparison of primordialism with instrumentalism and constructivism is provided in Tilley (1997). For a controversial discussion of Shils and Geertz see Eller and Coughlan (1993).

4

Modernism

Man is an animal suspended in webs of significance he himself
has spun.

Clifford Geertz, *The Interpretation of Cultures*

What is Modernism?

Modernism emerged as a reaction to the primordialism of the
older generations who tacitly accepted the basic assumptions of the
nationalist ideology. According to Smith, classical modernism
achieved its canonical formulation in the 1960s, above all in the
model of 'nation-building' which had a wide appeal in the social
sciences in the wake of the movement of decolonization in Asia
and Africa (1998: 3). This was followed by a variety of models and
theories, all of which regarded nations as historically formed constructs. Modernist explanations soon became the dominant orthodoxy in the field. Despite sustained criticisms by ethno-symbolists
since the early 1980s, many scholars today still subscribe to some
form of modernism.

The common denominator of all these studies is a belief in the
modernity of nations and nationalism. According to this perspective, both appeared in the last two centuries, that is in the wake of
the French Revolution, and they are the products of specifically
modern processes like capitalism, industrialism, the emergence of
the bureaucratic state, urbanization and secularism (Smith 1994:
377; 1995: 29). In fact, they become a sociological necessity only
in the modern world: there was no room for nations or national-

ism in the pre-modern era. In short, 'nationalism comes before nations. Nations do not make states and nationalisms but the other way round' (Hobsbawm 1990: 10).

Apart from this basic belief, modernists have very little in common. They all stress different factors in their accounts of nationalism. With this in mind, I will refrain from treating modernist scholars as a 'monolithic' category, and I will divide them into three categories in terms of the key factors – economic, political and social/cultural – they have identified. At first glance, this classification may seem overly simplistic: it might be argued that none of these theorists rely on a single factor in their accounts of nationalism. Nevertheless, most of the theories we will discuss below, whatever their degree of sophistication, emphasize one set of factors at the expense of others. In fact, this is what lies behind the major charge brought against modernist interpretations, namely the charge of 'reductionism' (Smith 1983; Calhoun 1997). Moreover, the classification I am introducing here does not consist of 'mutually exclusive' categories. Scholars are classified on the basis of the factor they 'prioritize' in explaining nationalism. This does not imply that they have identified a single factor in their theories, but that they have attached a 'greater weight' to one set of factors as opposed to others.

Economic Transformation

I will begin my critical review with neo-Marxist scholars who stress economic factors in their theories. The late 1960s and 1970s were very crucial in Marxist thinking about nationalism for a variety of reasons. The orthodox Marxist position was beginning to be challenged with the emergence of anti-colonial nationalist movements in many parts of the Third World. The majority of left-wing intellectuals were sympathetic to these movements and some were even actively involved in them. It was increasingly avowed that the fight against 'neo-imperialism', 'economic imperialism' or 'international capital' was first a national one (Zubaida 1978: 65–6).

Another development that induced many Marxists to 'come to terms' with their creed was the recent 'ethnic revival' in Europe and North America. The proliferation of 'fissiparous' nationalist movements, based on seemingly primordial attachments which were thought to be long-forgotten by liberals and Marxists alike, was now threatening the unity of the established nation-states of the Western world (James 1996: 105–7). Traditional Marxism was ill-prepared to cope with these developments. It was in such a context that attempts to reform the orthodox credo came to the fore. The new generation of Marxists, who were not intent on 'dismantling the old edifice' in James' words, attached a greater weight to the role of culture, ideology and language in their analyses (*ibid.*: 107). The New Left had a much more ambivalent attitude *vis-à-vis* nationalism. Probably the most important statement of such a position was Tom Nairn's *The Break-up of Britain* (1981).

Tom Nairn and 'Uneven Development'

The Scottish Marxist intellectual Tom Nairn taught social science and philosophy at Birmingham University and Hornsey College of Art. He was sacked from the latter in 1968 for participating in the student rebellions of the same year. He returned to academic life in 1993–94, and since then he has been teaching nationalism at Edinburgh University.

Nairn was heavily influenced by Gramsci's writings. He had read Gramsci in 1957–58 when he was studying at the Scuola Normale Superiore of Pisa. In 1963, he published a Gramscian analysis of English class history entitled 'La nemesi borghese' in *Il Contemporaneo* (Forgacs 1989: 75). This analysis was to underlie a series of articles on the British state and the labour movement, published mainly in the *New Left Review* whose editorial board he joined in 1962. Together with similar essays by Perry Anderson, another influential figure of the New Left, these became known as 'Nairn–Anderson theses' and led to a major debate with Edward Thompson in the 1960s. In 1975, he published a book-length polemic against the British Left's opposition to the Common Market. This was the harbinger of a long-term engagement with issues of nationalism, which resulted in *The Break-up of Britain: Crisis and Neo-Nationalism* (1981), originally published in 1977 (Eley and Suny 1996b: 78).

Though he never abandoned Marxism, Nairn is quite sympathetic to the claims of the Scottish National Party (SNP). For him, this reflects 'the dilemma of an insecure national identity' (1981:

397). Gellner, who thinks that Nairn's theory of nationalism is sub-
stantially correct but is puzzled as to how Nairn could think his
theory was at all compatible with Marxism, interprets this dilemma
in a different way. The passage, reflecting Gellner's exceptionally
witty style, is worth quoting in full:

> The Christians have passed through at least three stages: the
> first, when they really believed what they said, when the actual
> message and its promise of salvation was what attracted them to
> it, and when the historic continuity with earlier believers was an
> irrelevancy; the second, when they had to struggle to retain their
> faith in the face of increasingly pressing grounds for unbelief,
> and many fell by the wayside; and the third, that of modernist
> theology, when the 'belief' has acquired negligible (or sliding-
> scale) content, when the claim to continuity with their purely
> nominal predecessors becomes the only real psychic reward and
> significance of adherence, and it is doctrine which is played
> down as irrelevancy. Marxists seem doomed to pass through the
> same stages of development. When they reach the third stage
> (some already have), their views also will be of no intellectual
> interest. Tom Nairn is still in the second stage . . . His struggles
> with or for faith are still passionate, troubled and sincere, which
> is what gives the book some of its interest. (1979: 265–6)

Nairn's stated aim in *The Break-up of Britain* is not to provide a
theory of nationalism, but to present 'the scantiest outline' of how
this might be done. He begins with the following contention: 'the
theory of nationalism represents Marxism's great historical failure'
(1981: 329). This failure, which can be observed either in theory
or in political practice, was inevitable. Moreover, it was not peculiar to Marxists: nobody could or did provide a theory of nationalism at that period simply because the time was not yet ripe for
it. However, Nairn maintains, nationalism can be understood in
materialist terms. The primary task of the theorist is to find the
right explanatory framework within which nationalism can be
properly evaluated.

According to Nairn, the roots of nationalism should not be
sought in the internal dynamics of individual societies, but in the
general process of historical development since the end of the
eighteenth century. Thus, the only explanatory framework which

is of any utility is that of 'world history' as a whole. Nationalism, in this sense, is 'determined by certain features of the world political economy, in the era between the French and Industrial Revolutions and the present day' (1981: 332). Here, we can see that Nairn's views on the subject have been greatly influenced by the 'dependency school', especially the work of André Gunder Frank, Samir Amin and Immanuel Wallerstein on the international system of capitalist exploitation (Zubaida 1978: 66).

On the other hand, the origins of nationalism are not located in the process of development of the world political economy as such – in other words, nationalism is not simply an inevitable concomitant of industrialization – but the 'uneven development' of history since the eighteenth century. For many centuries, it was believed that the opposite would indeed be the case, that is that material civilization would develop evenly and progressively. According to this view, characteristic of the Enlightenment thought, Western European states have initiated the capitalist development process and accumulated the necessary capital for perpetuating this process for a long period of time. The idea of 'even development' maintained that 'this advance could be straightforwardly followed, and the institutions responsible for it copied – hence the periphery, the world's countryside, would catch up with the leaders in due time' (Nairn 1981: 337). But history did not unfold as expected by Western Philosophers. Capitalist development was not experienced 'evenly'.

Instead, the impact of the leading countries was experienced as domination and invasion. This was in a way inevitable because the gap between the core and the periphery was too great and 'the new developmental forces were not in the hands of a beneficent, disinterested elite concerned with Humanity's advance' (*ibid.*: 338). The peoples of backward countries learned quickly that '[p]rogress in the abstract meant domination in the concrete, by powers which they could not help apprehending as foreign or alien'. However, popular expectations were not thwarted by the recognition of this fact. Since these expectations were always racing ahead of material progress itself, 'the peripheric elites had no option but to try and satisfy these demands by taking things into their own hands' (*ibid.*: 339). For Nairn, 'taking things into one's own hands' denotes a great deal of the substance of nationalism. The elites had to persuade the masses to take the short cut. They had to contest the concrete form assumed by progress as they were setting out to progress themselves. They wanted factories, schools and parliaments, so they had to copy the leaders somehow; but they had to do this in a way which rejected the direct intervention of these countries. 'This meant the conscious formation of a militant, inter-class community rendered strongly (if mythically) aware of its own separate identity *vis-à-vis* the outside forces of domination' (*ibid.*: 340). There was no other way of doing it. 'Mobilization had to be in terms of what was there; and the whole point of the dilemma was that there was nothing there'. Or more exactly, there was only the people with its speech, folklore, skin colour and so on. Under these circumstances, 'the new middle-class intelligentsia of nationalism had to invite the masses into history; and the invitation-card had to be written in a language they understood' (*ibid.*).

In short, the socio-historical cost of the rapid implantation of capitalism into world society was 'nationalism'. However, that was not the whole story. Of course, it was possible to end the story here and deduce from all this a theory of anti-imperialism whereby nationalism could be seen in a positive moral light, that is as the motor force of peripheric struggles against the imperialist forces of the West. But the story was dialectical. The process did not end with the emergence of nationalism in the peripheral countries under the impact of uneven development; once successful, nationalism reacted upon the core countries and they too fell under its spell. These countries did not invent nationalism; they did not need to since they were in front and 'possessed the things nationalism is really about' (*ibid.*: 344). But once the nation-state had been transformed into a compelling norm, or the 'new climate of world politics', the core countries were bound to become nationalist. In short, ' "uneven development" is not just the hard-luck tale of poor countries' (*ibid.*). The 'founder-members' and the '*parvenus*' were forcing each other to change continuously. In the long term, core area nationalism was as inevitable as peripheric nationalism.

This picture, Nairn contends, shows clearly that it is not meaningful to make a distinction between 'good' and 'bad' nationalisms. All nationalisms contain the seeds of both progress and regress. In fact, this ambiguity is its historical *raison d'être*:

It is through nationalism that societies try to propel themselves forward to certain kinds of goal (industrialization, prosperity, equality with other peoples, etc.) *by a certain sort of regression* – by looking inwards, drawing more deeply upon their indigenous resources, resurrecting past folk heroes and myths about themselves and so on. (*Ibid.*: 348)

It follows that the substance of nationalism is always morally and politically ambiguous. Nationalism can in this sense be pictured as the old Roman god Janus, who stood above gateways with one face looking forward and one backwards. Nationalism is standing over the passage to modernity: 'As human kind is forced through its strait doorway, it must look desperately back into the past, to gather strength wherever it can be found for the ordeal of "development"' (*ibid.*: 349).

Orthodox Marxism's greatest failure was the conviction that class is always more important in history than national differences. But, Nairn claims, the uneven – imperialist – spread of capitalism has insured that the fundamental contradiction was not that of class struggle, but that of nationality (Zubaida 1978: 68). 'As capitalism spread, and smashed the ancient social formations surrounding it, these always tended to fall apart along the fault-lines contained inside them. It is a matter of elementary truth that these lines of fissure were nearly always ones of nationality' (Nairn 1981: 353).

Now the time was ripe for the formulation of a Marxist theory of nationalism. Marxism should get rid of its Enlightenment foundations and become an 'authentic world-theory', that is a theory that focuses on the social development of the whole world. The 'enigma of nationalism' had displayed Marxism's Eurocentric nature. However, it could not see – and overcome – these theoretical limitations until they had been undermined in practice. The events of the 1960s and 1970s were crucial in that respect since they enabled Marxism to come to terms with its own failures. It was finally possible to separate out the durable – the 'scientific' historical materialism – from the ideology, 'the grain from the husks represented by the defeat of Western Philosophy' (*ibid.*: 363).

Such were Nairn's basic arguments, as articulated in *The Break-up of Britain*. Nairn perseveres with the general thrust of this account in his subsequent writings – developing, however, a much more sympathetic attitude towards 'primordialism' (1997, 1998). Let me now turn to the major criticisms raised against Nairn's theory. These can be summarized as follows: Nairn's theory does not fit the facts; it perpetuates the classical Marxist distinction between 'historic' and 'historyless' nations; it is 'essentialist'; it does not provide an adequate account of the origins of nations and nationalism; it is 'reductionist'; finally, it pretends that nationalisms are always successful.

Nairn's Theory Does Not Fit the Facts

Breuilly argues that Nairn's theory, although plausible in the abstract, does not fit the facts. He holds that Nairn inverts the actual sequence of events by placing the origins of nationalism within the less developed countries. For Breuilly, nationalism originates in Europe before the establishment of colonial empires in overseas areas. Hence, anti-colonial nationalisms, which can be seen as a reaction to imperialism, postdate European nationalisms. Moreover, it is not possible to account for the first nationalist movements in terms of economic exploitation or backwardness. Breuilly cites the example of Magyar nationalism in the Habsburg Empire to support this assertion. He notes that the Magyars, who developed the first strong nationalist movement in the Habsburg Empire, were not a backward or exploited group; to the contrary, they had a number of privileges. Breuilly argues that Magyar nationalism was a reaction to the oppressive control exercized by Vienna. There were other nationalist movements as well, especially among the non-Magyar groups exploited by Magyars, but, Breuilly insists, this was a later development (1993a: 412–3). Similarly, Smith argues that locating the origins of nationalism in the periphery constitutes a historical error since the first nationalist sentiments and movements occurred in the 'core' areas of England, France, Holland, Spain and so on. (1983: xvii).

Orridge multiplies the number of examples. He remarks that Catalonia and the Basque country, where there are strong nationalist movements, were and are the most developed regions of Spain. Similarly, Bohemia, 'the heartland of nineteenth century Czech nationalism' in Orridge's words, was the most developed part of the Habsburg Empire. Finally, Belgium was highly industrialized at the time it separated from the Netherlands in the 1830s (Orridge 1981b: 181–2). As Orridge reminds us, Nairn tries to avoid these criticisms by arguing that 'uneven development' can sometimes operate in reverse and produce highly developed peripheries within backward states. However, Orridge notes, there are also 'instances of nationalism not accompanied by any great differences in developmental level from their surroundings' (*ibid.*: 182). Thus, there was no significant difference – as far as their developmental level is concerned – between Norway and Sweden or Finland and Russia, when the smaller countries developed their nationalisms. Similarly, when the Balkan nations won their independence in the course of the nineteenth century, they were not more developed or backward than the core region of the Ottoman Empire. Orridge maintains that it is more difficult to accommodate these cases within Nairn's theory (*ibid.*).

A further difficulty with Nairn's account is that there are instances of 'uneven development' without strong nationalist movements. Orridge asks why there is no counterpart to the nationalisms of Scotland and Wales in Northern England or Southern Italy (*ibid.*). Breuilly goes one step further and argues that it is difficult to correlate the strength and intensity of a nationalist movement with the degree of economic exploitation and backwardness. He notes that nationalisms have often developed fastest in the least exploited or backward areas and that there were no significant nationalist movements in areas where the most naked forms of exploitation took place (1993a: 413).

Nairn Perpetuates the Classical Marxist Distinction between 'Historic' and 'Historyless' Nations

Nairn tends to treat the original formation of the 'historic' nations like France and England as a historical given (James 1996: 111). In other words, he does not question the origins of 'core' nations: he just notes that they owe their nationalisms to a dialectical process whereby peripheric nationalisms react upon them, forcing them to become nationalist. He remains silent as to how these nations have come into being in the first place. This tendency manifests itself clearly in his attitude towards Scotland, his 'homeland'. As Benedict Anderson – another *New Left Review* writer – notes, Nairn treats 'his "Scotland" as an unproblematic, primordial given' (1991: 89). But Scotland presents an anomaly for Nairn's theory because Scottish nationalism develops at a relatively later date (Tiryakian 1995: 221). Nairn explains this by pointing to the fact that Scotland had been incorporated into the British state before the great period of industrialization. Therefore, it did not experience economic exploitation until very recently (Nairn 1974).

Nairn's Theory is 'Essentialist'

Nairn's tendency to treat the existence of 'historic' nations as a given brings us to the third criticism levelled against his theory, namely that of essentialism. Zubaida rightly asks how, without assuming the existence of essential nations, could 'nationality' constitute the 'fault-lines' of fissure contained within the ancient social formations (1978: 69; see the relevant quotation from Nairn above). Nairn seems to confirm this observation when he claims that England was 'a country of ancient and settled nationality' (1981: 262) or that 'nationalism, *unlike nationality or ethnic variety*, cannot be considered a "natural" phenomenon' (*ibid.*: 99, emphasis added). Clearly, then, nationality or ethnic variety are 'natural' phenomena for Nairn.

Drawing on these examples, Zubaida argues that Nairn falls prey to the fundamental assumptions of the nationalist discourse. Nairn considers nations to be 'historical super-subjects' which 'mobilize', 'aspire', 'propel themselves forward' and so on. However, Zubaida notes, 'there must be a way of systematically determining "a nation" for the fault-lines to be considered to be those of nationality' (1978: 69). MacLaughlin joins Zubaida by arguing that Nairn accords a higher degree of historical agency and explanatory power to factors such as ethnicity and nationalist ideology than would appear to be justified by the evidence (1987: 14).

This point leads Orridge to question the relationship between 'uneven development' and pre-existing ethnic identities. He raises the following question: 'Does uneven development alone create the sense of separateness or does it need a strong pre-existing sense of distinctiveness to work on' (1981b: 188)? Orridge claims that Nairn is not very clear about this point and goes on to argue that no modern European nationality has been distinguished from its environment by uneven development alone. According to

Orridge, uneven development should be joined by other distinguishing features such as religion or language for discontent to take the form of nationalism. This can also explain why there are no nationalist movements in Northern England or Southern Italy (*ibid.*: 188–9). This ethno-symbolist (primordialist?) criticism is also expressed by Llobera who argues that the effects of capitalism were felt at a time when national identities were already there (1994: 215).

Nairn stands much closer to 'essentialism' in his recent writings. Thus, in a talk given to students at Edinburgh in early 1997, Nairn stressed the need for a new paradigm which will combine sociology and biology to study nationalism. This new paradigm – what he calls a 'life science' – 'depends . . . on establishing a more plausible link between biology and kinship on one hand, and the world of political nation-states and resurgent nationality on the other' (1997: 13). Elsewhere, he asserts that 'the kind of remaking which features in modern nationalism is not creation *ex nihilo*, but a reformulation constrained by determinate parameters of [a particular] past' (1998: 121). Clearly, Nairn has not made much progress as far as 'essentialism' is concerned. It seems that Scottish nationalism has triumphed over Marxism!

Nairn's Theory Does Not Provide an Adequate Account of the Origins and Spread of Nationalism

According to Orridge, Nairn's theory explains why there should be a developmental difference between core and peripheral areas and why those at the periphery should object to this state of affairs, but it does not explain why this reaction takes the form of nationalism. The peripheral elites may well choose to reform their traditional institutions instead of creating new ones. Nationalism, Orridge argues, is not simply a reaction against subjection and superiority: 'it is an attempt to construct a particular kind of political order and has its own subjective content' (1981b: 183). For him, what underlies this failure is the absence of a theory of the nation-state in Nairn's writings. Obviously, it might not be necessary for a theory of nationalism to explain the emergence of nation-states, but it must surely explain 'why, once in existence, this form of political organization has proved so attractive' (*ibid.*: 184).

In short, uneven development may tell us that the world is divided into smaller units, but it does not explain why these units take the form of nation-states.

Nairn's Theory is 'Reductionist'

A common objection raised against all neo-Marxist and most modernist theories of nationalism concerns their 'reductionism'. At the heart of this objection lies the belief that nationalism is too complex to be explained in terms of a single factor. Thus, Smith argues that Nairn's formula is too simple and crude to encompass the variety and timing of nationalisms. Moreover, 'we cannot simply reduce ethnic "sentiments" to "real" class interests, if only because sentiments are equally "real" and nationalism involves a good deal more than sentiments' (1983: xvii–xviii; see also Orridge 1981b: 190).

Nairn's Nationalisms are Always Successful

This criticism comes from Zubaida. In Nairn's account, the masses are always mobilized by nationalism as it offers them 'something real and important – something that class consciousness could never have furnished' (1981: 22). For Zubaida, this constitutes another aspect of Nairn's participation in the nationalist myths. Zubaida argues that nationalist movements are highly variable in terms of their contents and goals. The nature of the relationship between nationalist leaders and mass support cannot be assumed, but has to be shown in relation to each particular case (1978: 69–70).

Michael Hechter and 'Internal Colonialism'

Michael Hechter's *Internal Colonialism: The Celtic Fringe in British National Development, 1536–1966* (1975) was another influential contribution to the growing literature on nationalism from the neo-Marxist camp. Hechter's book was particularly important in two respects. First, it introduced Lenin's concept of 'internal colonialism' to the study of nationalism. Before that, the concept was used in other contexts, notably by Gramsci to discuss the Italian

Mezzogiorno and, more recently, by Latin American sociologists to describe the Amerindian regions of their societies (Hechter 1975: 9). Second, unlike many of his predecessors – a notable exception is Deutsch (1966) – Hechter made sustained use of quantitative data and multivariate statistical analysis to support his thesis. The book led to a variety of studies on both sides of the Atlantic either challenging it or following in its footsteps (Tiryakian 1985: 6). Hechter later revised his original assumptions in response to the criticisms questioning the factual adequacy of his theory (1985). More recently, he moved to a 'rational choice' analysis of the changing fortunes of ethnoregional political parties, which in turn led him 'to raise microsociological questions about the nature of group solidarity' (Tiryakian 1985: 6; Hechter and Levi 1979). Hechter currently teaches sociology at the University of Arizona.

Hechter's point of departure was the problems of ethnic conflict and assimilation which preoccupied American politics since the 1960s. Broadly speaking, there were two alternative ways of solving these problems in the scholarly literature on intergroup relations: 'assimilationism' and 'nationalism'. Hechter notes that the majority of academics endorsed the assimilationist position at that time. Briefly, assimilationists held that ethnic/racial minorities were poor and frustrated because they were isolated from the national culture. The norms and values of ghetto communities were dysfunctional in the wider society. This implied a solution: if the governments were to invest the necessary resources to educate and socialize the ghetto children, then the problems of maladjustment and the so-called 'culture of poverty' would cease (1975: xiv–xv).

According to Hechter, a particular model of national development underlies the assimilationist perspective. He calls this the 'diffusion model of development'. This model identifies three stages in the process of national development. The first stage is pre-industrial. At this stage, there is no relationship between the core and the periphery: they exist in virtual isolation from one another. Moreover, there are fundamental differences in their economic, cultural and political institutions. Increased contact between the core and peripheral regions leads to the second stage of national development. The second stage was generally associated with the process of industrialization. 'As a rule, the diffusionist view holds that from interaction will come commonality'

(1975: 7). It was believed that the institutions of the developing core will, after some time, 'diffuse' into the periphery. The cultural forms of the periphery, evolved in complete isolation from the rest of the world, will renew, or in Hechter's words 'up-date' themselves as a result of increased contact with the modernizing core. True, massive social dislocation brought about by industrialization and expansion of regional interaction might initially lead to an increased sense of cultural separateness in the periphery, inducing those who suffer from this process of rapid change to cling to their familiar cultural patterns. However, this 'traditional behaviour' is temporary: it will tend to decline as industrialization promotes the general welfare and reduces the initial regional differences. The model posits that the core and peripheral regions will become culturally homogeneous in the long run as the economic, political and cultural bases of ethnic differentiations will disappear. In the third and final stage, regional wealth will become equal; cultural differences will no longer be socially meaningful; and political processes will be conducted within a framework of national parties (*ibid.*: 7–8).

Hechter argues that this is an 'over-optimistic' model of social change. For him, the model which seems to be more realistic is what he calls the 'internal colonial model'. This model holds that an altogether different relationship will ensue from increased core–periphery contact. The core will dominate the periphery politically and exploit it economically. With the exception of a small number of cases, industrialization and increased regional contact will not lead to national development (*ibid.*: 8–9).

The main assumptions of this model can be summarized as follows. The uneven wave of modernization over state territories creates two kinds of groups: 'advanced' and 'less advanced' groups. As a result of this initial fortuitous advantage, resources and power are distributed unequally between the two groups. The more powerful group, or the core, tries to 'stabilize and monopolize its advantages though policies aiming at the institutionalization of the existing stratification system' (*ibid.*: 9). The economy of the core is characterized by a diversified industrial structure, whereas the peripheral economy is dependent and complementary to that of the core:

Peripheral industrialization, if it occurs at all, is highly specialized and geared for export. The peripheral economy is, therefore, relatively sensitive to price fluctuations in the international market. Decisions about investment, credit, and wages tend to be made in the core. As a consequence of economic dependence, wealth in the periphery lags behind the core. (*Ibid.*: 9–10)

On the other hand, the advanced group regulates the allocation of social roles in such a way that the more prestigious roles are reserved for its members. Conversely, the members of the less advanced group are denied access to these roles. Hechter calls this stratification system the 'cultural division of labour'. This system may be enforced *de jure*, when the state actively intervenes to deny certain roles to the members of the disadvantaged collectivity. Alternatively, it may be preserved *de facto*, through discriminatory policies, that is by providing differential access to institutions conferring status in the society, such as educational, religious or military institutions (*ibid.*: 39–40). The cultural division of labour leads individuals to identify themselves with their groups and contributes to the development of distinctive ethnic identification. 'Social actors come to define themselves and others according to the range of roles each may be expected to play. They are aided in this categorization by the presence of visible signs' (*ibid.*: 9). Such visible signs increase group solidarity and unite them around a certain commonality of definitions.

Drawing on Marxism, Hechter identifies two further conditions for the emergence of group solidarity. First, there must be substantial economic inequalities between individuals such that these individuals may come to see this inequality as part of a pattern of collective oppression. But this in itself is not sufficient for the development of collective solidarity since there must also be 'an accompanying social awareness and definition of the situation as being unjust and illegitimate', hence the second condition: there must be adequate communication among members of the oppressed group (*ibid.*: 42). These general observations can be summed up by three propositions:

1. The greater the economic inequalities between collectivities, the greater the probability that the less advantaged collectivity will be status solidary, and hence, will resist political integration.
2. The greater the frequency of intra-collectivity communication, the greater the status solidarity of the peripheral collectivity.

3. The greater the intergroup differences of culture, particularly in so far as identifiability is concerned, the greater the probability that the culturally distinct peripheral collectivity will be status solidary (*Ibid.*: 43).

In short, when objective cultural differences are superimposed upon economic inequalities, leading to a cultural division of labour, and when an adequate degree of intra-group communication exists, the chances for successful political integration of the peripheral collectivity into the national society are minimized (*ibid.*). The members of the disadvantaged group may start to assert that their culture is equal or superior to that of the advantaged group, claim the separateness of their nation and seek independence (*ibid.*: 10).

The picture drawn by the model of internal colonialism is in many ways similar to that of the overseas colonial situation. The peripheral/colonial economy is forced into complementary development to that of the core/metropolis and therefore becomes dependent on international markets. The movement of labour in the periphery/colony is determined by the decisions made in the core/metropolis. This economic dependence is reinforced through political and military measures. There is a lower standard of living in the periphery/colony and a stronger sense of deprivation. Discrimination on the basis of language, religion or other cultural forms are routine, daily occurrences (*ibid.*: 31–4).

Hechter maintains that the internal colonial model provides a much more adequate explanation of the process of national development than the diffusion model. It accounts for the persistence of backwardness in the midst of industrial society and the volatility of political integration. Moreover, by linking economic and occupational differences between groups to their cultural differences, it suggests an explanation for the resilience of peripheral cultures (*ibid.*: 34).

The model of internal colonialism developed by Hechter has been subject to a number of criticisms – some of which will be reviewed below (Page 1978; Brand 1985; Kellas 1991). The most important objection to the theory concerned its factual (in)adequacy: certain cases did not seem to fit the model. In particular, Scotland constituted a real anomaly for Hechter's account since the Scots were not relegated to inferior social positions in Britain, and Scotland has been as industrialized as Britain from the eighteenth century onwards (Kellas 1991: 40). In the light of these criticisms, Hechter made an important amendment to his theory (1985).

The inspiration for the amendment came from American Jews. As might be recalled, Hechter argued in his original theory that economic inequalities increase group solidarity. On the other hand, the Jews in America also had high solidarity, but 'in no sense could they be regarded as materially disadvantaged' (1985: 21). Hechter explains this anomaly by pointing to the high degree of 'occupational specialization' among the Jews. The clustering of Jews in specific occupational niches contributed to group solidarity by promoting status equality and a commonality of economic interests within group boundaries. Drawing on this observation, Hechter concludes that the cultural division of labour had at least two separate and independent dimensions: 'a hierarchical dimension, in which the various groups were vertically distributed in the occupational structure, and a segmental one, in which the groups were occupationally specialized at any level of the structure' (*ibid.*: 21).

Hechter holds that this second dimension enables us to make sense of the Scottish case. Scotland did not experience internal colonialism to any great degree, but instead had a high level of 'institutional autonomy'. According to The Act of Union signed in 1707 between England and Scotland, the latter had the right to establish its own educational, legal and ecclesiastical institutions. Hechter argues that this institutional autonomy created a potential basis for the development of a 'segmental' cultural division of labour. The Scots were clustered in the specific occupational niches created by Scotland's institutional autonomy. Let alone being discriminated against for their cultural distinctiveness, they often owed their very jobs to the existence of this distinctiveness. Moreover, these jobs were not less prestigious than the ones found in England. The existence of these institutions helped those in the periphery to identify with their culture and provided a strong incentive for the reproduction of this culture through history (*ibid.*: 21–2).

As I have mentioned above, this model has been criticized on many grounds. If we leave the methodological ones aside (Page 1978: 303–15), these criticisms converge on two aspects of Hechter's account: its factual inadequacy and its reductionism.

Hechter's Model of 'Internal Colonialism' Does Not
Fit the Facts

The most obvious examples are Catalonia and Scotland. Catalonia
has never been an internal colony. On the contrary, it was – and
still is – the strongest regional economy in Spain. Brand notes that
Catalonia was the only industrial economy in Spain when nationalism acquired mass support, 'second only to Britain in its productive capacity and technical superiority in the textile industry'
(1985: 277). Scotland, on the other hand, was a case of 'over-
development': 'The Scots had long been innovators in the British
context – in education, finance, technology, and the physical and
social sciences' (Hechter 1985: 20). We have already discussed
Hechter's attempt to amend his theory by adding a second dimension to the cultural division of labour, namely 'segmental' dimension, whereby the members of the disadvantaged groups cluster in
specific occupational niches. In the Scottish case, this segmental
division of labour operates through the mechanism of 'institutional autonomy': the Scots, finding jobs in specifically Scottish
institutions, developed a higher degree of group solidarity than
would be predicted by the original theory.

However, this amendment does not save Hechter's theory. Brand
argues that the initial version was tied into a wider Marxist model
of society. But the new version bears no relation to the original
theory put forward by Lenin. Hence, Brand concludes, 'it makes
no sense to call this "internal colonialism"' (1985: 279). More
importantly, the conditions of segmentation, adduced specifically
to cope with exceptional cases such as Scotland or Catalonia, did
not exist in these countries.

First, the proportion of Scots working in the institutions created
by the Settlement of 1707 was very small. Secondly, 'even if we allow
that their centrality outweighs their small size, there is very little
evidence that they were important in the early regionalist and
nationalist organizations' (Brand 1985: 281). Brand notes that
these specifically Scottish institutions have not been sympathetic
to nationalism. For instance, The Church of Scotland only started
to support Home Rule after the Second World War and by this
time, it was a rapidly waning force in Scottish society. Finally, a considerable number of Scots were employed in the colonial and
administrative services of the British empire (Smith 1983: xvi). The

case of Catalonia was not more promising. As mentioned above, Catalonia was a highly industrialized region. However, 'the industrial workers of Catalonia, especially those of Barcelona, were the most difficult to recruit for the Catalan cause' (Brand 1985: 282).

On the other hand, Brand notes that the occupational breakdown of the population in Scotland does not have the feature which Hechter identified among American Jews. A large proportion of Scots were engaged in agriculture. For occupational clustering to produce greater group solidarity, there must be sufficient communication among the members of the group in question. However, of all occupations, agricultural workers are the most difficult to organize. Brand holds that much of this has to do with sheer geography since two hundred men in the factory can be contacted in half an hour, whereas this may take three weeks in the countryside (1985: 280). But the heart of the matter lies elsewhere. It may be conceded that individuals concentrated in particular occupations will meet regularly and share opinions. From this interaction, a point of view will probably emerge. However, 'this does not answer the question as to why a nationalist point of view specifically should grow up' (Brand 1985: 282).

Hechter's Model is Reductionist

Despite the amendment to the earlier model, Hechter's theory continues to explain cultural cleavages and ethnic sentiments by purely economic and spatial characteristics. Such an account reduces nationalism to discontent caused by regional economic inequalities and exploitation. We have only to consider the cases of ethnic revival among the scattered Armenians, Jews, Blacks and Gypsies to realize the shallowness of this view. According to Smith, economic exploitation can only exacerbate a pre-existing sense of ethnic grievance (1983: xvi; cf. Orridge 1981b: 188–9).

Moreover, Smith contends, explaining nationalism by a single factor, that is 'internal colonialism', inevitably limits the utility of the model. As such the model cannot explain why there has been cases of national revival in areas where the impact of capitalism, let alone industrialization, has been minimal (Eritreans); why there has been a long time-interval between the onset of industrialization and nationalist revival within the Western states; and why there has been no ethnic revival or a strong nationalist movement in economically backward areas like Northern England or Southern Italy (1983: xvi).

Political Transformation

Another variant of modernism has been propounded by scholars who focus on the transformations in the nature of politics, for example the rise of the modern bureaucratic state, or the extension of suffrage, to explain nationalism. Here, I will discuss the contributions of three scholars who espoused this standpoint, namely John Breuilly, Paul R. Brass and Eric J. Hobsbawm. As criticisms levelled against these theories tend to converge on a number of assumptions shared by all three scholars, I will review them at the end of the section.

John Breuilly and Nationalism as a Form of Politics

John Breuilly's *Nationalism and the State* has become established as one of the key general works on nationalism since its initial publication in 1982. Breuilly's massive historical survey differs from the historical studies of earlier periods, which were mainly chronological narratives of particular nationalisms, by its insistence in combining historical perspectives with theoretical analysis. Through the comparative analysis of a wide variety of examples, Breuilly introduces a new conception of nationalism, that is nationalism as a form of politics, and constructs an original typology of nationalist movements. The breadth of his book (he reviews more than 30 individual cases of nationalism from different continents and historical periods) is even appreciated by critical reviewers, who concede that the book is a 'valuable and useful' source of information (Symmons-Symonolewicz 1985b: 359). Breuilly currently teaches history at the University of Birmingham.

It should be stressed at the outset that Breuilly's historical analysis does not amount to a 'theory of nationalism'. His aim, declared in the introduction, is to outline and apply a general procedure for the study of nationalism (1993a: 1). He states clearly that he is sceptical of 'grand' theories or studies which develop a general argument, using examples only in an illustrative fashion. He believes that such examples are unrepresentative and removed from their historical context. For him, a general framework of analysis is only acceptable if it permits an effective analysis of particular cases. Breuilly argues that this requires two procedures. First, it is necessary to develop a typology of nationalism since nationalisms are too varied to be explained by a single method of investigation. Thus, any study should begin by identifying various types of nationalism which can be considered separately. Second, each type should be investigated by the method of comparative history (*ibid*.: 2). In the light of these observations, Breuilly first develops a typology of nationalism, then selects a few cases from each category and analyses them at length, using the same methods and concepts. This procedure, he argues, enables him to compare and contrast these various types systematically.

Breuilly uses nationalism to refer to 'political movements seeking or exercising state power and justifying such action with nationalist arguments'. A nationalist argument in turn is a political doctrine built upon three basic assertions:

1. There exists a nation with an explicit and peculiar character.
2. The interests and values of this nation take priority over all other interests and values.
3. The nation must be as independent as possible. This usually requires at least the attainment of political sovereignty. (*Ibid*.: 2).

Breuilly notes that nationalism has been variously explained in the literature by reference to ideas, class interest, economic modernization, psychological needs or culture. But for him, although particular nationalisms can be illuminated with respect to this or that class, idea or cultural achievement, none of these factors can help us understand nationalism generally. He contends that all these approaches overlook a crucial point, namely that nationalism is above all about politics and politics is about power. 'Power, in the modern world, is principally about control of the state'. Our central task therefore is 'to relate nationalism to the objectives of obtaining and using state power. We need to understand why nationalism has played a major role in the pursuit of those objectives' (*ibid*.: 1). In other words, we need to find out what it is about modern politics that makes nationalism so important. Only then might we go on to consider the contributions of other factors such as class, economic interests or culture. It follows that the first step in formulating an analytical framework to study nationalism is to consider it as a form of politics. Breuilly argues that such an approach will also enable us to assess the importance of the subject, since it is possible to ask how much support nationalist movements are able to tap within their society, whereas it is very difficult to estimate the significance of ideas or sentiments (1996: 163).

The next step consists of relating nationalism to the process of modernization. Breuilly conceives of modernization as involving a fundamental change in the 'generic division of labour'. The most important stage of this change is the transition from a 'corporate' to a 'functional' division of labour. The former exists in a society where a collection of functions are performed by particular institutions, usually on behalf of some distinct group. Breuilly refers to guilds as an example of such institutions. An ideal-typical guild will perform economic functions (regulating production and distribution of goods and services); cultural functions (education of apprentices, organizing recreational or ceremonial activities for the members of the guild); and political functions (running courts which impose sanctions upon unruly behaviour, sending members to town governments). In such an order, churches, lordships, peasant communes and even the monarchs are multifunctional. Breuilly argues that this order was increasingly criticized from the eighteenth century onwards and was crumbling in many parts of Western and Central Europe. The new order was based on a different division of labour, with each major social function carried out by a particular institution. Economic functions were handed over to individuals or firms competing in a free market; churches became free associations of believers; and political power was delegated to specialized bureaucracies controlled by elected parliaments or enlightened despots (*ibid.*: 163–4).

Historically, this transformation was not smooth. It developed at different paces and in different ways. The linking of this transformation to nationalist politics constitutes the third step of Breuilly's general framework. He argues that this requires focusing on one aspect of the transformation, namely the development of the modern state (*ibid.*: 164).

According to Breuilly, the modern state originally developed in a liberal form. Thus, 'public' powers were handed over to specialized state institutions (parliaments, bureaucracies) and many 'private' powers were left under the control of non-political institutions (free markets, private firms, families and so on). This involved a double transformation: 'institutions such as the monarchy lost "private" powers ... other institutions such as churches, guilds, and lordships lost their "public" powers to government' (1993b: 22). In this way, Breuilly continues, the distinction between the state as 'public' and civil society as 'private' became clearer.

On the other hand, with the breakdown of corporate division of labour, there was now a new emphasis upon people as individuals rather than as members of particular groups. Under such circumstances, the main problem was how to establish the state–society connection, or to put it differently, how to reconcile the public interests of citizens and the private interests of selfish individuals. It was precisely at this juncture that nationalist ideas came on the scene. Breuilly holds that the answers provided to this critical question took two major forms and nationalism played a crucial role in both (1996: 165; 1993b: 23).

The first answer was 'political' and rested on the idea of citizenship. In this case, Breuilly observes, the society of individuals was simultaneously defined as a polity of citizens. According to this view, commitment to the state could only be generated by participating in democratic and liberal institutions. The 'nation' was simply the body of citizens and only the political rights of the citizens – not their cultural identities – mattered. Breuilly claims that such a conception of nationality underlayed the programmes of eighteenth century patriots. In its most extreme form, it equated freedom with the implementation of the 'general will' (1996: 165).

The second answer, on the other hand, was 'cultural': it consisted of stressing the collective character of society. This was initially formulated by political elites confronted both by an intellectual problem (how did one legitimize state action?) and by a political problem (how could one secure the support of the masses?). Subsequently, this solution was standardized and became the major way of providing an identity to members of different social groups (*ibid.*).

Breuilly maintains that liberalism's inability to cope with collec-

tive or community interests was very crucial in this context. Moreover, many groups were not attracted to liberalism, 'the first major
political doctrine of modernity' in Breuilly's words, since the
system it gave birth to was largely based on socially structured
inequality. According to Breuilly, such groups were easy prey for
nationalist ideologues. But the picture was not that simple. What
complicated matters further was the 'modern' need to develop
political languages and movements which could appeal to a wide
range of groups. This could best be done by nationalism which has
been a 'sleight-of-hand ideology' connecting the two solutions, that
is the nation as a body of citizens and as a cultural collectivity,
together (*ibid.*: 166; 1993b: 23–4).

Breuilly argues that the general picture sketched so far does not
enable us to analyse particular nationalist movements, mainly
because, being politically neutral, nationalism has assumed a bewildering variety of forms. To investigate all these different forms, a
typology and auxiliary concepts which draw our attention to the
different functions performed by nationalist politics are required
(1996: 166). Breuilly concentrates on two aspects of nationalist
movements when developing his typology. The first of these concerns the relationship between the movement and the state to
which it either opposes or controls. In a world where the basic
source of political legitimacy was not yet the nation, such movements were necessarily oppositional:

> it was only at a later stage that governments, either formed by
> the success of nationalist oppositions or taking on board the
> ideas of those oppositions, would themselves make nationalist
> arguments the basis of their claims to legitimacy. (*Ibid.*)

The second aspect concerned the goals of nationalist movements:
hence, a nationalist opposition can strive to break away from the
present state (separation), to reform it in a nationalist direction
(reform) or to unite it with other states (unification) (1993a: 9).
In addition to these two aspects, Breuilly notes, the state which is
opposed may or may not define itself as a nation-state. The typology should mirror this distinction as well since this will have certain
implications for the nature of the conflict between the state and
the relevant nationalist movement. Having made these specifica-
tions, Breuilly introduces his typology (*ibid.*):

	Opposed to non-nation states	Opposed to nation-states
Separation	Magyar, Greek, Nigerian	Basque, Ibo
Reform	Turkish, Japanese	Fascism, Nazism
Unification	German, Italian	Arab, Pan-African

Finally, Breuilly identifies three different functions performed by nationalist ideas: 'coordination', 'mobilization' and 'legitimacy'. By coordination he means that 'nationalist ideas are used to promote the idea of common interests amongst a number of elites which otherwise have rather distinct interests in opposing the existing state'. By mobilization he means 'the use of nationalist ideas to generate support for the political movement from broad groups hitherto excluded from the political process'. And by legitimacy he means 'the use of nationalist ideas to justify the goals of the political movement both to the state it opposes and also to powerful external agents, such as foreign states and their public opinions' (1996: 166–7).

Having outlined this framework, Breuilly examines the development of nationalism in a number of cases. As I have alluded to above, he covers a wide range of nationalist movements from Europe to the Arab world, from Africa to the Indian sub-continent and a large time span, that is from the eighteenth century to 1989. Since a review of his findings will be beyond the scope of this book, I will now turn to Brass' analysis of nation-formation.

Paul R. Brass and Instrumentalism

Professor of Political Science and South Asian Studies at the University of Washington-Seattle, Paul R. Brass is best known in the literature on nationalism for his studies stressing the 'instrumental' nature of ethnicity. Broadly speaking, instrumentalists hold that ethnic and national identities are convenient tools at the hands of competing elite groups for generating mass support in the universal struggle for wealth, power and prestige (Smith 1986: 9). In stark contrast to primordialists who treat ethnicity as a 'given' of the human condition, they argue that ethnic and national attachments are continually redefined and reconstructed in response to changing conditions and the manipulations of political elites. It follows that

> the study of ethnicity and nationality is in large part the study of politically induced cultural change. More precisely, it is the study of the process by which elites and counter-elites within ethnic groups select aspects of the group's culture, attach new value and meaning to them, and use them as symbols to mobilize the group, to defend its interests, and to compete with other groups. (Brass 1979: 40–1)

These views led Brass to a fierce debate with Francis Robinson about the role of political elites in the process culminating in the formation of two separate nation-states in the Indian sub-continent, India and Pakistan. Leaving this highly polemical exchange to the section on criticisms, I will now turn to Brass' account of nationalism, which can be considered as the 'quintessential' illustration of the instrumentalist position.

Brass' theoretical framework is built upon a few basic assumptions. The first concerns the variability of ethnic identities. Brass holds that there is nothing inevitable about the rise of ethnic identities and their transformation into nationalism. To the contrary, the politicization of cultural identities is only possible under specific conditions which need to be identified and analysed carefully. Secondly, ethnic conflicts do not arise from cultural differences, but from the broader political and economic environment which also shapes the nature of the competition between elite groups. Thirdly, this competition will also influence the definition of the relevant ethnic groups and their persistence. This is because the cultural forms, values and practices of ethnic groups become political resources for elites in their struggle for power and prestige. They are transformed into symbols which can facilitate the creation of a political identity and the generation of greater support; thus, their meanings and contents are dependent on political circumstances. Finally, all these assumptions show that the process of ethnic identity formation and its transformation into nationalism is reversible. Depending on political and economic circumstances, elites may choose to downplay ethnic differences and seek cooperation with other groups or state authorities (Brass 1991: 13–16).

Having laid down his basic assumptions, Brass sets out to develop a general framework of analysis that focuses on processes of identity-formation and identity-change. He begins by defining what he calls an 'ethnic category'. In the words of Brass,

> any group of people dissimilar from other peoples in terms of objective cultural criteria and containing within its membership, either in principle or in practice, the elements for a complete division of labour and for reproduction forms an ethnic category. (*Ibid.*: 19)

However, Brass is quick to stress that these 'objective cultural criteria' are not fixed: on the contrary, they are susceptible to change and variation. Moreover, he adds, in pre-modern societies where the process of ethnic transformation (into nationalism) has not yet begun or in postindustrial societies where a great deal of cultural assimilation has taken place, the boundaries separating various ethnic categories are not so clear.

The boundaries in question become clearer and sharper in the process of ethnic transformation. In this process, which should be distinguished from the mere persistence of ethnic differences in a population,

> cultural markers are selected and used as a basis for differentiating the group from other groups, as a focus for enhancing the internal solidarity of the group, as a claim for a particular social status, and, if the ethnic group becomes politicized, as justification for a demand for either group rights in an existing political system or for recognition as a separate nation. (1991: 63)

Brass notes that the existence of objective cultural markers – here, read ethnic differences – in a given population is a necessary, but not a sufficient condition for the process of ethnic transformation to begin.

Another necessary, but still not sufficient condition, is the presence of elite competition for the leadership of an ethnic group or for control over various tangible and/or intangible resources. According to Brass, competition for local control may take four different forms: those between local land controllers and alien authorities, between competing religious elites, between local religious elites and collaborationist native aristocracies, and between native religious elites and alien aristocracies. Another general type of competition arises from the uneven processes of modernization and takes the form of competition for jobs in the government, industry and universities (*ibid.*).

However, as stressed above, neither the existence of ethnic differences nor elite competition are sufficient conditions for the inception of the process of ethnic transformation. The sufficient conditions, Brass argues, are

> the existence of the means to communicate the selected symbols of identity to other social classes within the ethnic group, the existence of a socially mobilized population to whom the symbols may be communicated, and the absence of intense class cleavage or other difficulties in communication between elites and other social groups and classes. (*Ibid.*)

Brass cites growth in literacy rates, the development of media of mass communication, particularly newspapers, the standardization of local languages, the existence of books in local languages and the availability of schools where the medium of instruction is the native language among the factors necessary to promote such interclass communication. Referring to Deutsch, he contends that the growth of communication facilities should be complemented by the emergence of new groups in the society who are 'available' for more intense communication and who demand education and new jobs in the modern sectors of the economy. In short, demand is as important as supply.

Brass notes in passing that a high degree of communal mobilization will be achieved most easily in two types of situations: (a) where there is a local religious elite controlling the temples, shrines or churches and the lands attached to them as well as a network of religious schools; and (b) where the local language has been recognized by the state authorities as a legitimate medium of education and administration, thereby providing the native intelligentsia the means to satisfy the new social groups aspiring to education and job opportunities (*ibid.*: 63–4).

According to Brass, the necessary and sufficient conditions for ethnic transformation are also the preconditions for the development of a successful nationalist movement. He claims that nationalism as an elite phenomenon may arise at any time, even in the early stages of ethnic transformation. However, for it to acquire a mass base, it should go beyond mere elite competition:

> The mass base for nationalism may be created when widespread intraclass competition occurs brought about by the movement of large numbers of people from either a previously over-whelmingly rural group or from a disadvantaged group into eco-nomic sectors occupied predominantly by other ethnic groups. If such a movement is resisted by the dominant group, sup-ported openly or tacitly by state authorities, then the aspirant group will be easily mobilized by nationalist appeals that chal-lenge the existing economic structure and the cultural values associated with it. (*Ibid.*: 65)

On the other hand, if the dominant group perceives the aspira-tions of the disadvantaged group as a threat to its status, then it may develop a nationalist movement of its own. Brass argues that uneven distribution of ethnic groups in urban and rural areas may exacerbate the situation since this will lead to a fierce competition over scarce resources and/or for control of the state structure.

While the mass base of nationalism is provided by ethnic com-petition for economic opportunities, or what Brass calls 'sectorally-based competition for control over state power', the demands that are articulated and the success of a nationalist movement depend on political factors. Brass cites three such factors: the existence of and the strategies pursued by nationalist political organizations, the nature of government response to ethnic group demands, and the general political context (*ibid.*).

Political Organization

According to Brass, nationalism is by definition a political move-ment. Thus, it requires healthy organization, skilled leadership and resources to compete effectively in the system. Brass puts forward five propositions with regard to political organizations. First, organizations that control community resources are likely to be more effective than those that do not. Secondly, organizations that succeed in identifying themselves with the community as a whole are likely to be more effective than those that 'merely' represent the community or those pursuing their own interests. Thirdly, effective nationalist organizations must be able to shape the identity of the groups they lead. Fourthly, they must be able to provide continuity and to withstand changes in leadership. Finally, for a nationalist movement to be successful, one political organization must be dominant in representing the interests of the ethnic group against its rivals (*ibid.*: 48–9).

Government Policies

Brass maintains that institutional mechanisms in a given polity and the responses of governments to ethnic demands may be very crucial in determining a particular group's capacity to survive, its self-definition and its ultimate goals. The strategies adopted by governments to prevent the 'rekindling of ethnic fires' display a great diversity. They range from the most extreme forms of repression (genocide, deportation) to policies designed to undermine the mass base of ethnic groups (assimilation through schooling, integration of ethnic group leaders into the system). Alternatively, governments may attempt to satisfy ethnic demands by following explicitly pluralist policies. These may include the establishment of political structures such as federalism or some special concessions such as the right to receive education in the native language (*ibid.*: 50).

Political Context

The third factor that may influence the success of nationalist movements is the general political context. According to Brass, three aspects of the political context are particularly important: 'the possibilities for realignment of political and social forces and organizations, the willingness of elites from dominant ethnic groups to share power with aspirant ethnic group leaders, and the potential availability of alternative political arenas' (1991: 55).

Brass notes that the need for political realignment may not arise in early modernizing societies where the first groups to organize politically are ethnic groups, or where the leading organizations articulate local nationalisms. Such a need arises when existing political organizations are not able to cope with social changes that erode their support bases or in times of revolutionary upheaval.

Brass argues that a general political realignment will lead to the establishment of new nationalist organizations and present them with new opportunities to secure mass support.

On the other hand, the willingness of elites from dominant ethnic groups to share political power determines the way ethnic conflicts are resolved: '[w]here that willingness does not exist, the society in question is headed for conflict, even civil war and secessionism. However, where such willingness does exist, the prospects for pluralist solutions to ethnic group conflicts are good' (*ibid.*: 57–8).

The third crucial aspect of the general political context is the availability of alternative political arenas and the price to be paid by ethnic groups for shifting to such arenas. Brass contends that unitary states containing geographically concentrated minorities will definitely face at some point demands for administrative and/or political decentralization, if the political needs of these minorities are not adequately satisfied by the state authorities. Under such circumstances, governments may opt for the reorganization of old political arenas or the construction of new ones to satisfy ethnic demands. According to Brass, the use of these strategies work best under the following conditions:

• where there is a relatively open system of political bargaining and competition;
• where there is a rational distribution of power between the federal and local units so that the capture of power at one level by one ethnic group does not close all significant avenues to power;
• where there is more than two or three ethnic groups;
• where ethnic conflicts do not overlap with ideological disagreements between unitarists and federalists; and
• where external powers are not willing to intervene (*ibid.*: 60–1).

Brass claims that where any of these conditions are lacking, pluralist (or federalist) solutions may fail and civil war or secession may ensue. However, Brass adds, secessionism is a high-cost strategy which most political elites will not adopt unless all other alternatives are exhausted and there is a reasonable prospect of external intervention in their favour (*ibid.*: 61). As a result of this, secession has been the least adopted strategy of ethnic conflict resolution in the period following the Second World War (see also Mayall 1990).

It is hard to do justice to this sophisticated theory in a few pages. Suffice it to say that for Brass, or in that respect for any 'instrumentalist', elite competition and manipulation provide the key to an understanding of nationalism.

Eric J. Hobsbawm and the 'Invention of Tradition'

The distinguished Marxist historian Eric J. Hobsbawm is another scholar who stressed the role of political transformations in his analysis of nationalism. Born in the year of the Bolshevik Revolution, Hobsbawm grew up in Vienna as the threat of Nazism moved across central Europe. Living through state-fascism's destruction, he has become 'the most outspoken critic of the "new nationalisms" of Europe, arguing that the Mazzinian age in which nationalism was integrative and emancipatory has long passed' (Anderson 1996: 13). It should also be noted that Hobsbawm's theory of nationalism is part of his broader project of writing the history of modernity: hence his account of nationalism as an outgrowth of the industrial revolution and the political upheavals of the last two centuries. Hobsbawm assembled his theses in *The Invention of Tradition* (1983) which he co-edited with Terence Ranger and, more recently, in *Nations and Nationalism since 1780: Programme, Myth, Reality* (1990) which consists of the Wiles Lectures he delivered at the Queen's University of Belfast in 1985.

According to Hobsbawm, both nations and nationalism are products of 'social engineering'. What deserves particular attention in this process is the case of 'invented traditions' by which he means

> a set of practices, normally governed by overtly or tacitly accepted rules and of a ritual or symbolic nature, which seek to inculcate certain values and norms of behaviour by repetition, which automatically implies continuity with the past. (1983: 1)

Hobsbawm argues that 'the nation' and its associated phenomena are the most pervasive of such invented traditions. Despite their historical novelty, they establish continuity with a suitable past and 'use history as a legitimator of action and cement of group cohesion' (*ibid.*: 12). For him, this continuity is largely factitious. Invented traditions are 'responses to novel situations which take the form of reference to old situations' (*ibid.*: 2). Hobsbawm cites the deliberate choice of the Gothic style for the rebuilt British parliament in the nineteenth century to illustrate this point.

Hobsbawm distinguishes between two processes of invention, namely the adaptation of old traditions and institutions to new situations, and the deliberate invention of 'new' traditions for quite novel purposes. The former can be found in all societies, including the so-called 'traditional' ones as was the case with the Catholic Church faced with new ideological and political challenges or professional armies faced with conscription. The latter, however, occurs only in periods of rapid social change when the need to create order and unity becomes paramount. This explains the importance of the idea of 'national community' which can secure cohesion in the face of fragmentation and disintegration caused by rapid industrialization (Hobsbawm and Ranger 1983: chapter 7; Smith 1991b: 355).

According to Hobsbawm, the period from 1870 to 1914 can be considered as the apogee of invented traditions. This period coincides with the emergence of mass politics. The incursion of hitherto excluded sections of the society into politics created unprecedented problems for the rulers who found it increasingly difficult to maintain the obedience, loyalty and cooperation of their subjects – now defined as citizens whose political activities were recognized as something to be taken into account, if only in the form of elections (Hobsbawm and Ranger 1983: 264–5). The 'invention of tradition' was the main strategy adopted by the ruling elites to counter the threat posed by mass democracy. Hobsbawm singles out three major innovations of the period as particularly relevant: the development of primary education; the invention of public ceremonies (like the Bastille Day); and the mass production of public monuments (*ibid.*: 270–1). As a result of these processes, 'nationalism became a substitute for social cohesion through a national church, a royal family or other cohesive traditions, or collective group self-presentations, a new secular religion' (*ibid.*: 303). And since

so much of what subjectively makes up the modern 'nation' consists of such constructs and is associated with appropriate and,
in general, fairly recent symbols or suitably tailored discourse
(such as 'national' history), the national phenomenon cannot
be adequately investigated without careful attention to the
'invention of tradition'. (*Ibid.*: 14)

In the light of these observations, Hobsbawm concurs with
Gellner's definition of nationalism in his later work; that is, 'a principle which holds that the political and national unit should be
congruent' (1990: 9; Gellner 1983: 1). For him, this principle also
implies that the political duties of citizens to the nation override
all other obligations. This is what distinguishes modern nationalism from earlier forms of group identification which are less
demanding. Such a conception of nationalism overrules 'primordialist' understandings of the nation which treat it as a 'given' and
unchanging category. Hobsbawm argues that nations belong to a
particular, historically recent, period. It does not make sense to
speak of nations before the rise of the modern territorial state;
these two are closely related to each other (1990: 9–10). Here,
Hobsbawm once again refers to Gellner:

Nations as a natural, God-given way of classifying men, as an
inherent though long-delayed political destiny, are a myth;
nationalism, which sometimes takes pre-existing cultures and
turns them into nations, sometimes invents them, and often
obliterates pre-existing cultures: *that* is a reality, and in general
an inescapable one. (Gellner 1983: 48–9)

In short, 'nations do not make states and nationalisms but the
other way round' (Hobsbawm 1990: 10).

On the other hand, Hobsbawm holds that the origins of nationalism should be sought at the point of intersection of politics,
technology and social transformation. Nations are not only the
products of the quest for a territorial state: they can come into
being in the context of a particular stage of technological and economic development. For instance, national languages cannot
emerge as such before the invention of printing and the spread of
literacy to large sections of the society, hence mass schooling

(*ibid.*). According to Hobsbawm, this shows that nations and nationalism are dual phenomena,

> constructed essentially from above, but which cannot be under-
> stood unless also analysed from below, that is in terms of the
> assumptions, hopes, needs, longings and interests of ordinary
> people, which are not necessarily national and still less nation-
> alist. (*Ibid.*)

Hobsbawm finds Gellner's account wanting in that respect since it does not pay adequate attention to the view from below. Obviously, the views and needs of ordinary people are not easy to discover. But, Hobsbawm continues, it is possible to reach preliminary con-clusions from the writings of social historians. He suggests three such conclusions. First, official ideologies of states and movements are not reliable guides as to what ordinary people – even the most loyal citizens – think. Second, we cannot assume that for most people national identification is always or ever superior to other forms of identification which constitute the social being. And thirdly, national identification and what it means to each indi-vidual can shift in time, even in the course of short periods (*ibid.*: 10–11).

Broadly speaking, Hobsbawm identifies three stages in the his-torical evolution of nationalism. The first stage covers the period from the French Revolution to 1918 when nationalism was born and gained rapid ground. Hobsbawm makes a distinction between two kinds of nationalism in this stage: the first, which transformed the map of Europe between 1830 and 1870, was the democratic nationalism of the 'great nations' stemming from the ideals of the French Revolution; and the second, which came to the fore from 1870 onwards, was the reactionary nationalisms of the 'small nations', mostly against the policies of the Ottoman, Habsburg and Tsarist empires (1990: chapter 1; Smith 1995: 11).

Hobsbawm's second stage covers the period from 1918 to 1950. For him, this period was the 'apogee of nationalism', not because of the rise of fascism, but the upsurge of national sentiment on the left – as exemplified in the course of the Spanish Civil War. Hobs-bawm claims that nationalism acquired a strong association with the left during the anti-fascist period, 'an association which was subsequently reinforced by the experience of anti-imperial strug-

gle in colonial countries' (1990: 148). For him, militant nationalism was nothing more than the manifestation of despair, the utopia
of 'those who had lost the old utopias of the age of Enlightenment'
(*ibid.*: 144).

The late twentieth century constitutes Hobsbawm's last stage. He
argues that the nationalisms of this period were functionally different from those of the earlier periods. Nationalisms of the nineteenth and early twentieth centuries were 'unificatory as well as
emancipatory' and they were a 'central fact of historical transformation'. However, nationalism in the late twentieth century was no
longer 'a major vector of historical development' (*ibid.*: 163). They
are

> essentially negative, or rather divisive . . . In one sense they may
> be regarded as the successors to, sometimes the heirs of, the
> small-nationality movements directed against the Habsburg,
> Tsarist and Ottoman empires . . . Time and again they seem to
> be reactions of weakness and fear, attempts to erect barricades
> to keep at bay the forces of the modern world. (*ibid.*: 164)

Hobsbawm cites Québec, Welsh and Estonian nationalisms to illustrate this claim and argues that 'in spite of its evident prominence,
nationalism is historically less important'. After all, the fact that historians are now making rapid progress in analysing nationalism
means that the phenomenon is past its peak. He concludes: 'The
owl of Minerva which brings wisdom, said Hegel, flies out at dusk.
It is a good sign that it is now circling round nations and nationalism' (*ibid.*: 181, 183).

*   *   *

So far, I have tried to summarize the theories/approaches of three
scholars who focus on the role of political transformations to
explain nationalism. A brief recapitulation of their main arguments will be helpful here in terms of setting the scene for criticisms. Breuilly treats nationalism primarily as a form of politics and
tries to make sense of it in the context of the development of the
modern state. Pouring scorn on 'general theories', he develops a
typology of nationalism and explores each type by the method of
comparative history. Brass, on the other hand, provides an 'instrumentalist' account of nationalism which stresses the role of elite
competition in the genesis of ethnic and national identities. He

holds that the cultural forms, values and practices of ethnic groups become political resources for elites who are engaged in an endless struggle for power and/or economic advantage. Hence, the study of ethnicity and nationality should be the study of 'politically-induced cultural change'. Finally, Hobsbawm regards the nation and its associated phenomena as products of 'social engineering', more specifically as traditions invented by ruling elites who felt threatened by the incursion of the masses into politics. Their aim was to secure the obedience and loyalty of their subjects, now redefined as citizens, in an age when other forms of legitimacy like religion or dynasty were rapidly losing ground. By establishing continuity with a suitable historical past, they smoothed the transition to a new kind of society.

For the sake of a more systematic presentation, I will divide the criticisms raised against political explanations into two categories. The first category will be devoted to 'general' criticisms which concentrate on the assumptions common to all three accounts. I will identify four such criticisms: theories of 'political transformation' are misleading so far as the date of first nations is concerned; they fail to account for the persistence of pre-modern ethnic ties; they cannot explain why so many people are prepared to die for their nations; and finally, they put too much emphasis on one set of factors at the expense of others. The second category on the other hand, will be reserved for more 'specific' criticisms, that is criticisms levelled against particular aspects of each theory. Three such criticisms will be singled out: state-building should not be equated with nation-building; instrumentalists exaggerate the part played by elites in shaping national identities; and Hobsbawm fails in his predictions about the future of nationalism. Let me now discuss each of these criticisms in more detail.

General Criticisms

Theories of 'Political Transformation' are Misleading so far as the Date of First Nations is Concerned

Mostly articulated by ethno-symbolists, this 'counter-argument' suggests that the first examples of nationalism can be found much earlier than the eighteenth century. For example Smith, while conceding that nationalism as an ideology and a movement is a fairly

recent phenomenon, argues that the origins of national sentiments can be traced back to the fifteenth and sixteenth centuries
in many states of Western Europe. According to Smith, the small
clerical and bureaucratic classes of France, England, Spain and
Sweden began to feel a strong attachment to their nation – which
they conceived as a territorial-cultural community – from the fifteenth century onwards. And a wider 'middle-class' nationalism
was already in place by the sixteenth century, especially in England
and the Netherlands (1995: 38). Similarly, Greenfeld locates the
emergence of national sentiment in England in the first third of
the sixteenth century (1992: 42). Hastings goes one step further
and contends that 'English nationalism of a sort was present
already in the fourteenth century in the long wars with France'
(1997: 5). However, he admits that the most intense phase of that
nationalism should be located in the late sixteenth century.

Such Theories Fail to Account for the Persistence of Pre-modern
Ethnic Ties

Ethno-symbolists also argue that political modernists cannot
explain the continuing relevance of pre-modern ethnic attachments. Holding that traditional structures have been eroded by the
revolutions of modernity, the modernists fail to notice that the
impact of these revolutions has been more marked in certain areas
than others and has penetrated some strata of the population more
profoundly than others. Smith argues that religion and ethnicity
in particular have resisted assimilation to the 'dominant and
secular ethos of modernity' (1995: 40–1). For him, theories which
do not take the durability of ethnic ties into consideration cannot
answer the following questions: 'Can such manipulations hope to
succeed beyond the immediate moment? Why should one
invented version of the past be more persuasive than others? Why
appeal to the past at all, once the chain of tradition is seen to be
beyond repair?' (1991b: 357).

Drawing on these observations, Smith objects to Hobsbawm's
notion of 'invented traditions' and claims that these turn out to be
more akin to 'reconstruction' or 'rediscovery' of aspects of the
ethnic past. He notes that although the past can be interpreted in
different ways, it is not any past, but rather the 'past of that particular community, with its distinctive patterns of events, person-

ages and milieux'. This past acts as a constraint on the manipulations of elites, hence on invention (*ibid.*: 358). 'New' traditions will
be accepted by the masses in so far as they can be shown to be continuous with the living past. Lieven makes a similar point, arguing
that from a practical, non-academic point of view 'it is of secondary
importance where nationalist ideas . . . came from, how "genuine"
or "artificial" they may be, or how recently they were generated'.
The real test is: do they work? In other words, do they succeed in
mobilizing the people to which they appeal? Do they make them
willing to fight and die? (1997: 16).

These Theories Cannot Explain Why So Many People are Prepared to Die for Their Nations

Another criticism voiced by ethno-symbolist writers concerns the
instrumentalism of these theories. For them, such accounts are
unable to explain why millions of women and men have sacrificed
their lives for their nations. Smith argues that this failure stems
from the 'top-down' method employed by most modernist theorists: 'They concentrate, for the most part, on elite manipulation
of "the masses" rather than on the dynamics of mass mobilisation
per se' (1995: 40). As a result of this, they do not pay enough attention to the needs, interests, hopes and longings of ordinary people.
They fail to notice that these needs and interests are differentiated
by class, gender, religion and ethnicity (*ibid.*). This also applies
to Hobsbawm who criticizes Gellner for ignoring 'the view
from below'. Koelble notes that Hobsbawm 'does not himself
provide much of an analysis of the effects of modernization on the
lower classes' (1995: 78). As I have alluded to earlier, for ethno-
symbolist writers the answer lies in the subjective 'ethno-history'
which continues to shape our identity and helps to determine our
collective goals and destinies. Thus, they prefer to focus on the
ways in which these groups have been mobilized by their own cultural and political traditions, their memories, myths and symbols
(Smith 1991b: 358).

Strikingly enough, Breuilly expresses a similar complaint about
the instrumentalist approach. He argues that this approach cannot
explain why – and how – nationalism convinces those who have no
interest – or those who actually go against their own interests – in
supporting it (1993b: 21). Actually, all these criticisms revolve

around one simple question: how does nationalism succeed in per-suading so many people to lay down their lives for their country? To put it differently, how do we explain the emotional appeal or the 'charm' of nationalism?

These Theories Put Too Much Emphasis on One Set of Factors at the Expense of Others

This final criticism concerns the modernists' portrayal of recent history. Some ethno-symbolist writers argue that the modernists depict the last two centuries as shaped by a single decisive transi-tion. Political revolutions, industrial take-off and the decline of religious authority were the main features of this transition. Hutchinson calls this the 'revolutionary' model of modernization (1994: 23). For scholars who espouse some version of the revolu-tionary model, nationalism is one of the by-products – albeit an important one – of this momentous transition to modernity. Hutchinson contends that this model cannot explain the much more evolutionary formation of national states in Western Europe. According to him, this process needs to be examined in *la longue durée*, that is by focusing on a much larger time span. In other words, post-eighteenth century nationalism can only be under-stood within the framework of 'a wider theory of ethnic formation that refers to the factors that may be common to the premodern and modern periods' (*ibid.*: 24; see also Llobera 1994).

Smith puts this in a different way. He argues that modernist approaches underestimate the significance of local cultural and social contexts. For him, what determines the intensity, character and scope of nationalism is the interaction between the tidal wave of modernization and these local variations. He accepts that modernity played its part in generating Aboriginal nationalisms in Australia just as it had done in France and Russia; but this does not tell us much about the timing, scope and character of these completely different nationalisms (1995: 42).

Specific Criticisms

State-building Should Not be Equated with Nation-building

Smith holds that state-building is not to be confused with the forging of a national identity among culturally homogeneous

populations, because the establishment of incorporating state institutions is no guarantee that the population will identify with these
institutions and the national myth they promote. On the contrary,
the formulation of an assimilative myth by the ruling elites may
alienate those groups who refuse to identify with it (Smith 1995:
38). He refers to the experiences of the new states of Asia and
Africa to illustrate this point and argues that in many cases 'there
has been not the fusion of *ethnies* through a territorial national
identity but the persistence of deep cleavages and ethnic antagonisms that threaten the very existence of the state' (*ibid.*: 39). In
other cases, attempts by state authorities to create a homogeneous
national identity were perceived as repression, even 'ethnocide' or
genocide by the victimized groups who in turn resorted to mass
resistance, if not outright revolt, to counter them. In short, then,
the role of the modern state in the genesis of nationalism should
not be exaggerated. There are other forces which may predispose
populations to nationalist programmes (*ibid.*).

Instrumentalists Exaggerate the Part Played by Elites in Shaping National Identities

This criticism led to a memorable exchange between Francis
Robinson and Paul R. Brass on the relative weight to be attached
to Islamic values and to elite manipulation in the process leading
up to the formation of two separate states in the Indian sub-
continent (Brass 1977, 1979; Robinson 1977, 1979). Accusing Brass
for exaggerating the role of elite manipulation in this process,
Robinson holds that the values and religio-political ideas of
Islam, especially those that stress the existence of a Muslim community, limited the range of actions open to Muslim elite groups.
These ideas formed 'their own apprehensions of what was possible
and of what they ought to be trying to achieve' and thus acted
as a constraining factor on Hindu–Muslim cooperation (1979:
106).

For Robinson, the religious differences between Muslims and
Hindus in the nineteenth century were too great to allow peaceful coexistence: in a way, they were predisposed to live as separate
national groups. Brass does not ignore these differences, or more
generally pre-existing cultural values that may influence the ability
of elites to manipulate particular symbols. But for him, the crucial
question is:

given the existence in a multi-ethnic society of an array of cultural distinctions among peoples and of actual and potential cultural conflicts among them, what factors are critical in determining which of those distinctions, if any, will be used to build political identities? (1991: 77)

Here, Brass turns to the role of political elites, the balance between rates of social mobilization and assimilation between ethnic groups, the building of political organizations to promote group identities and the influence of government policies. Clearly, the answer to this question has broader theoretical implications with regard to the most fundamental divide of the literature on nationalism, namely that between the 'primordialists' and 'instrumentalists'. Both writers agree that these are extreme positions and that the answer lies between the two (Brass 1991: chapter 3; Robinson 1979: 107). As the above discussion shows, Brass veers towards the instrumentalist position, whereas Robinson insists that 'the balance of the argument should shift more towards the position of the primordialists' (1979: 107).

Hobsbawm Fails in his Predictions about the Future of Nationalism

We have seen that for Hobsbawm nationalism no longer constitutes the major vector of historical development: it has rapidly lost ground in the late twentieth century *vis-à-vis* the forces of globalization. The fragments of ethnic and linguistic nationalisms we witness today are no more than ephemeral reactions of weakness and fear of those who feel threatened by the processes of modernization (1990: chapter 6). Some scholars argued that this was a rather 'naive' prediction as the events of the last decade, especially the post-1989 'nationality boom', have revealed. Tiryakian, for example, asserts that 'the keenest historian was no more prescient about the impending implosion of the Soviet Empire than anybody else' (1995: 213).

Smith makes the same point with the help of examples. He argues that nationalism continues to flourish, if in sometimes less violent forms, in some of the most advanced industrial societies such as France, Canada, Spain and the United States (1995: 42–3). There is also the recent problem of xenophobia and ethnic violence against immigrants, *Gastarbeiter* and asylum-seekers. Smith remarks that this takes both popular and official forms. Given the continuing power of ethnicity, he concludes, 'it would be folly to predict an early supersession of nationalism and an imminent transcendence of the nation' (*ibid*.: 160).

Social/Cultural Transformation

The last group of theories I will consider in this chapter stresses the importance of social/cultural transformations in understanding national phenomena. The influential analyses of Ernest Gellner and Benedict Anderson will be reviewed in this section. The chapter will then conclude with an assessment of Hroch's account of the rise of national movements among the 'small nations' of Central/Eastern Europe.

Ernest Gellner and 'High Cultures'

Tom Nairn once made the important point that 'personal biography and life experience have been a major determinant of what and how nationalism gets studied' (cited in McCrone 1998: 172). Nothing illustrates this better than the work of the Czech polymath Ernest Gellner. The circumstances of Gellner's life made it utterly impossible for him to neglect nationalism (Hall 1998: 1; see also Hall and Jarvie 1996a; Gellner 1997; McCrone 1998). Born in Paris in 1925, he grew up in Prague which was then a multicultural and highly cosmopolitan city. Both his parents were lower middle class Bohemians of Jewish background, who shifted their allegiance from the German to the Czech community (Hall 1998: 1). Gellner himself spoke German with his parents, Czech with his sister and friends, and learned English after he was sent to the Prague English Grammar School.

In the late 1930s, when the Nazi threat became obvious, the family fled the country, crossing Germany by train: 'not all their relatives managed to escape in time' (Gellner 1997: viii). Later, he joined the Czech brigade who fought as part of the British army and saw active service in northern Europe in 1944 and 1945. As a member of the brigade, he took part in the victory parades in

Pilsen and Prague in May 1945. These experiences led Gellner to theorize nationalism. We might note in passing that much theorizing on nationalism has been done by scholars from similar backgrounds, that is coming from cosmopolitan urban settings destroyed by the rise of nationalism – like Hans Kohn, Karl W. Deutsch, Miroslav Hroch, Eric J. Hobsbawm and Elie Kedourie.

Gellner's theory is generally considered as the most important attempt to make sense of nationalism. The originality of his analysis is conceded even by his most staunch critics. Thus, the Marxist Tom Nairn calls Gellner's 1964 essay 'the most important and influential recent study in English' (1981: 96). Another critic, Gavin Kitching, praises Gellner's 'trenchant clarity' in *Nations and Nationalism* (1985: 98). Finally, Anthony D. Smith, who wrote his PhD dissertation under the auspices of Gellner in 1966, considers his theory to be 'one of the most complex and original attempts to come to grips with the ubiquitous phenomenon of nationalism' (1983: 109).

The originality of Gellner's analysis lies in its broad theoretical sweep. The theses he advanced in the seventh chapter of *Thought and Change* (1964) surpassed those of its predecessors in terms of both scope and detail. However, the sweep of his analysis also made him the target of a large number of criticisms. It is indeed true that Gellner was not modest when presenting his model:

> A theoretical model is available which, starting from generalizations which are eminently plausible and not seriously contested, in conjunction with available data concerning the transformation of society in the nineteenth century, does explain the phenomenon in question. (1996a: 98)

After providing a brief summary of his model, he continues:

> The argument . . . seems to me virtually Euclidean in its cogency. It seems to me impossible to be presented with these connections clearly and not to assent to them . . . As a matter of regrettable fact, an astonishing number of people have failed to accept the theory even when presented with it. (*Ibid.*: 110–11)

Gellner's analysis (in particular the original version formulated in *Thought and Change*) set the terms of the debate in subsequent years and provoked a large body of work critically evaluating his contribution to the study of nationalism (see for example Hall and Jarvie 1996b; Hall 1998). In the meantime, Gellner continued to refine his model and to defend it in the face of ever-growing criticisms. He divided his last years between Cambridge and Prague where he set up a Center for the Study of Nationalism – in the former Prague College of the Central European University. He passed away prematurely on 5 November 1995, one month before a conference organized by the Central European University to mark the occasion of his seventieth birthday. Gellner's 'last words' on nationalism are compiled in a small volume which saw the light of day in 1997.

Gellner's theory of nationalism can be better understood within the context of a long-lasting sociological tradition whose origins go back to Durkheim and Weber. The cardinal feature of this tradition is a basic distinction between 'traditional' and 'modern' societies. Following in the footsteps of the founding fathers of sociology, Gellner posited three stages in human history: the hunter-gatherer, the agro-literate and the industrial. This distinction forms the basis of Gellner's explanation which he presents as an alternative to 'false theories of nationalism'. He identifies four such theories:

1. the nationalist theory which sees nationalism as a natural, self-evident and self-generating phenomenon;
2. Kedourie's theory which treats it as 'an artificial consequence of ideas which did not need ever to be formulated, and appeared by a regrettable accident';
3. 'The Wrong Address Theory' favoured by Marxists which holds that the 'awakening message was intended for *classes*, but by some terrible postal error was delivered to *nations*'; and
4. 'Dark Gods Theory' shared by both lovers and haters of nationalism which regards it as 'the re-emergence of the atavistic forces of blood or territory' (1983: 129–30).

For Gellner, on the other hand, 'nationalism is primarily a political principle which holds that the political and the national unit should be congruent' (*ibid.*: 1). It is also a fundamental feature of the modern world since in most of human history political units were not organized along nationalist principles. The boundaries of city-states, feudal entities or dynastic empires rarely coincided with those of nations. In pre-modern times, the nationality of the rulers was not important for the ruled. What counted for them was whether the rulers were more just and merciful than their predecessors (1964: 153). Nationalism became a sociological necessity only in the modern world. And the task of a theory of nationalism is to explain how and why did this happen (1983: 6; 1996a: 98).

Gellner tries to account for the absence of nations and nationalisms in pre-modern ages by referring to the relationship between power and culture. He does not dwell too much on the first, hunter-gatherer, phase as there are no states at this stage, hence no room for nationalism which intends to endow the national culture with a political roof. Agro-literate societies, on the other hand, are characterized by a complex system of fairly stable statuses: 'the possession of a status, and access to its rights and privileges, is by far the most important consideration for a member of such a society. A man is his rank' (1996a: 100–1). In such a society, power and culture, two potential partners destined for each other according to nationalist theory, do not have much inclination to come together: the ruling class, consisting of warriors, priests, clerics, administrators and burghers, uses culture to differentiate itself from the large majority of direct agricultural producers who are confined to small local communities where culture is almost invisible (1983: 9–10, 12). Communication in these self-enclosed units is 'contextual', in contrast to the 'context-free' communication of the literate strata. Thus, this kind of society is marked by 'a discrepancy, and sometimes conflict, between a high and a low culture' (1996a: 102). There is no incentive for rulers to impose cultural homogeneity on their subjects: on the contrary, they derive benefit from diversity. The only class that might have an interest in imposing certain shared cultural norms is the clerisy, but they do not have the necessary means for incorporating the masses in a high culture (1983: 11). The overall conclusion for Gellner is quite simple: since there is no cultural homogenization in agro-literate societies, there can be no nations.

Gellner postulates an altogether different relationship between power and culture in industrial societies. Now, 'a high culture pervades the whole of society, defines it, and needs to be sustained by the polity' (1983: 18). Shared culture is not essential to the preservation of social order in agro-literate societies since status, that is an individual's place in the system of social roles, is ascriptive. In such societies, culture merely underlines structure and reinforces existing loyalties. Conversely, culture plays a more active role in industrial societies which are characterized by high levels of social mobility – and in which roles are no longer ascribed. The nature of work is quite different from that of agro-literate societies:

> Physical work in any pure form has all but disappeared. What is still called manual labour does not involve swinging a pick-axe or heaving soil with a spade . . . it generally involves controlling, managing and maintaining a machine with a fairly sophisticated control mechanism. (1996a: 106)

This has profound implications for culture in that the system can no longer tolerate the dependence of meaning on 'local dialectical idiosyncrasy', hence the need for impersonal, context-free communication and a high level of cultural standardization. For the first time in history, culture becomes important in its own right: it 'does not so much underline structure: rather it replaces it' (Gellner 1964: 155; see also O'Leary 1996).

There is, however, another factor making for the standardization of culture. Industrial society is based on the idea of 'perpetual growth' and this can only be sustained by a continuous transformation of the occupational structure: 'this society simply cannot constitute a stable system of ascribed roles, as it did in the agrarian age . . . Moreover, the high level of technical skill required for at least a significant proportion of posts . . . means that these posts have to be filled "meritocratically"' (Gellner 1996a: 108). The immediate upshot of this is 'a certain kind of egalitarianism'. The society is egalitarian because it is mobile and in a way, it has to be mobile. The inequalities that continue to exist tend to be camouflaged rather than flouted.

On the other hand, the industrial society is also a highly-specialized society. However, the distance between its various specialisms is far less great. This explains why we have 'generic training' before any specialized training on and for the job:

> A modern society is, in this respect, like a modern army, only more so. It provides a very prolonged and fairly thorough training for all its recruits, insisting on certain shared qualifications:

literacy, numeracy, basic work habits and social skills . . . The assumption is that anyone who has completed the generic train-ing common to the entire population can be re-trained for most other jobs without too much difficulty. (1983: 27–8)

This system of education is quite different from the one-to-one or on-the-job principle found in pre-modern societies: 'men are no longer formed at their mother's knee, but rather in the *école mater-nelle*' (1996a: 109). A very important stratum in agro-literate soci-eties was that of the clerks who can transmit literacy. In industrial society where exo-education becomes the norm, every man is a clerk: they are and must be 'mobile, and ready to shift from one activity to another, and must possess the generic training which enables them to follow the manuals and instructions of a new activ-ity or occupation' (1983: 35). It follows that

> the employability, dignity, security and self-respect of individuals . . . now hinges on their *education* . . . A man's education is by far his most precious investment, and in effect confers identity on him. Modern man is not loyal to a monarch or a land or a faith, whatever he may say, but to a culture. (*Ibid.*: 36)

Obviously, this educational infrastructure is large and exceedingly expensive. The only agency capable of sustaining and supervising such a vast system is the central state:

> Given the competition of various states for overlapping catch-ment areas, the only way a given culture can protect itself against another one, which already has its particular protector-state, is to acquire one of its own, if it does not already possess one. Just as every girl should have a husband, preferably her own, so every culture must have its state, preferably its own. (1996a: 110)

This is what brings state and culture together: 'The imperative of exo-socialization is the main clue to why state and culture *must* now be linked, whereas in the past their connection was thin, fortuitous, varied, loose, and often minimal. Now it is unavoidable. That is what nationalism is about' (1983: 38).

In short, nationalism is a product of industrial social organiza-tion. This explains both its weakness and its strength. It is weak in the sense that the number of potential nations far exceeds the number of those that actually make the claim. Most cultures enter the age of nationalism without even the 'feeblest effort' to benefit from it themselves (*ibid.*: 47). They prefer to remain as 'wild' cultures, producing and reproducing themselves spontaneously, without conscious design, supervision or special nutrition. By contrast, the cultures that characterize the modern era are 'cultivated' or 'garden' cultures which are usually sustained by literacy and specialized personnel and would perish if deprived of their distinctive nourishment (*ibid.*: 50; see also Smith 1996d: 132–3).

On the other hand, nationalism is strong because 'it determines the norm for the legitimacy of political units in the modern world' (Gellner 1983: 49). The modern world can be depicted as a kind of 'giant aquarium' or 'breathing chamber' designed to preserve superficial cultural differences. The atmosphere and water in these chambers are specifically tailored to the needs of a new species, the industrial man, which cannot survive in the nature-given atmosphere. But the maintenance of this life-preserving air or liquid is not automatic: 'it requires a special plant. The name for this plant is a national educational and communications system' (*ibid.*: 51–2).

That is what underlies Gellner's contention that 'nations can be defined only in terms of the age of nationalism'. Nations can emerge 'when general social conditions make for standardized, homogeneous, centrally sustained high cultures, pervading entire populations and not just elite minorities'. Hence, 'it is nationalism which engenders nations, and not the other way round' (*ibid.*: 55; see also Smith 1996d: 132):

> Nationalism is, essentially, the general imposition of a high culture on society, where previously low cultures had taken up the lives of the majority, and in some cases of the totality, of the population . . . It is the establishment of an anonymous, impersonal society, with mutually substitutable atomized individuals, held together above all by a shared culture of this kind. (*ibid.*: 57)

How do the small local groups become conscious of their own 'wild' culture and why do they seek to turn it into a 'garden' culture? Gellner's answer to this question is simple: labour migration and bureaucratic employment disclosed 'the difference between dealing with a co-national, one understanding and sympathizing with their culture, and someone hostile to it. This very concrete experience taught them to be aware of their culture, and to love it (or, indeed, to wish to be rid of it)' (*ibid.*: 61) Thus, in conditions of high social mobility, 'the culture in which one has been *taught* to communicate becomes the core of one's identity' (*ibid.*).

This is also one of the two important principles of fission in industrial society. Gellner calls this 'the principle of barriers to communication', barriers based on pre-industrial cultures. The other principle is what he terms 'entropy-resistant traits' like skin colour, deeply engrained religious and cultural habits which tend not to become, even with the passage of time, evenly dispersed throughout the entire society (*ibid.*: 64). Gellner holds that in the later stages of industrial development, when 'the period of acute misery, disorganization, near-starvation, total alienation of the lower strata is over', it is the persistent 'counter-entropic' traits (whether they be genetic or cultural) which become the source of conflict. In the words of Gellner, 'resentment is now engendered less by some objectively intolerable condition . . . it is now brought about above all by the non-random social distribution of some visible and habitually noticed trait' (*ibid.*: 74–5). This conflict may give rise to new nations organized around either a high or a previously low culture.

I have tried to offer a relatively full account of Gellner's theory by concentrating mostly on *Nations and Nationalism*, referring to the earlier chapter in *Thought and Change* and other writings only where appropriate. Gellner later reworked his theory and made some important refinements to it. One such refinement concerns the transition from an agrarian to a full-grown industrial society. Observing that the original version of his theory remained silent on this issue, Gellner postulated five stages on the path from a world of non-ethnic empires and micro-units to one of homogeneous nation-states (1995a, 1996a):

1. *Baseline.* At this stage, ethnicity is not yet important and the idea of a link between it and political legitimacy is entirely absent.

2. *Nationalist Irredentism.* The political boundaries and structures of this stage are inherited from the previous era, but ethnicity – or nationalism – as a political principle begins to operate. The old borders and structures are under pressure from nationalist agitation.

3. *National Irredentism triumphant and self-defeating.* At this stage, multi-ethnic empires collapse and the dynastic-religious principle of political legitimation is replaced by nationalism. New states emerge as a result of nationalist agitation. But, Gellner contends, this state of affairs is self-defeating since these new states are just as 'minority-haunted' as the larger ones they replaced.

4. *Nacht und Nebel.* This is an expression used by the Nazis to depict some of their secret operations in the course of the Second World War. At this stage, all moral standards are suspended and the principle of nationalism, which demands homogeneous national units, is implemented with a new ruthlessness. Mass murder and forcible transplantation of population replace more benign methods such as assimilation.

5. *Post-industrial stage.* This is the post-1945 period. High level of satiation of the nationalist principle, accompanied by general affluence and cultural convergence, leads to a diminution, though not the disappearance, of the virulence of nationalism (1996a: 111–12).

For Gellner, these five stages represent a plausible account of the transition from a non-nationalist order to a nationalist one. However, this schema is not universally applicable, even in Europe. He observes that the stages he postulated played themselves out in different ways in various time zones. He identifies four such zones in Europe:

• Going from West to East, there is first the Atlantic sea-coast. Here, from pre-modern times, there were strong dynastic states. The political units based on Lisbon, London, Paris and Madrid corresponded roughly to homogeneous cultural-linguistic areas. Thus, when the age of nationalism came, relatively little redrawing of frontiers was required. In this zone, one hardly finds 'ethnographic nationalism', that is 'the study, codification, idealization of peasant cultures in the interest of forging a new national culture' (1995a: 29). The problem was rather that of turning peasants into citizens, not so much that of inventing a new culture on the basis of peasant idiosyncrasy (*ibid.*: 29; 1996a: 127–8).

- The second time zone corresponds to the territory of the erstwhile Holy Roman Empire. This area was dominated by two well-endowed high cultures which existed since the Renaissance and the Reformation, namely the German and Italian cultures. Thus, those who tried to create a German literature in the late eighteenth century were merely consolidating an existing culture – and not creating a new one. In terms of literacy and self-awareness, the Germans were not inferior to the French and a similar relationship existed between the Italians and the Austrians. All that was required here was to endow the existing high culture with its political roof (1995a: 29–30; 1996a: 128–9).

- Things were more complicated in the third time zone further east. This was the only area where all five stages played themselves out to the full. Here, there were neither well-defined high cultures, nor states to cover and protect them. The area was characterized by old non-national empires and a multiplicity of folk cultures. Thus, for the marriage between culture and polity required by nationalism to take place, both partners had to be created. This made the task of the nationalists more difficult and 'hence, often, its execution more brutal' (1995a: 30; 1996a: 129).

- Finally, there is the fourth time zone. Gellner maintains that this zone shared the trajectory of the previous one until 1918 or the early 1920s. But, then, the destinies of the two zones diverged. While two of the three empires covering the fourth zone, the Habsburg and Ottoman empires, disintegrated, the third one was dramatically revived under a new management and in the name of a new, inspiring ideology. Gellner notes that the victorious advance of the Red Army in 1945 and the incorporation of a considerable portion of zone three into zone four complicated matters still further. The new regime was able to repress nationalism at the cost of destroying civil society. Hence, when the system was dismantled, nationalism emerged with all its vigour, but few of its rivals. Having been artificially frozen at the end of the second stage, the fourth time zone can resume its normal course at stage three (irredentist nationalism), four (massacres or population transfers) or five (diminution of ethnic conflict). Which of these options will prevail – that is the crucial question facing the territories of the former Soviet Union (1995a: 30–1; 1996a: 129–32).

As I have mentioned earlier, the theoretical sweep of his model and the assertive tone with which he presented it made Gellner the target of a great deal of criticism. Here, I will confine myself to the standard criticisms raised against his theory, which can be summarized as follows: Gellner's model is too functionalist; he misreads the relationship between industrialization and nationalism; he fails to account for the resurgence of ethnic and nationalist sentiments within advanced industrialized societies; his model cannot explain the passions generated by nationalism; the processes underlying his explanation are too general and vacuous.

Gellner's Theory is Too Functionalist

Many scholars reject the stark functionalism of Gellner's theory. It is indeed true that Gellner tries to account for nationalism on the basis of the consequences it generates. More specifically, 'nationalism is "explained" by reference to an historical outcome (the emergence of Industrial Society) which chronologically follows it' (Kitching 1985: 102). For Gellner, nationalism is required by industrial society which could not 'function' without it: thus, nationalism is beneficial for modernizing states. In such a picture, nationalism is unintended by the actors producing modernization as they are unaware of the causal relationship between these two processes (O'Leary 1996: 85). O'Leary contends that

> Gellner's argument displays all the vices of functionalist reasoning – in which events and processes occur which are implausibly treated as wholly beyond the understanding of human agents, in which consequences precede causes, and in which suspicions arise that supra-individual and holistic entities are being tacitly invoked to do explanatory work. (*Ibid.*: 86)

Breuilly, on the other hand, notes that there are a multitude of functions which it is suggested nationalism can serve. For some, nationalism facilitates the process of modernization; for others, it helps the preservation of traditional identities and structures. For some, it is a function of class interest; for others, of identity need. Since there is no universally accepted interpretation, it makes no sense to explain nationalism in terms of the 'function' it serves (Breuilly 1993a: 419).

Minogue goes one step further and argues that functional explanations patronize in the sense of treating the researcher/theorist as a kind of omniscient being. Such explanations imply that what people are doing is actually different from what they believe they are doing and the theorist is in a position to perceive the reality. Hence, nationalists may think that they are liberating the nation, but Gellner knows that what they are really doing is in fact facilitating the transition to an industrial society. The olympian theorist spots the real causes of what is happening and reveals them to the readers (Minogue 1996: 117). Minogue also criticizes Gellner – and functional explanations in general – for underestimating the full conditions of human agency. He maintains that individuals respond rationally to the situations in which they find themselves in the light of the understanding they have of it. According to Minogue, 'different ideas, like the fluttering of the famous butterfly's wing that produces tempest on the other side of the globe, can lead to quite unpredictable consequences' (*ibid.*: 118). Discarding these ideas may doom a theory to extrapolation.

Gellner's functionalism does not manifest itself only in his portrayal of the relationship between nationalism and industrialization. His account of the rise of mass education displays similar functionalist overtones. The theory postulates that the new educational system based on generic training is a product of the new societal conditions. But again a process – here, the emergence of standardized educational systems – is explained by reference to a function which it is purported to play. Breuilly asks: 'education may eventually function in this way but does that explain its development' (1985: 68)? His answer is negative: 'unless one specifies either a deliberate intention on the part of key groups to produce this result or some feed-back mechanism which will "select" generic training patterns of education against other patterns, this cannot count as an explanation' (*ibid.*).

In addition to these theoretical complications, Gellner's functionalism also creates some factual difficulties. This brings us to the second criticism.

Gellner Misreads the Relationship between Industrialization and Nationalism

This is probably the most common charge brought against Gellner's theory. Many scholars cast doubt on Gellner's assumptions by pointing to a series of 'counter-examples'. First, it is argued that many nationalist movements flourished in societies which had not yet undergone industrialization. For instance, Kedourie asserts that nationalism as a doctrine was articulated in German-speaking lands in which there was as yet hardly any industrialization (1994: 143). Kitching makes a similar point for Britain, claiming that the emergence of nationalism in the British Isles precedes even early industrialism by 150–200 years (1985: 106). Minogue suggests the opposite by contending that Britain industrialized without having nationalism at all, and concludes that nationalism is not a necessary condition of industrial society (1996: 121). Kedourie concurs with Minogue and argues that the areas where industrialism first appeared and made the greatest progress, that is Great Britain and the United States, are precisely those areas where nationalism is unknown (1994: 143). However, this disagreement does not save Gellner's theory. Counter-examples abound. Areas like Greece, the Balkans and parts of the Ottoman Empire fell prey to nationalist ideology when they were innocent of industrialization (Kedourie 1994: 143).

Breuilly notes that one can find broadly shared national sentiments in parts of the world which have still not reached this stage. According to him, commercial agriculture, mass education and modern systems of communication can all produce the effects Gellner relates to industrialism. Thus, he concludes, there are other means of diffusing a national culture in non-industrial societies (1996: 162). Anti-imperialist or post-colonial nationalisms are another case in point. Gandhi's nationalism, for example, was quite explicitly hostile to industrialism. In Russia, a regime deeply hostile to nationalism took over the empire in 1917 and proceeded to supply just the conditions Gellner takes to be necessary to an industrial society (Minogue 1996: 120). A final difficulty is created by Nazi Germany, Italy in the Fascist era, and Japan in the 1920s and 1930s which produced the most frenzied nationalist movements despite their high level of industrialization (Kedourie 1994: 143). To sum up, nationalism preceded industrialization in many places; and in still others, nationalism was not a concomitant of the process of industrialization.

It is worth noting that Gellner tries to counter these criticisms by arguing that 'industrialism casts a long shadow' before its actual reality and that at any rate it was only the intellectuals who were nationalists (BBC radio discussion with Kedourie, cited in Minogue 1996: 120). On the other hand, he explicitly admits that Balkan nationalism constitutes a problem for his theory (1996c: 630).

Gellner's Theory Fails to Account for the Resurgence of Ethnic and Nationalist Sentiments within Advanced Industrialized Societies

As might be recalled, one of Gellner's core arguments was that the late industrial society is going to be one in which nationalism persists, but in a muted, less virulent form (1983: 122). This argument was an inevitable consequence of the industrialism/nationalism link he postulated in his theory. Kellas questions the validity of this assumption by pointing to the contemporary nationalist movements that have erupted in long-industrialized countries such as Britain, Spain and Belgium (1991: 44). Similarly, Hutchinson argues that Gellner's theory cannot explain the revival of 'ferocious terrorist nationalisms' within the heartlands of Europe, for instance among the relatively prosperous Basques and Catalans in Spain (1994: 22). On the other hand, Smith makes the same point by invoking the popular reaction to the Maastricht Treaty in countries like France, Britain and Denmark. According to him, the popular doubts and resistance we have witnessed in these countries suggest that we should not overlook the continuing importance of national traditions and experiences (1996d: 141).

Gellner's Model Cannot Explain the Passions Generated by Nationalism

As Gellner himself notes, this point has been raised by various critics from opposed ends of the ideological spectrum (1996c:

625). For instance, Perry Anderson, a leading figure of the New Left, contends that Gellner's theory cannot explain the emotional power of nationalism and adds: '[w]here Weber was so bewitched by its spell that he was never able to theorize nationalism, Gellner had theorized nationalism without detecting the spell' (1992: 205). O'Leary and Minogue, who have nothing to do with Marxism, make much the same point: while O'Leary accuses Gellner for relying on 'culturally and materially reductionist accounts of the political motivations which produce nationalism', Minogue is critical of his neglect of the power of identity (O'Leary 1996: 100; Minogue 1996: 126).

As we saw earlier, this point also forms one of the core arguments of the ethno-symbolist critique of modernist theories. Smith, the leading exponent of the ethno-symbolist approach, begins by asking the following question: why should people ardently identify with an invented high culture and be willing to lay down their lives for it (1996d: 134)? Gellner seeks the answer in modern systems of mass education. However, Smith notes, the ardour of the early nationalists, those who create the nation in the first place, cannot be the product of a national mass education system which has not at that date come into being (1996d: 135). It is not possible to establish a 'national' educational system without first determining who the 'nation' is. Who will receive the education? In which language? To explain the nationalism of those who propose answers to these questions, that is those who 'construct' the nation, by mass education is to fall, once again, into the trap of functionalism. According to Smith, the solution to this problem lies in pre-existing ethnic cultures, the elements of which (its myths, symbols and traditions) have been incorporated into the nascent national cultures.

Gellner rejects these charges by arguing that they are based on a misreading of his theory. He stresses that the model does not explain nationalism by the use it has in legitimating modernization, but by the fact that 'individuals find themselves in very stressful situations, unless the nationalist requirement of congruence between a man's culture and that of its environment is satisfied' (1996c: 626). He contends that without such a congruence, life would be hell: hence the deep passion which is thought to be absent from the theory. The passion, he continues, is not a means to an end, 'it is a reaction to an intolerable situation' (*ibid.*). It is best to end this sub-section with Gellner's reply to Anderson:

Perry gets it absolutely wrong: I *am* deeply sensitive to the spell of nationalism. I can play about thirty Bohemian folk songs (or songs presented as such in my youth) on my mouth organ. My oldest friend, whom I have known since the age of three or four and who is Czech and a patriot, cannot bear to hear me play them because he says I do it in such a schmaltzy way, 'crying into the mouth organ'. I do not think I could have written the book on nationalism which I did write, were I not capable of crying, with the help of a little alcohol, over folk songs, which happen to be my favourite form of music. (*ibid*.: 624–5)

The Processes Underlying his Explanation are Too General and Vacuous

According to Zubaida, all general theories of nationalism assume a 'sociological homogeneity', that is that there are common social structures and processes which underlie the ideological/political phenomena (1978: 56). He notes that all these theories share a basic structure despite their conceptual and terminological variations. To illustrate this structure, he focuses on Gellner's theory which can be regarded as the clearest example of such theories. The main elements of the narrative are: a world historical process (modernization/industrialization); traditional societies which this process hits at a differential pace, leading to differences in the degree of development and resulting in the breakdown of traditional ties and structures; particular social groups (intelligentsia and proletariat for Gellner) taking up the double fight against tradition and against external enemies. The story ends with the establishment of national states. That is followed by the struggle to replace traditional loyalties with national ones among the population at large. For Gellner, this is generated by an educational system which produces citizens with the needed qualifications (*ibid*.: 57).

According to Zubaida, the reality is much more complex. He argues that the sociological explanations of nationalist movements are based on processes and groups which are not generalizable or comparable between the various social contexts. For instance, the term 'industry' does not have the same meaning everywhere: it covers a wide range of forms of production, in scale from small workshops to nuclear power stations. Moreover, the consequences of industrial development are not uniform: factors like capital intensivity, the stratification or segmentation of labour markets, the source, nature and duration of capital investment, the relationship of industry to the agricultural sector may influence the outcome of industrialization and lead to very different socioeconomic configurations. In short, industrialization may not lead to nationalism in all these societies. Gellner's theory – or in that respect any general theory of nationalism – overlooks regional and historical variations (1978: 58–9). In his review of Gellner's *Nations and Nationalism*, Breuilly makes a similar point by arguing that a more differentiated model is needed to explain nationalism (1985: 70).

Benedict Anderson and 'Imagined Communities'

The year 1983 saw the publication of yet another very influential book on nationalism – along with Gellner's *Nations and Nationalism* and Hobsbawm and Ranger's *The Invention of Tradition* – namely *Imagined Communities: Reflections on the Origin and Spread of Nationalism*. Its author, Benedict R. O'G. Anderson, was a Southeast Asia specialist who had done extensive fieldwork in Indonesia, Siam and the Philippines. The initial impetus for writing this book, Anderson later recalls, came from 'the triangular Third Indochina War that broke out in 1978–79 between China, Vietnam, and Cambodia' (1998: 20). More generally, Anderson was intrigued by the fact that 'since World War II every successful revolution has defined itself in *national* terms' and sought to explain how this state of affairs came into being, focusing mainly, but not exclusively, on the cultural sources of nationalism – particularly the transformations of consciousness that made presently existing nations thinkable (Eley and Suny 1996b: 242).

Anderson's point of departure is that nationality and nationalism are cultural artefacts of a particular kind. In order to understand them properly, we need to find out how they have come into being, in what ways their meanings have changed over time and why they command such profound emotional legitimacy. Anderson argues that nationalism emerged towards the end of the eighteenth century as a result of the 'spontaneous distillation of a complex "crossing" of discrete historical forces' and once created, they became models which could be used in a great variety of social terrains, by a correspondingly wide variety of ideologies (1991[1983]: 4). For him, a persuasive explanation of nationalism should not confine itself to specifying the cultural and political factors which facilitate the growth of nations. The real challenge lies in showing why and how these particular cultural artefacts have aroused such deep attachments. In other words, the crucial question is: 'what makes the shrunken imaginings of recent history (scarcely more than two centuries) generate such colossal sacrifices' (*ibid.*: 7)? Before addressing this question, however, he considers the concept of 'nation' and tries to offer a workable definition.

For Anderson, the terminological confusion surrounding the concept of nation is partly caused by the tendency to treat it as an ideological construct. Things would be easier if it is seen as belonging to the same family as 'kinship' or 'religion'; hence his definition of the nation as 'an imagined political community – and imagined as both inherently limited and sovereign'. It is imagined because 'the members of even the smallest nation will never know most of their fellow-members, meet them, or even hear of them, yet in the minds of each lives the image of their communion'. It is imagined as limited because each nation has finite boundaries beyond which lie other nations. It is imagined as sovereign because it is born in the age of Enlightenment and Revolution, when the legitimacy of divinely-ordained, hierarchical dynastic realm was rapidly waning: the nations were dreaming of being free, and if under God, then at least directly so. Finally, it is imagined as a community because, 'regardless of the actual inequality and exploitation that may prevail in each, the nation is always conceived as a deep, horizontal comradeship'. According to Anderson, it is ultimately this sense of fraternity which makes it possible for so many millions of people to willingly lay down their lives for their nation (*ibid.*: 6–7).

Here, it is worth stressing that for Anderson, 'imagining' does not imply 'falsity'. He makes this point quite forcefully when he accuses Gellner for assimilating 'invention' to 'fabrication' and 'falsity', rather than to 'imagining' and 'creation' with the intention of showing that nationalism masquerades under false pretences. Such a view implies that there are 'real' communities which can be advantageously compared to nations. In fact, however, all communities larger than small villages of face-to-face contact (perhaps even these) are imagined. Communities, Anderson concludes, should not be distinguished by their falsity/genuineness, but by the style in which they are imagined (*ibid.*: 6).

Anderson then turns to the conditions which give rise to such imagined communities. He begins with the cultural roots of nationalism, arguing that 'nationalism has to be understood by aligning it, not with self-consciously held political ideologies, but with the large cultural systems that preceded it, out of which – as well as against which – it came into being' (*ibid.*: 12). He cites two such systems as relevant, the religious community and the dynastic realm. Both of these systems held sway over much of Europe until the sixteenth century. Their gradual decline, which began in the seventeenth century, provided the historical and geographical space necessary for the rise of nations.

The decline of the 'great religiously imagined communities' was particularly important in this context. Anderson emphasizes two reasons for this decline. The first was the effect of the explorations of the non-European world which widened the general cultural and geographical horizon, and showed the Europeans that alternative forms of human life were also possible. The second reason was the gradual decay of the sacred language itself. Latin was the dominant language of a pan-European high intelligentsia; in fact, it was the only language taught in medieval Western Europe. But by the sixteenth century all this was changing fast. More and more books were coming out in the vernacular languages and publishing was ceasing to be an international enterprise (1991: 12–19).

What was the significance of all these developments for the emergence of the idea of nation? The answer lies, Anderson argues, in the crucial role played by traditional religions in human life. First and foremost, they soothed the sufferings resulting from the contingency of life ('Why is my best friend paralysed? Why is my daughter retarded?') by explaining them away as 'destiny'. At a more spiritual level, on the other hand, they provided salvation from the arbitrariness of fatality by turning it into continuity (life after death), by establishing a link between the dead and the yet unborn. Predictably, the ebbing of religious world-views did not lead to a corresponding decline in human suffering. In fact, now, fatality was more arbitrary than ever. 'What then was required was a secular transformation of fatality into continuity, contingency into meaning'. Nothing was better suited to this end than the idea of nation which always looms out of an immemorial past, and more importantly, glides into a limitless future: '[i]t is the magic of nationalism to turn chance into destiny' (*ibid.*: 11, 12).

It would be too simplistic, however, to suggest that nations grew out of and replaced religious communities and dynastic realms. Beneath the dissolution of these sacred communities, a much more fundamental transformation was taking place in the modes of apprehending the world. This change concerns the medieval Christian conception of time which is based on the idea of simultaneity. According to such a conception, events are situated simultaneously in the present, past and future. The past prefigures the future, so that the latter 'fulfils' what is announced and promised in the former. The occurrences of the past and the future are linked neither temporally nor causally, but by Divine Providence which alone can devise such a plan of history. In such a view of things, Anderson notes, 'the word "meanwhile" cannot be of real significance' (*ibid.*: 24). This conception of 'simultaneity-along-time' was replaced by the idea of 'homogeneous empty time', a term Anderson borrows from Walter Benjamin. Simultaneity is now understood as being transverse, cross-time, marked by temporal coincidence and measured by clock and calendar. The new conception of time made it possible to 'imagine' the nation as a 'sociological organism' moving steadily down (or up) history (*ibid.*: 26). To illustrate this point, Anderson examines two popular forms of imagining, the novel and the newspaper.

He first considers a simple novel-plot consisting of four characters: a man (A) has a wife (B) and a mistress (C), who in turn has a lover (D). Assuming that (C) has played her cards right and that (A) and (D) never meet, what actually links these two characters? First, that they live in 'societies' (Lübeck, Los Angeles): '[t]hese societies are sociological entities of such firm and stable reality that their members (A and D) can even be described as passing each other on the street, without ever becoming acquainted, and still be connected' (*ibid.*: 25). Second, that they are connected in the minds of the readers. Only the readers could know what (A) and (D) are doing at a particular moment in time. According to Anderson, that all these acts are performed at the same clocked, calendrical time, but by actors who may be largely unaware of one another, shows the novelty of this imagined world conjured up by the author in his readers' mind. (*Ibid.*: 26)

This has profound implications for the idea of nation. An American would probably never meet, or even know the names of more than a handful of his fellow-Americans. He would have no idea of what they are doing at any one time. Yet he has complete confidence in their existence and their 'steady, anonymous, simultaneous activity' (*ibid.*).

A similar link is established by the newspaper which embodies a profound fictiveness. If we take a quick glance at the front page of any newspaper, we will discover a number of, seemingly independent, stories. Anderson asks: what connects them to each other? First, calendrical coincidence. The date at the top of the newspaper provides the essential connection: 'Within that time, "the world" ambles sturdily ahead'. If, for example, Mali disappears from the front pages of newspapers, we do not think that Mali has disappeared altogether. 'The novelistic format of the newspaper assures them that somewhere out there the "character" Mali moves along quietly, awaiting its next appearance in the plot' (*ibid.*: 33).

The second connection is provided by the simultaneous mass consumption of newspapers. In that sense, the newspaper can be considered as an 'extreme form of the book', a 'book sold on a colossal scale' or 'one-day best-sellers' (*ibid.*: 33–4). We know that a particular edition will be read between this and that hour, only on this day, not that. This is, in a way, a mass ceremony, a ceremony performed in silent privacy, '[y]et each communicant is well aware that the ceremony he performs is being replicated simultaneously by thousands (or millions) of others of whose existence he is confident, yet of whose identity he has not the slightest notion' (*ibid.*: 35). It is difficult to envision a more vivid figure for the secular, historically clocked imagined community. Moreover, observing that the exact replicas of his own newspaper are consumed by his neighbours, in the subway or barbershop, the reader is continually reassured that the imagined world is rooted in everyday life: 'fiction seeps quietly and continuously into reality, creating that remarkable confidence of community in anonymity which is the hallmark of modern nations' (*ibid.*: 36).

To recapitulate, the cultural origins of the modern nation could be located historically at the junction of three developments: a change in the conceptions of time, the decline of religious communities and of dynastic realms. But the picture is not complete yet. The missing ingredient is provided by commercial book-publishing on a wide scale, or what Anderson calls 'print-capitalism'. This made it possible, more than anything else, for rapidly growing numbers of people to think of themselves in profoundly new ways.

The initial market for capitalist book-publishing was the thin stratum of Latin-readers. This market, Anderson notes, was saturated in 150 years. However, capitalism needed markets, hence profit. The inherent logic of capitalism forced the publishers, once the elite Latin market was saturated, to produce cheap editions in the vernaculars with the aim of reaching the monoglot masses. This process was precipitated by three factors. The first was a change in the character of Latin. Thanks to the Humanists, the literary works of pre-Christian antiquity were discovered and spread to the market. This generated a new interest in the sophisticated writing style of the ancients which further removed Latin from ecclesiastical and everyday life. Second was the impact of the Reformation, which owed much of its success to print-capitalism. The coalition between Protestantism and print-capitalism quickly created large reading publics and mobilized them for political/religious purposes. Third was the adoption of some vernaculars as administrative languages. Anderson remarks that the rise of administrative vernaculars predated both print and the Reformation, hence must be regarded as an independent factor. Together, these three factors led to the dethronement of Latin and created large reading publics in the vernaculars (*ibid.*: 38–43).

Anderson argues that these print-languages laid the bases for national consciousnesses in three ways. First, they created 'unified fields of exchange and communication below Latin and above the spoken vernaculars'. Second, print-capitalism gave a new fixity to language which helped to build the image of antiquity so central to the idea of the nation. And third, print-capitalism created languages-of-power of a kind different from the earlier administrative vernaculars. In short, what made the new communities imaginable was 'a half-fortuitous, but explosive, interaction between a system of production and productive relations (capitalism), a technology of communications (print), and the fatality of human diversity' (*ibid.*: 42–4).

Having specified the general causal factors underlying the rise of nations, Anderson turns to particular historical/cultural contexts with the aim of exploring the 'modular' development of nationalism. He begins by considering Latin America. This section contains one of the most interesting – and controversial – arguments of the book, namely that the *creole* communities of the Americas developed their national consciousnesses well before most of Europe. According to Anderson, two aspects of Latin American nationalisms separated them from their counterparts in Europe. First, language did not play an important role in their formation since the colonies shared a common language with their respective imperial metropoles. Second, the colonial national movements were led by creole elites and not by the intelligentsia. On the other hand, the factors that incited these movements were not limited to the tightening of Madrid's control and the spread of the liberalizing ideas of the Enlightenment. Each of the South American Republics had been an administrative unit between the sixteenth and eighteenth centuries. This led them to develop a 'firmer reality' over time, a process precipitated by 'administrative pilgrimages', or what Anderson calls the 'journey between times, statuses and places'. Creole functionaries met their colleagues ('fellow-pilgrims') from places and families they have scarcely heard of in the course of these pilgrimages and, in experiencing them as travelling-companions, developed a consciousness of connectedness (why are *we . . . here . . . together?*) (*ibid.*: 50–6).

The close of the era of successful national movements in the Americas, Anderson argues, coincided with the onset of the age of nationalism in Europe. The earlier examples of European nationalisms were different from their predecessors in two respects: national print-languages were an important issue in their formation and they had 'models' they could aspire to from early on. Anderson cites two developments which speeded up the rise of classic linguistic nationalisms. The first was the discovery of distant 'grandiose' civilizations, such as the Chinese, Japanese, Indian, Aztec or Incan, which allowed Europeans to think of their civilizations as only one among many, and not necessarily the Chosen or the best (*ibid.*: 69–70).

The second was a change in European ideas about language.

Anderson observes that the scientific comparative study of languages got under way from the late eighteenth century onwards. In this period, vernaculars were revived; dictionaries and grammar books were produced. This had profound implications for the old, sacred languages which were now considered to be on an equal footing with their vernacular rivals. The most visible manifestation of this egalitarianism was 'bilingual dictionaries', for 'whatever the political realities outside, within the covers of the Czech–German/German-Czech dictionary the paired language had a common status' (*ibid.*: 71). Obviously, this 'lexicographic revolution' was not experienced in a vacuum. The dictionaries or grammar books were produced for the print-market, hence consuming publics. The general increase in literacy rates, together with a parallel growth in commerce, industry and communications, created new impulses for vernacular linguistic unification. This, in turn, made the task of nationalism easier.

On the other hand, these developments created increasing political problems for many dynasties in the course of the nineteenth century because the legitimacy of most of them had nothing to do with 'nationalness'. The ruling dynastic families and the aristocrats were threatened with marginalization or exclusion from the nascent 'imagined communities'. This led to 'official nationalisms', a term Anderson borrows from Seton-Watson, which was

> a means for combining naturalization with retention of dynastic power, in particular over the huge polyglot domains accumulated since the Middle Ages, or, to put it another way, for stretching the short, tight, skin of the nation over the gigantic body of the empire. (*Ibid.*: 86)

Anderson stresses that official nationalisms developed after, and in reaction to, the popular national movements proliferating in Europe since the 1820s. Thus, they were historically 'impossible' until after the appearance of the latter. Moreover, these nationalisms were not confined to Europe. Similar policies were pursued in the vast Asian and African territories subjected in the course of the nineteenth century. They were also picked up and imitated by indigenous ruling elites in areas which escaped subjection (*ibid.*: 109–10).

This brings Anderson to his final stop, namely anti-colonial nationalisms in Asia and Africa. This 'last wave' of nationalisms, he contends, was largely inspired by the example of earlier movements in Europe and the Americas. A key part was played in this process by official nationalisms which transplanted their policies of 'Russification' to their extra-European colonies. Anderson claims that this ideological tendency meshed with practical exigencies as the late nineteenth century empires were too large and too far-flung to be ruled by a handful of nationals. Moreover, the state was rapidly multiplying its functions in both the metropoles and the colonies. What, then, was required was well-educated subordinate cadres for state and corporate bureaucracies. These were generated by the new school systems, which in turn led to new pilgrimages, this time not only administrative, but also educational.

On the other hand, the logic of colonialism meant that the natives were invited to schools and offices, but not to boardrooms. Result: 'lonely, bilingual intelligentsias unattached to sturdy local bourgeoisies' which became the key spokesmen for colonial nationalisms (*ibid.*: 140). As bilingual intelligentsias, they had access to models of nation and nationalism, 'distilled from the turbulent, chaotic experiences of more than a century of American and European history'. These models could be copied, adapted and improved upon. Finally, the improved technologies of communication enabled these intelligentsias to propagate their messages not only to illiterate masses, but also to literate masses reading different languages (*ibid.*). In the conditions of the twentieth century, nation-building was much easier than before.

It is hard to do justice to Anderson's sophisticated analysis in a few pages. Suffice it to say that it constitutes one of the most original accounts of nationalism to date. Before proceeding, it needs to be noted that Anderson's theory has not been immune to the general criticisms raised against modernist explanations of nationalism. I will not repeat them here since they were discussed in detail in previous sections. Apart from these general points, it is possible to identify five specific objections to Anderson's account: it is culturally reductionist; his arguments concerning the relationship between nationalism and religion do not work for certain cases; his thesis that nationalism is born in the Americas runs counter to available evidence; his examples of official nationalism are not correct; he misinterprets the rise of anti-colonial-nationalisms.

Anderson's Account is Culturally Reductionist

Anderson's emphasis on the way in which nations as 'imagined communities' come to be constructed through cultural representations led some scholars to accuse him of 'cultural reductionism'. Breuilly, for instance, criticizes Anderson for underestimating the political dimension of nationalism, and more specifically, for exaggerating the importance of cultural nationalism in nineteenth century Europe (1985: 71–2). According to Breuilly, Anderson's theses, while plausible in eighteenth century America, falter when he moves to Europe: he cannot tackle the thorny problem of the lack of congruence between 'cultural' and 'political' nationalism in certain cases (*ibid.*). To illustrate this point, Breuilly points to the 'political' unification of Germany which was not accompanied by a 'cultural' unification. The political dimension plays a more significant role even in the case of the liberation movements that developed in eighteenth century America, for which Anderson's argument works better. Most of these movements, Breuilly notes, worked within the territorial framework set down by the colonial system.

In general, Breuilly concurs with Anderson that the cultural dimension is important for understanding nationalism, but adds that this dimension can only explain why certain small groups might be disposed to imagine themselves as a nation and act politically on the basis of this assumption. Anderson's theory, he continues, cannot provide an answer to the question of 'why are those groups important': in other words, 'why does anyone either above (in power) or below (in the society claimed to be national) take these arguments seriously' (*ibid.*: 73). Breuilly contends that Gellner's theory is more satisfactory in this respect since it tries to pinpoint some basic changes in the social structure which might underpin the type of cultural processes Anderson considers. He concludes by claiming that a closer examination of the links between the modern state and nationalism might provide a solution to this problem.

Balakrishnan makes a similar point when he argues that the cultural affinities generated and shaped by print-capitalism do not seem sufficient to explain the colossal sacrifices that peoples are at times willing to make for their nation. It is easier to understand the sacrifices people make for their religion since 'weightier issues than mere life on this earth hang in the balance' (1996a: 208). It is harder to see how societies operating in a vernacular could ever inspire the same pathos. At this stage, Balakrishnan points to the impact of wars in shaping national consciousness and blames Anderson for neglecting the role of domination and force in history (*ibid.*: 208–11). Smith agrees with Balakrishnan and calls attention to the needs of the 'state-at-war' which antedate both print and expanding capitalism in Western Europe (1991b: 363).

Anderson's Arguments Concerning the Relationship between Nationalism and Religion Do Not Work for Certain Cases

Kellas claims that religion is not always replaced by nationalism: he refers to the examples of Ireland, Poland, Armenia, Israel and Iran, where religious institutions have reinforced nationalism, to support this argument. There are also cases where nationalism and religion thrive together. Therefore, it is difficult to relate the rise of nationalism to the decline of religion (1991: 48).

Greenfeld goes one step further and argues that '[n]ationalism emerged in a time of ardent religious sentiment, when questions of religious identity grew more, rather than less acute, and faith became more significant – the time of the Reformation' (1993: 49). According to Greenfeld, nationalism was able to develop and become established with the support of religion. Even at later stages, when it replaced it as the governing passion, it incorporated religion as a part of the national consciousness in many cases.

The same point is raised by Smith who observes that religious nationalism, 'or the superimposition (or uneasy coexistence) of mass religion on nationalism', has made a remarkable come back in the Islamic world, the Indian sub-continent and in parts of Europe and the Soviet Union. For Smith, this is hardly surprising since world religions have often served as repositories of popular myths, symbols and memories which often form the basis of modern nations (1991b: 364).

His Thesis that Nationalism is Born in the Americas Runs Counter to Available Evidence

As noted above, Anderson's contention that the national liberation movements in the Americas constitute the earliest examples of modern nationalism has been the subject of much controversy. The first examples of nationalism have been identified variously as appearing in England (Greenfeld 1992; Hastings 1997), France (Alter 1989), Germany (Kedourie 1994). Anderson, on the other hand, asserts that 'it is an astonishing sign of the depth of Eurocentrism that so many European scholars persist, in the face of all the evidence, in regarding nationalism as a European invention' (1991: 191, note 9). Anderson's argument about nationalism's 'place of birth' has not been attacked directly until recently. This silence ended in 1997, when Hastings stated that Anderson does not explain why the first wave of nation-making was the American. According to Hastings, Anderson offers no explanation 'as to why the growth in books did not have in the sixteenth century the effect he postulates for the late eighteenth' (1997: 11).

Anderson's Examples of Official Nationalism are Not Correct

This criticism comes from Breuilly, who argues that Anderson brackets some genuine cases of official nationalism (Russia, Siam) with cases that should be understood in quite different ways (1985: 72). He cites Magyar nationalism as an example. According to Breuilly, Magyar nationalism cannot be understood as an aristocratic response to nationalist threats from subordinate groups. In fact, Breuilly continues, the chronological sequence is the other way around: it was the development of Magyar nationalism which helped promote nationalist movements among subordinate groups. Breuilly notes that these movements did take on the character of an 'official nationalism' only at a later stage.

More complicated was the case of what Anderson calls a policy of official English nationalism in India. Breuilly admits that a policy of Anglicizing was pursued in India and that this was marked by assumptions of cultural superiority; but, he contends, this policy was never conceived of along national lines. This was similar to the Habsburg policy of adopting German as the official language of government which had nothing to do with nationalism, but rather with choosing the most suitable vehicle for the exercise of rational government. The real problem was (and this was underlined by Anderson as well) 'that the transfer of certain English . . . qualities to Indians was not envisaged as being synonymous with the transfer of "Englishness", and this led to cruel disillusionment amongst some Indians' (*ibid.*). Breuilly concludes by noting that the British government never tried to convince the Indians that they shared a common national identity with those in power. Thus, we cannot speak of a policy of 'official nationalism' in this case.

Anderson Misinterprets the Rise of Anti-colonial Nationalisms

This last objection is raised by Chatterjee. Drawing on Anderson's definition of the nation, Chatterjee asks:

> If nationalisms in the rest of the world have to choose their imagined community from certain 'modular' forms already made available to them by Europe and the Americas, what do they have left to imagine? History, it would seem, has decreed that we in the postcolonial world shall only be perpetual consumers of modernity. Europe and the Americas, the only true subjects of history, have thought out on our behalf not only the script of colonial enlightenment and exploitation, but also that of our anti-colonial resistance and postcolonial misery. Even our imaginations must remain forever colonized. (1996: 216)

Chatterjee rejects such an interpretation on the basis of the evidence provided by anti-colonial nationalisms. He holds that 'the most powerful as well as the most creative results of the nationalist imagination in Asia and Africa are posited not on an identity but rather on a *difference* with the "modular" forms of the national society propagated by the modern West' (*ibid.*). According to Chatterjee, this common error arises from taking the claims of nationalism to be a political movement much too literally and seriously. However, he claims, 'as history, nationalism's autobiography is fundamentally flawed' (*ibid.*: 217).

His own interpretation rests on the argument that anti-colonial nationalism creates its own domain of sovereignty within colonial society well before it begins its battle with the colonizer. It does this by dividing the social institutions and practices into two domains: the material and the spiritual. The material is the domain of the economy, statecraft, science and technology where the West is superior. In this domain, therefore, the superiority of the West has to be acknowledged and its success replicated. The spiritual domain, on the other hand, bears the essential marks of the nation's cultural identity. In this domain, the distinctness of one's culture needs to be preserved. As a result of this division, 'nationalism declares the domain of the spiritual its sovereign territory and refuses to allow the colonial power to intervene in that domain'. This does not mean that the spiritual domain is left unchanged. On the contrary, here nationalism launches its most creative and historically significant project: 'to fashion a "modern" national culture that is nevertheless not Western'. If the nation is an 'imagined community', then this is exactly where imagination works. The dynamics of this process, according to Chatterjee, are missed by conventional histories of nationalism (hence by Anderson) in which the story begins with the contest for political power (*ibid.*: 217–18).

Miroslav Hroch and the Three Phases of Nationalism

The last theoretical model I will discuss in this section is that of the Czech historian Miroslav Hroch. His work, compiled in *Die Vorkämpfer der nationalen Bewegungen bei den kleinen Völkern Europas: Eine vergleichende Analyse zur gesellschaftlichen Schichtung der patriotischen Gruppen* (Prague 1968) and *Obrození malých evropských národu. I: Národy severní a vychodní Evropy* [The Revival of the Small European Nations. I: The Nations of Northern and Eastern Europe] (Prague 1971), was pioneering in many respects. Hroch was the first scholar who undertook the quantitative social-historical analysis of nationalist movements in a systematic comparative framework. Second, he related nation-forming to the larger processes of social transformation, especially those associated with the spread of capitalism, but did so by avoiding economic reductionism, focusing on the effects of social and geographical mobility, more intense communication, the spread of literacy and generational change as mediating factors. Finally, he provided 'a socially and culturally grounded model of political development' (Eley and Suny 1996b: 59).

Strikingly enough, Hroch's pathbreaking studies were not translated into English until 1985. Until then, his findings were made accessible to a wider audience through the writings of Eric Hobsbawm (1972) and Tom Nairn (1974) who both treated Hroch's work as an excellent piece of comparative analysis. In a similar vein, Gellner commented that the publication of *Social Pre-conditions of National Revival in Europe* (1985) made it difficult for him to open his mouth for fear of making some mistake (cited in Hall 1998: 6). As Eley and Suny remark, his work still remains relatively little emulated and this is what makes it so 'important and exciting' (1996a: 16).

Hroch's point of departure is an empirical observation: at the beginning of the nineteenth century, there were eight 'state-nations' in Europe with a more or less developed literary language, a high culture and ethnically homogeneous ruling elites (including the aristocracy and an emerging commercial and industrial bourgeoisie). These eight state-nations – England, France, Spain, Sweden, Denmark, Portugal, the Netherlands and later Russia – were the products of a long process of nation-building that had started in the Middle Ages. There were also two emerging nations with a developed culture and an ethnically homogeneous elite, but without a political roof: the Germans and the Italians (Hroch 1993, 1995, 1996).

At the same time, there were more than 30 'non-dominant ethnic groups' scattered around the territories of multi-ethnic empires and some of the above-mentioned states. These groups lacked their own state, an indigenous ruling elite and a continuous cultural tradition in their own literary language. They usually occupied a compact territory, but were dominated by an 'exogenous', that is belonging to a different ethnic group, ruling class (Hroch 1995; 1996). Hroch notes that although these groups have come to be identified with Eastern and Southeastern Europe, there were many similar communities in Western Europe too (1993: 5). Sooner or later, some members of these groups became aware of their own ethnicity and started to conceive of themselves as a potential nation. Comparing their situation with that of the established nations, they detected certain deficits, which the future nation lacked, and began efforts to overcome them, seeking the support of their compatriots. Hroch observes that this national agitation started very early in some cases, that is around 1800 (the Greeks, Czechs, Norwegians, Irish), one generation later in others (the Finns, Croats, Slovenes, Flemish, Welsh), or even as late as the second half of the nineteenth century (Latvians, Estonians, Catalans, Basques) (1996: 37).

Hroch calls these 'organized endeavours to achieve all the attrib-

utes of a fully-fledged nation' a national movement. He argues that
the tendency to speak of them as 'nationalist' leads to serious confusion since nationalism *stricto sensu* is something else, namely that
'outlook which gives an absolute priority to the values of the nation
over all other values and interests' (1993: 6). In that sense, nationalism was only one of many forms of national consciousness to
emerge in the course of these movements. The term 'nationalist'
could be applied to such representative figures as the Norwegian
poet Wergeland who tried to create a language for his country or
the Polish writer Mickiewicz who longed for the liberation of his
homeland, but it cannot be suggested that all the participants of
these movements were 'nationalist' as such. Nationalism did of
course become a significant force in these areas, Hroch admits, but
as in the West, this was a later development. The programmes of
the classic national movements were of a different type. According
to Hroch, they included three groups of demands:

1. The development or improvement of a national culture based
    on the local language which had to be used in education,
    administration and economic life.
2. The creation of a complete social structure, including their
    'own' educated elites and entrepreneurial classes.
3. The achievement of equal civil rights and of some degree of
    political self-administration (1995: 66–7).

The timing and relative priority of these three sets of demands
varied but the trajectory of any national movement was only completed when all were fulfilled (1993: 6).

On the other hand, Hroch distinguishes three structural phases
between the starting-point of any national movement and its successful completion. During the initial period, which he calls Phase
A, activists committed themselves to scholarly inquiry into the linguistic, historical and cultural attributes of their ethnic group.
They did not attempt to mount a patriotic agitation or formulate
any political goals at this stage, in part because they were isolated
and in part they did not believe it would serve any purpose (1985:
23). In the second period, Phase B, a new range of activists
emerged who intended to win over as many of their ethnic group
as possible to the project of creating a nation. Hroch notes that

these activists were not very successful initially, but their efforts found a growing reception in time. When the national consciousness became the concern of the majority of the population, a mass movement was formed, which Hroch terms Phase C. It was only at this stage that a full social structure could be formed (1993: 7; 1995: 67). Hroch stresses that the transition from one phase to the next did not occur at one stroke: 'between the manifestations of scholarly interest, on the one hand, and the mass diffusion of patriotic attitudes, on the other, there lies an epoch characterized by active patriotic agitation: the fermentation-process of national consciousness' (1985: 23).

This periodization, Hroch continues, permits meaningful comparisons between national movements. For him, the most important criterion for any typology of national movements is the relationship between the transition to Phase B and then to Phase C on the one hand, and the transition to a constitutional society on the other. Combining these two series of changes, he identifies four types of national movements in Europe:

1. In the first type, national agitation began under the old regime of absolutism, but it reached the masses in a time of revolutionary changes. The leaders of Phase B formulated their national programmes in conditions of political upheaval. Hroch cites the case of Czech agitation in Bohemia and the Hungarian and Norwegian movements to illustrate this type. All these movements entered Phase B around 1800. The Norwegians obtained their independence (and a liberal constitution) in 1814; the Czech and Magyar national programmes were developed in the course of the revolutions of 1848.

2. In the second type, national agitation again started under the old regime, but the transition to Phase C was delayed until after a constitutional revolution. This shift resulted either from uneven economic development, as in Lithuania, Latvia, Slovenia or Croatia; or from foreign oppression, as in Slovakia or the Ukraine. Hroch maintains that Phase B started in Croatia in the 1830s, in Slovenia in the 1840s, in Latvia in the late 1850s and in Lithuania not before the 1870s. This delayed the transition to Phase C to the 1880s in Croatia, the 1890s in Slovenia and the revolution of 1905 in Latvia and Lithuania.

He argues that the policies of Magyarization held back the transition to Phase C in Slovakia until after 1867, as did forcible Russification in the Ukraine.

3. In the third type, a mass movement was already formed under the old regime, thus, before the establishment of a constitutional order. This model was confined to the territories of the Ottoman Empire in Europe – Serbia, Greece and Bulgaria.

4. In the final type, national agitation began under constitutional conditions in a more developed capitalist setting; this pattern was characteristic of Western Europe. In some of these cases the transition to Phase C was experienced quite early, as in the Basque lands and Catalonia, while in others it did so after a very long Phase B, as in Flanders, or not at all as in Wales, Scotland or Brittany (for these types see 1985: chapter 7; 1993: 7–8).

Hroch maintains that these patterns do not enable us to understand the origins and outcomes of various national movements as they are based on generalizations. Any satisfactory account has to be 'multi-causal' and establish the links between the structural phases we have identified above. In the light of these considerations, Hroch tries to provide answers to the following questions: how did the experiences (and structures) of the past affect the modern nation-building process? How and why did the scholarly interest of a small number of intellectuals transform into political programmes underpinned by strong emotional attachments? What accounts for the success of some of these movements and the failure of others? He begins by considering the 'antecedents to nation-building'.

According to Hroch, the experiences of the past, or what he calls 'the prelude to modern nation-building' (that is earlier attempts at nation-building), were not only important for the 'state-nations' of the West, but also for the non-dominant ethnic groups of Central and Eastern Europe. The legacy of the past embodied three significant resources that might facilitate the emergence of a national movement. The first of these were 'the relics of an earlier political autonomy'. The properties or privileges granted under the old regime often led to tensions between the estates and the 'new' absolutism, which in turn provided triggers for later national movements. Hroch points to the resistance of Hungarian,

Bohemian and Croatian estates to Josephine centralism to illustrate his argument. A second resource was 'the memory of former independence or statehood'. This could also play a stimulating role as the cases of Czech, Lithuanian, Bulgarian and Catalan movements demonstrate. Finally, the existence of 'a medieval written language' was crucial as this could make the development of a modern literary language easier. Hroch notes that the absence of this resource was much exaggerated in the nineteenth century, leading to a distinction between 'historical' and 'unhistorical' peoples. In fact, its salience was limited to the tempo at which the historical consciousness of the nation developed (1993: 8–9; 1995: 69).

Whatever the legacy of the past, the modern nation-building process always started with the collection of information about the history, language and customs of the non-dominant ethnic group. The ethnic archeologists of Phase A excavated the group's past and paved the way for the subsequent formation of a national identity. But, Hroch argues, their efforts cannot be called an organized political or social movement since they articulated no national demands as yet. The transformation of their intellectual activity into a movement seeking cultural and political changes was a product of Phase B. Hroch distinguishes three developments that precipitated this transformation:

1. a social and/or political crisis of the old order, accompanied by new tensions and horizons;
2. the emergence of discontent among significant elements of the population;
3. loss of faith in traditional moral systems, above all a decline in religious legitimacy, even if this only affected small numbers of intellectuals (1993: 10).

On the other hand, the initiation of national agitation (Phase B) by a group of activists did not guarantee the emergence of a mass movement. Mass support and the successful attainment of the ultimate goal, that is the forging of a modern nation, depended in turn on four conditions:

1. a crisis of legitimacy, linked to social, moral and cultural strains;

2. a basic volume of vertical social mobility (some educated people must come from the non-dominant ethnic group);
3. a fairly high level of social communication, including literacy, schooling and market relations;
4. nationally relevant conflicts of interest (*ibid.*: 12).

Hroch takes the second and the third conditions from Deutsch. He accepts that a high level of social mobility and communication facilitates the emergence of a national movement. However, his endorsement is not unqualified. He notes that these conditions do not work in at least two cases. First, he points to the case of the district of Polesie in interwar Poland where there was minimal social mobility, very weak contacts with the market and scant literacy. The same pattern prevailed in Eastern Lithuania, West Prussia, Lower Lusatia and various Balkan regions. In all these cases, the response to national agitation was quite ardent. On the other hand, in Wales, Belgium, Brittany and Schleswig, high levels of social mobility and communication were not sufficient to generate mass support for the respective national movements (1993: 11).

Drawing on these observations, Hroch argues that there must be another factor that helped the transition to Phase C. This is what he terms 'a nationally relevant conflict of interest', that is 'a social tension or collision that could be mapped onto linguistic (and sometimes also religious) divisions'. According to Hroch, the best example of such a conflict in the nineteenth century was the tension between new university graduates coming from a non-dominant ethnic group and a closed elite from the ruling nation that kept a hereditary grip on leading positions in state and society. There were also clashes between peasants from the non-dominant group and landlords from the dominant one, between craftsmen from the former and large traders from the latter. Hroch stresses that these conflicts of interest cannot be reduced to class conflicts since the national movements always recruited supporters from several classes (*ibid.*: 11–12).

Finally, Hroch asks the following question: 'why were social conflicts of this kind articulated in national terms more successfully in some parts of Europe than others' (*ibid.*: 12)? He claims that national agitation started earlier and made more progress in areas where the non-dominant ethnic groups lived under absolutist oppression. In such areas, the leaders of these groups – and the group as a whole – hardly had any political education and no political experience at all. Moreover, there was little room for alternative, more developed, forms of political discourse. Thus, it was easier to articulate hostilities in national categories, as was the case in Bohemia and Estonia. According to Hroch, this was precisely why these regions were different from Western Europe. The higher levels of political culture and experience in the West allowed the nationally relevant conflicts of interest to be articulated in political terms. This phenomenon was observed in the Flemish, Scottish and Welsh cases where the national programmes of the activists found it hard to win a mass following and in some cases never achieved a transition to Phase C. Hroch continues: 'The lesson is that it is not enough to consider only the formal level of social communication reached in a given society – one must also look at the complex of contents mediated through it' (*ibid.*). Phase C can be attained in a relatively short time if the goals articulated by agitators correspond to the immediate needs and aspirations of the majority of the non-dominant ethnic group. Let me conclude this brief review by a general observation from Hroch about the contemporary ethnic revival in Central and Eastern Europe:

> in a social situation where the old regime was collapsing, where old relations were in flux and general insecurity was growing, the members of the 'non-dominant ethnic group' would see the community of language and culture as the ultimate certainty, the unambiguously demonstrable value. Today, as the system or planned economy and social security breaks down, once again – the situation is analogous – language acts as a substitute for factors of integration in a disintegrating society. When society fails, the nation appears as the ultimate guarantee. (Cited in Hobsbawm 1996: 261)

Hroch's approach has been criticized on two grounds, namely for reifying nations and for downplaying the importance of political factors.

Hroch Reifies Nations

This criticism comes from Gellner who describes Hroch's approach as 'an interesting attempt to save . . . the nationalist vision of itself' by confirming that nations do really exist and express themselves through nationalist striving (1995a: 182). What lies behind this criticism is Hroch's distinction between established 'state-nations' and the 'non-dominant ethnic groups'. As we have seen above, Hroch argues that there were eight fully-fledged state-nations in Western Europe in the nineteenth century, which were the products of a long process of development that started in the Middle Ages. This argument led some scholars to suggest that Hroch's approach was a mixture of primordialism and modernism. Hence, for Hall, 'Hroch stands closer to Anthony Smith [the leading figure of ethno-symbolism] in insisting that nationalism would be ineffective were its appeal not directed at a pre-existing community' (1998: 6). Hroch, however, rejects such an interpretation, noting that he used the term 'revival' in a metaphorical sense – without implying that nations were eternal categories (1998: 94). Gellner's objections, Hroch comments, are based partly on misunderstanding and partly on an inadequate interpretation of the terms and concepts he used in his model (*ibid.*: 106, note 30). For him, the basic difference of opinion lies elsewhere:

> I cannot accept the view that nations are a mere 'myth', nor do I accept Gellner's global understanding of nationalism as an all-purpose explanation including categories of which the nation is a mere derivative. The relation between the nation and national consciousness (or national identity, or 'nationalism') is not one of unilateral derivation but one of mutual and complementary correlation, and the discussion about which of them is 'primary' can, at least for the present, be left to the philosophers and ideologues. (*Ibid.*: 104)

Hroch Downplays the Importance of Political Factors

Hroch's model was also criticized for ignoring the political determinants of nationalism (Hall 1993: 25). Hroch tries to redress the balance in his later work by focusing more on the political dimension. In a recent article on national self-determination, for example, he examines how the structure of national programmes was shaped by the political setting under which they operated and when political demands entered these national programmes

(1995). He basically argues that 'the strength and timing of the call for self-determination did not depend upon the intensity of political oppression and had no correlation with the level of linguistic and cultural demands'. Self-determination became more successful in movements 'which were based on a complete social structure of their non-dominant ethnic group and which could use some institutions or traditions of their statehood from the past' (*ibid.*: 79).

Further Reading

A stimulating (and highly critical) discussion of most theories reviewed in this chapter can be found in a recent book by Smith (1998). Smith's stated aim in this book is to provide an internal critique of what remains the dominant orthodoxy in the field, namely modernism. His unstated aim, however, is to promote his own 'ethno-symbolism'.

Where neo-Marxist theories are concerned, Nairn (1981) [1977] and Hechter (1975, 1985) are required reading. For a critical overview of Nairn's theory of 'uneven development' see James (1996), chapter 5. For other useful critiques of theories of economic transformation see Orridge (1981a, 1981b) and Brand (1985).

The most elaborate statement of Breuilly's approach is found in his *Nationalism and the State* (1993a) [1982]. For a concise summary see Breuilly (1996) [1994]. For an instrumentalist approach to ethnicity and nationalism see Brass (1991); for the theme of invention see Hobsbawm and Ranger (1983). Political theories of nationalism have been severely criticized by primordialist and ethno-symbolist writers. For an example of this critique, see Hastings (1997).

The earlier version of Gellner's theory appeared as chapter 7 of his *Thought and Change* (1964). Later, he expanded his theory to book length as *Nations and Nationalism* (1983). For a shorter and revised version of his theory see Gellner (1996a). On Gellner's theory, see also the books by Hall and Jarvie (1996b) and Hall (1998). The former is a general evaluation of the social philosophy of Gellner and contains articles which critically discuss his arguments on nationalism (see part II). The latter, on the other hand, is devoted solely to Gellner's theory of nationalism, and thus assesses every aspect of that theory.

For Anderson's theory see his *Imagined Communities* (1991) [1983]. For a critique of Anderson see the above-mentioned book by Smith (chapter 6) and an insightful essay by Chatterjee (1996) [1993]. An extended comparative review of Anderson and Gellner can be found in Breuilly (1985).

On Hroch's celebrated phase model see his *Social Preconditions of National Revival in Europe* (1985). For a concise statement of his theory see Hroch (1993). Hroch's work has been criticized most vigorously by Gellner (1995a). His reply to these criticisms can be found in Hroch (1998).

5
Ethno-symbolism

That is what the war is doing to us, reducing us to one dimension: the Nation. The trouble with this nationhood, however, is that whereas before, I was defined by my education, my job, my ideas, my character – and, yes, my nationality too – now I feel stripped of all that. I am nobody because I am not a person any more. I am one of 4.5 million Croats . . . I am not in a position to choose any longer . . . Something people cherished as part of their cultural identity has become their political identity and turned into something like an ill-fitting shirt. You may feel the sleeves are too short, the collar too tight. But there is no escape; there is nothing else to wear. One doesn't have to succumb voluntarily to this ideology of the nation – one is sucked into it. So right now, in the new state of Croatia, no one is allowed not to be a Croat.

Slavenka Drakulic, *The Balkan Express:*
Fragments from the Other Side of War

What is Ethno-symbolism?

Modernist arguments have been challenged in recent years by a number of scholars who focused on the role of pre-existing ethnic ties and sentiments in the formation of modern nations. In their determination to reveal the 'invented' or 'constructed' nature of nationalism, these scholars argued, modernists systematically overlooked the persistence of earlier myths, symbols, values and memories in many parts of the world and their continuing significance for large numbers of people (Smith 1996c: 361). We have already discussed the ethno-symbolist critique of modernism in the preceding chapter. In this chapter, I will abstain from repeating these criticisms and concentrate instead on their own account of the rise of nations and nationalisms.

The term 'ethno-symbolist' seems to be a good starting point. Broadly speaking, this term is used to denote scholars who aim to uncover the symbolic legacy of pre-modern ethnic identities for today's nations (Smith 1998: 224). Uneasy with both poles of the debate, that is, primordialism/perennialism and modernism, ethno-symbolists like John Armstrong, Anthony D. Smith and John Hutchinson proposed a third position, a compromise or a kind of 'midway' between these two approaches. However, the term has not been appropriated by the writers in question until recently. For example Armstrong, considered by many as the pioneer of this approach, never mentions the term in his studies. For Smith, Armstrong is a 'perennialist', while for Hutchinson, both Smith and Armstrong are 'ethnicists' (Smith 1984; Hutchinson 1994: 7).

The term mostly appears in the writings of researchers who sympathize with such views. Hence, in an article on the theories of nationalism, Conversi defines 'ethno-symbolism' as an approach which rejects the axiom that nations may be *ipso facto* invented, claiming that they rely on a pre-existing texture of myths, memories, values and symbols and which, by so doing, tries to transcend the polarization between primordialism and instrumentalism (1995: 73–4). The modernists, on the other hand, ignore the term altogether and regard ethno-symbolism as a less radical version of 'primordialism' (for example Breuilly 1996: 150). This confusion came to an end recently, when Smith explicitly acknowledged – and defined – the term (1996c, 1998).

Ethno-symbolists form a more homogeneous category than both the primordialists and the modernists. Guided by a common reverence for the past, they lay stress on similar processes in their explanations of national phenomena. According to them, the formation of nations should be examined in *la longue durée*, that is, a 'time dimension of many centuries' (Armstrong 1982: 4), for the emergence of today's nations cannot be understood properly without taking their ethnic forebears into account. In other words, the rise of nations needs to be contextualized within the larger phenomenon of ethnicity which shaped them (Hutchinson 1994:

7). The differences between modern nations and the collective cultural units of earlier eras are of degree rather than kind. This suggests that ethnic identities change more slowly than is generally assumed. Once formed, they tend to be exceptionally durable under 'normal' vicissitudes of history (such as migrations, invasions, intermarriages) and to persist over many generations, even centuries (Smith 1986: 16). In short, the modern era is no *tabula rasa*:

> On the contrary, it emerges out of the complex social and ethnic formations of earlier epochs, and the different kinds of *ethnie* [ethnic community], which modern forces transform, but never obliterate. The modern era in this respect resembles a palimpsest on which are recorded experiences and identities of different epochs and a variety of ethnic formations, the earlier influencing and being modified by the later, to produce the composite type of collective cultural unit which we call 'the nation'. (Smith 1995: 59–60)

Ethno-symbolists reject the stark 'continuism' of the perennialists and accord due weight to the transformations wrought by modernity. They also reject the claims of the modernists by arguing that a greater measure of continuity exists between 'traditional' and 'modern' or 'agrarian' and 'industrial' eras. Hence the need for a wider theory of ethnic formation that will bring out the differences and similarities between contemporary national units and premodern ethnic communities (Smith 1986: 13).

Smith contends that such an approach is more helpful than its alternatives in at least three ways. First, it helps to explain which populations are likely to start a nationalist movement under certain conditions and what the content of this movement would be. Second, this approach enables us to understand the important role of memories, values, myths and symbols. Nationalism, Smith argues, mostly involves the pursuit of symbolic goals such as education in a particular language, having a TV channel in one's own language or the protection of ancient sacred sites. Materialist and modernist theories of nationalism fail to illuminate these issues as they are unable to comprehend the emotive power of collective memories. Finally, the ethno-symbolist approach explains why and how nationalism is able to generate such a widespread popular

support. 'The intelligentsia may "invite the masses into history"
. . . But why do "the people" respond?' For the sake of material
benefits? According to Smith, the answer cannot be that simple.
Ethno-symbolist approaches try to shed light on this process
(1996c: 362).

In the following sub-sections, I will discuss the contributions of
two leading figures of ethno-symbolism, namely John Armstrong
and Anthony D. Smith. I will end the chapter by considering the
major criticisms levelled against ethno-symbolist arguments.

John Armstrong and 'Myth–symbol Complexes'

Professor Emeritus of Political Science at the University of
Wisconsin-Madison and former President of the American Association for the Advancement of Slavic Studies, John Armstrong is a
leading specialist in East European politics. He is the author of the
classic *Ukrainian Nationalism* (1963). However, his most important
work in the field – his *magnum opus* in the words of Hutchinson
and Smith (1994: 362) – is the pioneering *Nations before Nationalism* (1982). Probing into the process of ethnic identity formation
in pre-modern Islamic and Christian civilizations, this book has the
quality of being the first study to cast a shadow of doubt on modernist assumptions.

Armstrong's stated aim is to explore 'the emergence of the
intense group identification that today we term a "nation"' by
adopting what he calls an 'extended temporal perspective' that
reaches back to antiquity (1982: 3). Having examined ethnic
groups in the course of their long historical journey, he stops at
the 'threshold of nationalism', that is before the period when
nationalism becomes the dominant political doctrine (the eighteenth century). He justifies this by noting that he is more concerned with the persistence rather than the genesis of particular
patterns (*ibid.*: 4). This led many scholars – including Smith – to
call his approach 'perennialist', or even 'primordialist'. Nevertheless, it can be asserted that the arguments put forward in this study,
particularly Armstrong's overall perspective, have laid the groundwork for ethno-symbolism which established itself more firmly with
the work of Smith. It is worth noting that Armstrong is still
regarded as the 'founding father' of ethno-symbolism by a con-

siderable number of scholars. However, the author himself refrains from using a term to describe his viewpoint.

Armstrong softens this stance in his recent work. While standing firm on his belief that nations did exist before nationalism, he nevertheless agrees with Anderson and Hobsbawm that, like other human identities, national identity had been an invention. The only remaining disagreement, Armstrong contends, is 'over the antiquity of some inventions and the repertory of pre-existing group characteristics that inventors were able to draw upon' (1995: 36). On this point, he seems to concur with Greenfeld (1992) who has located the origins of nationalism in the English Civil War. Unfortunately, Armstrong does not provide an explanation for this change. This in turn made him the target of a great deal of criticism (see for example Rizman 1996: 339). Before discussing this, however, it is necessary to summarize Armstrong's main arguments as articulated in *Nations before Nationalism*.

For Armstrong, ethnic consciousness has a long history: it is possible to come across its traces in ancient civilizations, for example in Egypt and Mesopotamia. In this sense, contemporary nationalism is nothing but the final stage of a larger cycle of ethnic consciousness reaching back to the earliest forms of collective organization. The most important feature of this consciousness, according to Armstrong, is its persistence. Therefore, the formation of ethnic identities should be examined in a time dimension of many centuries, similar to the *longue durée* emphasized by the *Annales* school of French historiography. Only an extended temporal perspective can reveal the durability of ethnic attachments and the 'shifting significance of boundaries for human identity' (1982: 4).

This emphasis on boundaries suggests Armstrong's stance *vis-à-vis* ethnic identities. Adopting the social interaction model of the Norwegian anthropologist Fredrik Barth, he argues that 'groups tend to define themselves not by reference to their own characteristics but by exclusion, that is, by comparison to "strangers"' (*ibid.*: 5). It follows that there can be no fixed 'character' or 'essence' for the group; the boundaries of identities vary according to the perceptions of the individuals forming the group. Thus, it makes more sense to focus on the boundary mechanisms that distinguish a particular group from others instead of objective group characteristics. For Armstrong, Barth's attitudinal approach affords many advantages. First, it makes room for changes in the cultural and the biological content of the group as long as the boundary mechanisms are maintained. Secondly, it shows that ethnic groups are not necessarily based on the occupation of particular, exclusive territories. The key to understanding ethnic identification is the 'uncanny experience of confronting others' who remained mute in response to attempts at communication, whether oral or through symbolic gestures (*ibid.*). Inability to communicate initiates the process of 'differentiation' which in turn brings a recognition of ethnic belonging.

Such a conception of ethnic group, that is a group defined by exclusion, implies that there is no definitional way of distinguishing ethnicity from other types of collective identity. Ethnic ties will often overlap with religious or class loyalties. 'It is precisely this complex, shifting quality that has repelled many social scientists from analyzing ethnic identity over long periods of time' (*ibid.*: 6). Drawing on this observation, Armstrong declares that he is more concerned with the shifting interaction among class, ethnic and religious loyalties than with 'compartmentalizing definitions'. To do that, however, the focus of investigation must shift from internal group characteristics to symbolic boundary mechanisms that differentiate these groups, without overlooking the fact that the mechanisms in question exist in the minds of the subjects rather than as lines on a map or norms in a rule book (*ibid.*: 7).

I have already noted that Armstrong lays special emphasis on the durability and persistence of these symbolic boundary mechanisms. For him, '[m]yth, symbol, communication, and a cluster of associated attitudinal factors are usually more persistent than purely material factors' (*ibid.*: 9). What, then, are the factors that ensure this persistence? Armstrong tries to specify and analyse these factors in the rest of his book.

He begins with the most general factor, namely ways of life and the experiences associated with them. Two fundamentally different ways of life, the nomadic and the sedentary, are particularly important in this context, because the myths and symbols they embody – expressed, notably, in nostalgia – create two sorts of identities based on incompatible principles. Thus, the territorial principle and its peculiar nostalgia ultimately became the predominant form in Europe, while the genealogical or pseudo-genealogical principle has continued to prevail in most of the Middle East. The second factor, religion, reinforced this basic distinction. The two great universal religions, Islam and Christianity, gave birth to different civilizations and the myths/symbols associated with them shaped the formation of ethnic identities in their own specific ways. Armstrong's third factor is the city. The analysis of the effect of towns on ethnic identification requires, Armstrong argues, examination of a host of factors, ranging from the impact of town planning to the unifying or centrifugal effects of various legal codes, especially the Lübeck and Magdeburg law. Then he moves to the role of imperial polities. At this point, the central question is 'how could the intense consciousness of loyalty and identity established through face-to-face contact in the city-state be transferred to the larger agglomerations of cities and countryside known as empires' (*ibid.*: 13)? Here, Armstrong stresses the diverse effects of the Mesopotamian myth of the polity – what he calls '*mythomoteur*' – as a reflection of heavenly rule. He argues that this myth was used as a vehicle for incorporating city-state loyalties in a larger framework. For him, this might constitute the earliest example of 'myth transference for political purposes' (*ibid.*). Finally, Armstrong introduces the question of language and assesses its impact on identity-formation in the pre-nationalist era. Contrary to commonsense assumptions, Armstrong concludes, 'the significance of language for ethnic identity is highly contingent' in pre-modern eras (*ibid.*: 282). Its significance depended in the long run on political and religious forces and allegiances.

Armstrong's work, despite its almost exclusive focus on the medieval European and Middle Eastern civilizations, offers a much more comprehensive overview of the process of ethnic identification than other comparable studies in the field. In the words of Smith,

> No other work attempts to bring together such a variety of evidence – administrative, legal, military, architectural, religious, linguistic, social and mythological – from which to construct a set of patterns in the slow formation of national identity... By doing so, Armstrong makes a strong case for grounding the emergence of modern national identities on these patterns of ethnic persistence, and especially on the long-term influence of 'myth-symbol complexes'. (1998: 185)

It was Smith who explored these issues further and elaborated the framework of analysis developed by Armstrong.

Anthony D. Smith and 'the Ethnic Origins of Nations'

One of the few scholars to specialize in the study of ethnicity and nationalism, Anthony D. Smith is the leading exponent of ethno-symbolism in the field. In his numerous books and articles on the subject, Smith focused especially on the pre-modern roots of contemporary nations, departing from the prevailing modernist interpretations that spurn the past. His three-decades-long intellectual engagement with nationalism led some scholars to call him 'the main guide' in the field for readers of the English language (Hobsbawm 1990: 2). Smith's contribution to the study of nationalism is not confined to his writings; he also played an important part in establishing ASEN, an association concerned with advancing the study of ethnicity and nationalism, at the London School of Economics and Political Science where he still teaches nationalism. In a way, then, Smith is the last representative of a chain of scholars who contributed to what Gellner calls the 'LSE debate' (1995a: 61), continuing a tradition bequeathed to him by such distinguished scholars as Elie Kedourie, Kenneth Minogue and Ernest Gellner.

Yet, Smith differs from the generation that preceded him in one important respect. Most participants of the LSE debate, including Kedourie, Minogue and Gellner, were proponents of the modernist paradigm. Smith, on the other hand, bases his approach on a critique of modernism. His central thesis is that modern nations cannot be understood without taking pre-existing ethnic components into account, the lack of which is likely to create a serious impediment to 'nation-building' (1986: 17). Smith concedes that there are a variety of cases where there was little in the way of a rich ethnic heritage. But, he continues, such extreme cases are rare. 'Usually, there has been some ethnic basis for the construction of modern nations, be it only some dim memories and elements of culture and alleged ancestry, which it is hoped to revive' (*ibid.*). It follows that the rise of contemporary nations should be studied in the context of their ethnic background. This means

grounding our understanding of modern nationalism on an historical base involving considerable time-spans, to see how far its
themes and forms were pre-figured in earlier periods and how
far a connection with earlier ethnic ties and sentiments can be
established. (*Ibid.*: 13)

According to Smith, if we are to move beyond the sweeping generalizations of both modernism and primordialism, we need to
formulate clear working definitions of key terms like nation,
nation-state and nationalism, thereby breaking out of an impasse
which bedevils progress in the field (1994). He begins by proposing the following definition of the nation, derived to a large extent
from the images and assumptions held by most or all nationalists:
a nation is 'a named human population sharing an historic territory, common myths and historical memories, a mass, public
culture, a common economy and common legal rights and duties
for all members' (1991a: 14). Smith holds that such a definition
reveals the complex and abstract nature of national identity which
is fundamentally multi-dimensional.

On the other hand, the origins of nations are as complex as its
nature. We might begin to look for a general explanation by asking
the following questions:

1. *Who* is the nation? What are the ethnic bases and models of
    modern nations? Why did these particular nations emerge?
2. *Why* and *how* does the nation emerge? That is, what are the
    general causes and mechanisms that set in motion the process
    of nation-formation from varying ethnic ties and memories?
3. *When* and *where* did the nation arise? (1991a: 19).

For Smith, the answer to the first question should be sought in
earlier ethnic communities (he prefers to use the French term
ethnie) since pre-modern identities and legacies form the bedrock
of many contemporary nations. He posits six main attributes for
such communities: a collective proper name, a myth of common
ancestry, shared historical memories, one or more differentiating
elements of a common culture, an association with a specific
homeland, a sense of solidarity for significant sectors of the
population (*ibid.*: 21). As this list reveals, most of these attributes

have a cultural and historical content as well as a strong subjective component. This suggests, contrary to the rhetoric of nationalist ideologies, that the *ethnie* is anything but primordial. According to Smith, as the subjective significance of each of these attributes waxes and wanes for the members of a community, so does their cohesion and self-awareness (*ibid.*: 23).

If the *ethnie* is not a primordial entity, then how does it come into being? Smith identifies two main patterns of *ethnie*-formation: coalescence and division. By coalescence he means the coming together of separate units, which in turn can be broken down into processes of amalgamation of separate units such as city-states and of absorption of one unit by another as in the assimilation of regions. By division he means subdivision through fission as with sectarian schism or through 'proliferation' (a term he borrows from Horowitz), when a part of the ethnic community leaves it to form a new unit as in the case of Bangladesh (*ibid.*: 23–4).

Smith notes that *ethnies*, once formed, tend to be exceptionally durable (1986: 16). However, this should not lead us to the conclusion that they travel across history without undergoing any changes in their demographic composition and/or cultural contents. In other words, we should try to eschew the polar extremes of the primordialist–instrumentalist debate when assessing the recurrence of ethnic ties and communities. Smith admits that there are certain events that generate profound changes in the cultural contents of ethnic identities. Among these, he singles out war and conquest, exile and enslavement, the influx of immigrants and religious conversion (1991a: 26). Nevertheless, what really matters is how far these changes reflect on and disrupt the sense of cultural continuity that binds successive generations together. For Smith, even the most radical changes cannot destroy this sense of continuity and common ethnicity. This is partly due to the existence of a number of external forces that help to crystallize ethnic identities and ensure their persistence over long periods. Of these, state-making, military mobilization and organized religion are the most crucial.

In the light of these observations, Smith sets out to specify the main mechanisms of ethnic self-renewal. The first such mechanism is 'religious reform'. The history of the Jews is replete with many instances of this. Conversely, groups who fell prey to religious conservatism tried to compensate for the failure to introduce reforms by turning to other forms of self-renewal. This was the dilemma faced by the Greeks at the beginning of the nineteenth century. When the Orthodox hierarchy failed to respond to popular aspirations, the Greek middle classes turned to secular ideological discourses to realize their goals. The second mechanism is 'cultural borrowing', in the sense of controlled contact and selective cultural exchange between different communities. Here again, examples can be found from Jewish history. The lively encounter between Jewish and Greek cultures, Smith holds, enriched the whole field of Jewish culture and identity. The third mechanism is 'popular participation'. The popular movements for greater participation in the political system saved many *ethnies* from withering away by generating a missionary zeal among the participants of these movements. The final mechanism of ethnic self-renewal identified by Smith is 'myths of ethnic election'. According to Smith, *ethnies* that lack such myths tended to be absorbed by others after losing their independence (*ibid.*: 35–6).

Together, these four mechanisms ensure the survival of certain ethnic communities across the centuries despite changes in their demographic composition and cultural contents. These mechanisms also lead to the gradual formation of what Smith terms 'ethnic cores'. These 'cohesive and self-consciously distinctive *ethnies*' form the basis of states and kingdoms in later periods. Thus, locating the ethnic cores helps us a great deal to answer the question 'who is the nation?' Smith observes that most latter-day nations are constructed around a dominant *ethnie*, which annexed or attracted other ethnic communities into the state it founded and to which it gave a name and a cultural character (*ibid.*: 38–9).

However, this observation is not sufficient to justify our quest for the origins of nations in the pre-modern era since there are many cases of nations formed without immediate ethnic antecedents. In other words, the relationship between modern nations and prior ethnic cores is problematic. At this point, Smith lists three more reasons to support his case. To begin with, the first nations were formed on the basis of ethnic cores. Being powerful and culturally influential, these nations provided models for subsequent cases of nation-formation. The second reason is that this model sat easily on the pre-modern 'demotic' kind of community (which will be explained below). In the words of Smith, 'the ethnic model was sociologically fertile'. Finally, even when there were no ethnic antecedents, the need to fabricate a coherent mythology and symbolism became everywhere paramount to ensure national survival and unity (*ibid.*: 40–1).

The existence of pre-modern ethnic ties helps us to determine which units of population are likely to become nations, but it does not tell us why and how this transformation comes about. To answer the second general question raised above, that is, 'why and how does the nation emerge?', we need to specify the main patterns of 'identity-formation' and the factors that triggered their development. Smith begins by identifying two types of ethnic community, the 'lateral' (aristocratic) and the 'vertical' (demotic), noting that these two types gave birth to different patterns of nation-formation.

'Lateral' *ethnies* were generally composed of aristocrats and higher clergy, though in some cases they might also include bureaucrats, high military officials and richer merchants. Smith explains why he chose the term 'lateral' by pointing out that these *ethnies* were at once socially confined to the upper strata and geographically spread out to form close links with the upper echelons of neighbouring lateral *ethnies*. As a result, their borders were 'ragged', but they lacked social depth, 'and [their] often marked sense of common ethnicity was bound up with [their] *esprit de corps* as a high status stratum and ruling class' (1991a: 53). On the contrary, 'vertical' *ethnies* were more compact and popular. Their culture was diffused to other sections of the population as well. Social cleavages were not underpinned by cultural differences; 'rather, a distinctive historical culture helped to unite different classes around a common heritage and traditions, especially when the latter were under threat from outside' (*ibid.*). As a result of this, the ethnic bond was more intense and exclusive, and the barriers to admission were much higher.

As noted above, these two types of ethnic communities followed different trajectories in the process of becoming a nation. Smith calls the first, lateral, route 'bureaucratic incorporation'. The survival of aristocratic ethnic communities depended to a large extent on their capacity to incorporate other strata of the population within their cultural orbit. This was most successfully realized in Western Europe. In England, France, Spain and Sweden, the dominant *ethnie* was able to incorporate the middle classes and peripheral regions into the elite culture. According to Smith, the primary vehicle in this process was the newly emerging bureaucratic state. Through a series of 'revolutions' in the administrative, economic and cultural spheres, the state was able to diffuse the dominant culture down the social scale. The major constituents of the 'administrative revolution' were the extension of citizenship rights, conscription, taxation and the build-up of an infrastructure that linked distant parts of the realm. These developments were complemented by parallel 'revolutions' in economic and cultural spheres. Smith singles out two such processes as relevant to nation-formation, namely the movement to a market economy and the decline of ecclesiastical authority. The latter was particularly important in that it allowed the development of secular studies and of university learning. This, in turn, led to a 'boom' in popular modes of communication – novels, plays and journals. An important role was played in these processes by the intellectuals and professionals (*ibid.*: 59–60).

The second route of nation-formation, what Smith calls 'vernacular mobilization', set out from a vertical *ethnie*. The influence of the bureaucratic state was more indirect in this case mainly because vertical *ethnies* were usually subject communities. Here, the key mechanism of ethnic persistence was organized religion. It was through myths of chosenness, sacred texts and scripts, and the prestige of the clergy that the survival of communal traditions were ensured. But demotic communities had problems of their own, which surfaced at the initial stages of the process of nation-formation. To start with, ethnic culture usually overlapped with the wider circle of religious culture and loyalty, and there was no internal coercive agency to break the mould. Moreover, the members of the community simply assumed that they already constituted a nation, albeit one without a political roof. Under these circumstances, the primary task of the secular intelligentsia was to alter the basic relationship between ethnicity and religion. In other words, the community of the faithful had to be distinguished from the community of historic culture. Smith identifies three different orientations among the intellectuals confronted with this dilemma: a conscious, modernizing return to tradition ('traditionalism'); a messianic desire to assimilate to Western modernity ('assimilation' or 'modernism'); and a more defensive attempt to synthesize elements of the tradition with aspects of Western modernity, hence to revive a pristine community modelled on a former golden age ('reformist revivalism') (*ibid.*: 63–4).

The solution adopted by the intellectuals had profound implications for the shape, pace, scope and intensity of the process of nation-formation. But whatever the solution espoused, the main task of an ethnic intelligentsia was 'to mobilize a formerly passive community into forming a nation around the new vernacular historical culture it has rediscovered' (*ibid.*: 64). In each case, they had to provide 'new communal self-definitions and goals', construct 'maps and moralities out of a living ethnic past'. This could be done in two ways: by a return to 'nature' and its 'poetic spaces' which constitute the historic home of the people and the repository of their memories; and by a cult of golden ages. These two methods were frequently used by the 'educator-intellectuals' to promote a national revival.

It needs to be noted in passing that Smith identifies a third route of nation-formation in his later work, that of the immigrant nations which consist largely of the fragments of other *ethnies*, particularly those from overseas:

> In the United States, Canada and Australia, colonist-immigrants have pioneered a providentialist frontier nationalism; and once large waves of culturally different immigrants were admitted, this has encouraged a 'plural' conception of the nation, which accepts, and even celebrates, ethnic and cultural diversity within an overarching political, legal, and linguistic national identity. (1998: 194; see also 1995: chapter 4)

This brings us to the final question guiding Smith's explanatory framework, namely 'where and when did the nation arise'? 'It is at this point that nationalism enters the political arena'. Nationalism, Smith contends, does not help us to determine which units of population are eligible to become nations, nor why they do so, but it plays an important part in determining when and where nations will emerge (1991a: 99). The next step, then, is to consider the (political) impact of nationalism in a number of particular cases. But this cannot be done without clarifying the concept of nationalism itself.

Smith begins by noting that the term 'nationalism' has been used in five different ways:

1. the whole process of forming and maintaining nations;
2. a consciousness of belonging to the nation;
3. a language and symbolism of the 'nation';
4. an ideology (including a cultural doctrine of nations); and
5. a social and a political movement to achieve the goals of the nation and realize the national will (1991a: 72).

Smith stresses the fourth and the fifth meanings in his own definition. Hence, nationalism is 'an ideological movement for attaining and maintaining autonomy, unity and identity on behalf of a population deemed by some of its members to constitute an actual or potential "nation"' (*ibid.*: 73). The key terms in this definition are autonomy, unity and identity. Autonomy refers to the idea of self-determination and the collective effort to realize the true, 'authentic', national will. Unity denotes the unification of the national territory and the gathering together of all nationals within the homeland. It also signifies the brotherhood of all nationals in the nation. Finally, identity means 'sameness', that is, that the members of a particular group are alike in those respects in which they differ from non-members, but it also implies the rediscovery of the 'collective self' (or the 'national genius') (*ibid.*: 74–7).

On the other hand, the 'core doctrine' of nationalism consists of four central propositions:

1. The world is divided into nations, each with its own peculiar character, history and destiny.
2. The nation is the source of all political and social power, and loyalty to the nation has priority over all other allegiances.
3. Human beings must identify with a nation if they want to be free and realize themselves.
4. Nations must be free and secure if peace is to prevail in the world (*ibid.*: 74).

Smith then moves on to the types of nationalism. Drawing on Kohn's philosophical distinction between a more rational and a more organic version of nationalist ideology, he identifies two kinds of nationalism: 'territorial' and 'ethnic' nationalisms (based on 'Western', civic-territorial, and 'Eastern', ethnic-genealogical models of the nation respectively). On this basis, he constructs a provisional typology of nationalisms, taking into account the overall situation in which the movements find themselves before and after independence:

1. Territorial nationalisms

    (a) *Pre-independence* movements based on a civic model of the nation will first seek to eject foreign rulers, then establish a new state-nation on the old colonial territory: these are 'anti-colonial' nationalisms.
    (b) *Post-independence* movements based on a civic model of the nation will try to bring together often disparate ethnic populations and integrate them into a new political community replacing the old colonial state: these are 'integration' nationalisms.

2. Ethnic nationalisms

    (a) *Pre-independence* movements based on an ethnic/genealogical model of the nation will seek to secede from a larger political unit and set up a new 'ethno-nation' in its place: these are 'secession' and 'diaspora' nationalisms.
    (b) *Post-independence* movements based on an ethnic/genealogical model of the nation will seek to expand by including ethnic kinsmen outside the present boundaries and establish a much larger 'ethno-nation' through the union of culturally and ethnically similar states: these are 'irredentist' and 'pan' nationalisms (1991a: 82–3).

Smith admits that the typology he develops is not an exhaustive one. It does not include some well-known examples of nationalism like Maurras' 'integral' nationalism. However, he insists that such a basic typology helps us to compare nationalisms within each category. Let me end this sub-section by a simple diagrammatic representation of the two main routes of nation-formation postulated by Smith:

  I. Lateral (aristocratic) ethnies → bureaucratic incorporation → civic-territorial nations → territorial nationalisms (from above; usually led by the elites).

II. Vertical (demotic) ethnies → vernacular mobilization → ethnic-genealogical nations → ethnic nationalisms (from below; usually led by the intelligentsia).

A Critique of Ethno-symbolism

A quick glance at the literature will reveal that the framework of analysis developed by Armstrong and Smith had its fair share of criticisms. There are six main objections to ethno-symbolist inter-pretations: ethno-symbolist writers are conceptually confused; they underestimate the differences between modern nations and earlier ethnic communities; it is not possible to speak of nations and nationalisms in pre-modern eras; ethno-symbolists underesti-mate the fluidity and malleability of ethnic identities; the rela-tionship between modern national identities and the cultural material of the past is at best problematic; and their analysis of the process of ethnic consciousness-formation is misleading. Let us now consider each of these criticisms in more detail.

Ethno-symbolist Writers are Conceptually Confused

According to the proponents of this view, ethno-symbolist argu-ments constitute a typical illustration of the 'terminological chaos' that bedevils the study of nationalism. Connor, a stern critic of the conceptual licence in the field, notes that one of the most common manifestations of this confusion is the interutilization of the terms ethnicity, ethnic group and nation (1994: chapter 4). Smith and Armstrong are accused of falling into the same trap. O'Leary puts this very succinctly when he remarks that it is not too surprising to find nationalism in the 1500s if one grants the term such empiri-cal range. According to him, 'most of those who discuss "nations" before "nationalism" are in fact establishing the existence of cultural precedents, and ethnic and other materials, which are subsequently shaped and re-shaped by nationalists in pursuit of nation-building' (1996: 90). Symmons-Symonolewicz makes a similar point, arguing that this confusion is partly caused by the lack of a generally acceptable definition of the nation. For him, a nation is not simply a large ethnic group, nor every large ethnic group is a nation. To become a nation, he maintains, an ethnic group must undergo many changes which transform its structure and mentality. Moreover, in the course of their journey through history, nations absorb many alien elements and a neverending flux of influences from other cultures and societies (1985a: 220). This observation brings us to the second criticism levelled against ethno-symbolism.

Ethno-symbolists Underestimate the Differences between Modern Nations and Earlier Ethnic Communities

Symmons-Symonolewicz claims that Smith eliminates the differences between ethnic and national phenomena by attributing to all ethnic groups a fully developed group consciousness and a deep sense of history (1985a: 219). However, most pre-modern groups were not aware of the cultural idiosyncrasies that differentiated them from others. Even when a consciousness of this kind existed, it was mostly confined to an intellectual elite as the stage was not yet set for the diffusion of ethnic sentiments to the wider public (1981: 152). Breuilly concurs with Symmons-Symonolewicz by arguing that it is impossible to know what meaning such sentiments had for the majority of the people (1996: 151; *cf.* Hobsbawm 1990: 11). The main reason for that is the near absence of data on the ideas, feelings and opinions of the masses.

Breuilly spots another difference between modern nations and earlier ethnic communities in the light of Smith's own arguments. This concerns pre-modern identities' lack of institutional basis. Smith argues that the three fundamental elements of modern nationality, that is legal, political and economic identity, are absent in pre-modern *ethnies*. According to Breuilly, however, 'these are the principal institutions in which national identity can achieve form'. This leads to a contradiction in Smith's arguments because, Breuilly maintains, identities established outside institutions, particularly those which can bind together people across wide social and geographical spaces, are necessarily fragmentary, discontinuous and elusive (1996: 150–1). He notes that there were only two institutions in pre-modern epochs that could provide an institutional basis to ethnic allegiances, namely the church and the dynasty. However, these institutions usually carried at their heart an alternative, ultimately conflicting sense of identity to that of the ethnic group.

Yet another difference is highlighted by Calhoun who notes that nationalism is not simply a claim of ethnic similarity, but a claim that certain similarities should count as *the* definition of political community. For this reason, nationalism needs rigid boundaries in a way pre-modern ethnicity does not: 'Nationalism demands internal homogeneity throughout a putative nation, rather than gradual continua of cultural variation or pockets of subcultural distinction' (1993: 229). Most distinctively, nationalists generally assert that national identities are more important than other personal or group identities (such as gender, family or ethnicity) and link individuals directly to the nation as a whole. In stark contrast to this, most ethnic identities flow from family membership, kinship or membership in other immediate groups (*ibid.*).

Smith rejects these criticisms in his recent book (1998). He concedes that his definitions of the nation and of the *ethnie* are closely aligned. But, he argues, it is precisely those features of nations that *ethnies* lack, that is a clearly delimited territory, a public culture, economic unity and legal rights and duties for everyone, that ultimately differentiate nations from earlier *ethnies* (1998: 196). Smith claims that those who raise the charge of 'retrospective nationalism' confuse a concern with *la longue durée* with perennialism. For him, ethno-symbolists clearly separate off a modern nationalism from pre-modern ethnic sentiments. What they try to do, he comments, is to trace in the historical record 'the often discontinuous formation of national identities back to their pre-existing cultural foundations and ethnic ties – which is a matter for empirical observation rather than *a priori* theorising'. Finally, Smith acknowledges the important role institutions play as carriers and preservers of collective identities. Nevertheless, he argues that Breuilly's understanding of such institutions is narrowly modernist. Significant numbers of people were included in schools, temples, monasteries and a host of legal and political institutions. More important was their inclusion 'in linguistic codes and in popular literature, in rituals and celebrations, in trade fairs and markets, and in ethnic territories or "homelands", not to mention the corvée and army service' (*ibid.*: 197). Obviously, not all these institutions reinforced a sense of common ethnicity, but many did. Smith concludes by asserting that there are many more cases of ethnic identities in pre-

modern periods than Breuilly allows and that some of them do
have 'political significance', such as the ethnic states of hellenistic
antiquity.

It is Not Possible to Speak of Nations and Nationalisms in Pre-modern Eras

Can we, then, claim that there were nations and nationalisms in
pre-modern eras? For scholars who subscribe to some form of
modernism, the answer to this question is negative. Eley and Suny
argue that Greeks in the classical period or Armenians in the fifth
century were not (and could not be) nations in the modern sense
of the term. Whatever their degree of cohesion and consciousness,
these ethnoreligious formations did not make claims to territory,
autonomy or independence, nor could they, since these political
claims were only authorized in the age of nationalism (1996a: 11).
Hall makes a similar point by noting that most of the conditions
that facilitated the growth of nations such as effective communication, cheap transport, increase in literacy rates, were the products of modernization processes (1993: 3).

Symmons-Symonolewicz claims that there were only three kinds
of collective sentiments in the Middle Ages: religious, political and
ethnic. The first contained loyalty to the church or to various
heretic movements; the second included feudal, city-state, dynastic, monarchical and imperial loyalties; and the third consisted of
loyalty to the neighbourhood or the region. Some of these loyalties faded away in time; others were replaced by new loyalties; still
others provided the 'bricks and mortar' out of which the cultural
unity of the future nation was built. However, it is not possible to
know with certitude which of these sentiments was dominant in a
particular situation (1981: 158–63).

What all these scholars share is a belief in the modernity of
nations and nationalisms. Nationalism involves a new form of
group identity or membership (Calhoun 1993: 229). In this sense,
earlier histories of nations should not be read simply as pre-
histories, but 'as varied historical developments whose trajectories
remained open' (Eley and Suny 1996a: 11). Smith tries to counter
these criticisms by conceding that nationalism 'both as an ideology and movement, is a wholly modern phenomenon', but insists

that 'the "modern nation" in practice incorporates several features of pre-modern *ethnie* and owes much to the general model of ethnicity which has survived in many areas until the dawn of the "modern era"' (1986: 18).

Ethno-symbolists Underestimate the Fluidity and Malleability of Ethnic Identities

Modernist scholars do not share the ethno-symbolist belief in the persistence of ethnic identities. According to Kedourie, for instance, ethnic identity is not an inert or stable object. He observes that it has proved to be highly plastic and fluid over the centuries, and has been subject to far-reaching changes and revolutions. Hence, 'the pagan Roman citizen of North Africa becomes, through his biological descendant, the Christian subject of a Christian emperor, then a member of the Muslim *u m m a*, and today perhaps a citizen of the People's Democratic Republic of Algeria or the Libyan *Jamahiriya*' (1994: 141).

Calhoun, on the other hand, argues that nationalism fundamentally transforms pre-existing ethnic identities and gives new significance to cultural inheritances (1997: 49). He supports this argument by noting that the social and cultural significance of ethnic traditions is dramatically changed when they are written down, and sometimes again when they are reproduced through visual media (*ibid.*: 50).

The Relationship between Modern National Identities and the Cultural Material of the Past is at best Problematic

Modernists also question the significance of the cultural material of the past. Breuilly admits that nationalist intellectuals and politicians seize upon myths and symbols of the past and use them to promote a particular national identity. But, he continues, 'it is very difficult to correlate their degree of success with the "objective" importance of such myths and symbols' (1996: 151). He points to the fact that in many cases nationalists invent myths. Moreover, they ignore those which cut across their purposes. Hence, for every national myth that has been used, there are many others that have disappeared in the mists of history. Moreover, myths and symbols of the past can be put to various, often conflicting, uses. Finally, there are also many nationalist movements that have succeeded without having a rich ethno-history to feed upon (*ibid.*).

Calhoun concurs with Breuilly and argues that noticing the continuity in ethnic traditions does not explain either which of these traditions last or which become the basis for nations or nationalist claims (1997: 49). Furthermore, traditions are not simply inherited, they have to be reproduced:

> stories have to be told over and again, parts of traditions have to be adapted to new circumstances to keep them meaningful, what seem like minor updatings may turn out to change meanings considerably, and the 'morals' to the stories – the lessons drawn from them – sometimes change even while the narratives stay the same . . . To say too simply that nationalism is grounded in ethnic traditions, thus, obscures from our view important differences in scale and mode of reproduction. (*Ibid.*: 50)

Ethno-symbolists' Analysis of the Process of Ethnic Consciousness-formation is Misleading

This criticism comes from Zubaida who focuses on Smith's definition of ethnic community (or *ethnie*), or, more precisely, the element of 'solidarity' which appears in that definition (1989). He argues that this 'sense of solidarity' is a problematic notion in the context of Western Europe. Solidarity was not generated spontaneously by common communal existence, nor by kinship, neighbourhood or religious networks. These pertained to much smaller communities. Solidarity, Zubaida contends, was generated by political and socioeconomic processes and remained for a long time conditional upon their operation. This has profound implications for Smith's argument because it reveals that

> 'common ethnicity' and solidarity are not the product of communal factors *given* to modernity, but are themselves the product of the socio-economic and political processes which, in the West, were institutionalized into state and civil society. (1989: 330)

Zubaida elaborates this argument by noting that every society offers to its members a number of possible identifications, of which the 'national', if and when it exists, is only one. Which identification becomes the basis of political solidarities at a given point in time, he argues, is contingent upon particular processes and events. Hence, one can speak of a French or English *ethnie* by the fifteenth century; but, 'the question is under what conditions these became the foci of political solidarity as against other possible identifications, for whom, and with what degree of success' (*ibid.*: 331). According to Zubaida, once national identification is achieved, it has to be maintained. The success and endurance of national identities depended on economic and political achievements such as intensification of the division of labour (which is very effective in breaking up the mould of 'primordial' solidarities), extension of state institutions (which will guarantee the security of citizens), prosperity (which gives citizens a stake in the national entity). The success of the old Western nation-states was based on a long process of centralization and institutionalization. Common ethnicity and cultural homogeneity were the products of these processes and not their determinants (*ibid.*).

Further Reading

As far as ethno-symbolism is concerned, the best introduction is again Smith (1998), chapter 8. The classic works in this category are Armstrong (1982) and Smith (1986). Other books of general importance include Llobera (1994) and Hastings (1997).

For a modernist critique of ethno-symbolism see Breuilly (1996) [1994]. Two other useful critiques are Calhoun (1997), chapter 2, and Zubaida (1989). Here, we should also mention the remarkable exchange between Gellner and Smith on the relative importance of ethnic pasts for modern nations: see Gellner (1996b) and Smith (1996b, 1996c).

6

New Approaches to Nationalism

Consuetudine oculorum assuescunt animi, neque admirantur, neque requirunt rationes earum semper vident.

[The habits of the eyes are conducive to mental habits: we are not surprised by the things we see all the time, nor do we look for their reasons.]

Cicero (quoted in Montaigne 1982: 194)

Why 'New'?

One of the arguments of this book is that we have entered a new stage in the theoretical debate on nationalism since the late 1980s. This rather assertive argument was introduced and briefly discussed in Chapter 2, where a historical overview of the debate was provided. It is indeed true that the claim looks like an overstatement of the present situation given that a series of independent studies are treated as a separate category, which is then differentiated qualitatively from the whole body of work hitherto produced. In that sense, the argument needs to be sustained with more concrete evidence. But before that, one point requires further clarification. This claim is not based on the presupposition that the interventions of the last decade offer completely new, or 'revolutionary', insights into nationalism, invalidating everything that had been previously said on the subject. On the contrary, most scholars of the period are generally sympathetic to modernist arguments (Smith 1998: 220, 224).

The distinctive characteristic of this constellation of studies is their critical attitude *vis-à-vis* the mainstream scholarship on nationalism. Despite the fact that each highlights a different problem with earlier theories, they all question the fundamental assumptions of their predecessors, exploring the issues neglected (ignored?) by the latter. In short, the common denominator of these studies is their belief in the need to transcend the classical debate by proposing new ways of thinking about national phenomena. That explains the opening quotation from Cicero: scholars of the last decade question their visual habits and try to unearth what lies behind their commonsense assumptions. In a way, then, Cicero's words make up the slogan of the new era.

The rise of new theories was precipitated by a more general transformation in social sciences, which in turn reflected the developments in the real world, notably the rise of a women's movement, the writing of alternative histories which deny the homogeneity of national cultures and the changing nature of Western societies as a result of increasing migration. The growth of 'cultural studies' was particularly important in this context. The origins of this 'interdisciplinary incitement' go back to the late 1950s, when Richard Hoggart's *The Uses of Literacy* (1957) and Raymond Williams' seminal *Culture and Society* (1958) – among others – were published. The common aim of these scholars was to 'bring culture back' into social sciences (Eley and Suny 1996a: 20). In these studies, culture was not regarded as a coherent, harmonious whole, but as a deeply contested concept whose meaning is continually negotiated, revised and reinterpreted. In this sense, culture was not divorced from social fragmentation, class divisions, discrimination on the basis of gender and ethnicity, and relations of power: culture was more often not what people share, but what they choose to fight over (*ibid.*: 9).

The pioneering studies of Hoggart and Williams were soon followed by a rapidly growing body of work, focusing on questions of youth cultures and style, mass media, gender, race, popular memory and the writing of history. In Britain, it did not take long for cultural studies to acquire an institutional basis, first at the Birmingham Center for Contemporary Cultural Studies, then in various universities. In the United States, on the other hand, the impact of this emergent 'cross-disciplinary conversation' was more pronounced in areas like literary studies, film studies, anthropology and women's studies. The growing cultural studies literature made use of a wide range of theories, from Gramsci to psychoanalytic approaches, and incorporated the insights provided by alternative epistemological perspectives, notably feminism, postcolonialism and postmodernism (Eley and Suny 1996a; Eley 1996).

How was the study of nationalism affected by all these developments? It is possible to identify two broad influences in this context. First, the gender-blind, Eurocentric character of the mainstream literature was criticized; greater emphasis was put on internal (within nations) and external (among nations) hierarchies of power. Second, the interaction of the studies of nationalism with such developing fields as migration, race, multiculturalism, diasporas and the like increased. In other words, there was a renewed emphasis on the interdisciplinary nature of nationalism as a subject of investigation (*cf.* Smith 1998: xiii). Let me now elaborate each of these influences.

The common feature of the theories and approaches I have reviewed in previous chapters is their involvement in the reproduction of the dominant discourses. None of these theories took account of the experiences of the 'subordinated', for example the former European colonies and their postcolonial successors, or women, ethnic minorities and the oppressed classes. Even the Marxist and neo-Marxist scholars, who based their theories on the experiences of nations occupying a dependent (or peripheral) position within the world political economy, fell prey to Eurocentrism, concentrating on the experiences of countries like Scotland and Ireland, and ignoring the disillusionments of the dozens of former colonies in Asia and Africa. Taking this 'theoretical blindness' as their starting point, a number of scholars tried to formulate frameworks of analysis that stress the experiences of the subordinated. Among these, approaches emphasizing the differential participation of women into nationalist projects, the experiences of postcolonial societies and the everyday dimension of nationalism, as well as postmodernist analyses were the most important.

As McClintock rightly observes, 'theories of nationalism have tended to ignore gender as a category constitutive of nationalism itself' (cited in Eley and Suny 1996b: 259). This important gap was filled by scholars like Nira Yuval-Davis, Floya Anthias, Sylvia Walby, Deniz Kandiyoti and Cynthia Enloe, among others, who explored the gendered character of membership in the nation. Actually, women were – and are – never absent from the nationalist discourse: they figure as 'conquerors' mistresses, wartime rape victims, military prostitutes, cinematic soldier-heroes, pin-up models on patriotic calendars' and of course, as workers, wives, girlfriends and daughters waiting dutifully at home (Enloe 1993, cited in Eley and Suny 1996a: 27). The nation is invariably imagined as a big family and the homeland as a 'vulnerable' woman needing protection. Rape becomes a weapon in war and sexual assault on women is often interpreted as a direct assault on the identity of the entire community (McCrone 1998: 125; Enloe 1995). As a result,

> [a]nxieties about the health of the nation, or its demographic future and productive efficiencies, or the stabilities of the social fabric, commonly translate into a politics directed to and against women, whether through systems of mother-and-child welfare, through rhetorics of family values, or by policy offensives around reproductive health, the regulation of sexuality, or the direct control of women's bodies. (Eley and Suny 1996a: 26)

Yet, despite their centrality to nationalist discourse, women are excluded from the public sphere and confined to their homes. Hence, to analyse the marginalization (and the silencing) of women by the national body politic, we have to look in the family and household, in the unspectacular details of everyday life. That was precisely what feminist scholars were trying to do. They explored how women participate in various national projects, which roles they play – or are forced to play – within them, revealing the political/ideological constellations which underlie these roles and their allocation. In a way, then, they revolted against women's confinement to a secondary, always subordinate, position.

Another fundamental characteristic of mainstream writings on nationalism is their Eurocentric, or to use Yuval-Davis' term 'Westocentric' (1997: 3), outlook. The origins of this attitude go back to the Enlightenment tradition from which many of the concepts and ideas we associate today with democracy first descended. Imperialism and colonialism were the main ingredients of this tradition from the beginning. In many respects, the advance of democracy in Europe, for example the spread of universal citizenship, was contingent on the exploitation of people elsewhere. This complex

dialectical relationship between Europe and its 'others' was replicated inside Europe itself, between metropolitan and peripheral
cultures, city and countryside, dominant and subordinate nationalities, East and West (Eley and Suny 1996a: 28).

The exploration of these relationships and the deconstruction
of nationalism's negative codings, that is 'the ways in which even
the nation's most generous and inclusively democratic imaginings
entail processes of protective and exclusionary positioning against
others', was one of the most important theoretical gains of the last
decade (*ibid.*). Not surprisingly, this process of 're-reading' was initiated by scholars from outside Europe, notably by the Subaltern
Studies Group coming out of Indian Marxism. Scholars like Partha
Chatterjee and Ranajit Guha tried to reinterpret the history of
South Asia from the vantage point of the subordinated. Their aim
was to reveal how the hegemonic discourses of the West served to
suppress the voices of the 'subalterns'. The most important
Western instrument in this process was 'knowledge': thus, the
various ways in which knowledge was used to dominate the world
had to be unveiled. According to Chatterjee, Western ideas of ratio-
nality relegated non-Western cultures into 'unscientific traditionalism'. The relativist approach, on the other hand, which holds
that every culture is unique, was based on an essentialist conception of culture that precludes understanding from outside. Both
views, Chatterjee maintains, were reflections of power relations
(Chatterjee 1986, 1990; see also Eley and Suny 1996a: 29). For him,
anti/postcolonial nationalism, although a 'derivative discourse',
was never totally dominated by Western models of nationhood.
It could not imitate the West in every aspect of life, for then the
very distinction between the West and the East would vanish and
'the self-identity of national culture would itself be threatened'
(Chatterjee 1990: 237).

As explained in Chapter 4 (when considering Chatterjee's critique of Anderson), the nationalist resolution of this dilemma was
to separate the domain of culture into two spheres, the material
and the spiritual. 'What was necessary was to cultivate the material techniques of modern western civilization, while retaining and
strengthening the distinctive spiritual essence of the national
culture' (*ibid.*: 238). In short, the greatest contribution of scholars
like Chatterjee and Guha was to offer a 'non-Westocentric' interpretation of anti/postcolonial nationalisms.

A third issue neglected by mainstream scholarship on national-ism concerns the familiar terrain of 'everyday life'. Seeking after macro-explanations, traditional approaches paid little attention to the micro-level, that is, the everyday manifestations of nationalism. Yet, as Billig (1995) contends, nationalism has to be reproduced daily if it is to persist (see also Essed 1991; van Dijk 1993, 1998). This process of reproduction is not consciously registered by the participants since everyday life is also the domain of the 'uncon-scious': in other words, 'everyday awareness is naive' (Blaschke 1980, cited in Eley and Suny 1996a: 22). In short, to understand the continuing hold of nationalism, we must probe into the process by which ordinary people continue to imagine themselves as an abstract community. As McClintock observes, 'national fetishes' play an important role in this process:

> More often than not, nationalism takes shape through the visible, ritual organization of fetish objects – flags, uniforms, air-plane logos, maps, anthems, national flowers, national cuisines and architectures as well as through the organization of collec-tive fetish spectacle – in team sports, military displays, mass rallies, the myriad forms of popular culture and so on. (1996: 274)

This continual reminding, taken for granted by most people, trans-forms national identity into a form of life, a way of seeing and inter-preting the world, thereby securing the nation's existence (Yumul and Özkırımlı 1997).

The final stroke to the picture we have drawn so far comes from postmodernism. This is not the place to summarize all the debates around postmodernism or postmodernity, given that only a review of the definitions provided for these terms would require a sepa-rate volume. However, it is not possible to assess the impact of post-modernist approaches on the study of nationalism without first offering a working definition of the concept of postmodernity. Bauman's definition is quite helpful in this respect:

> Postmodernity is modernity coming of age: modernity looking at itself at a distance rather than from inside, making a full inven-tory of its gains and losses, psychoanalysing itself, discovering the intentions it never before spelled out, finding them mutually

cancelling and incongruous. Postmodernity is modernity coming to terms with its own impossibility: a self-monitoring modernity, one that consciously discards what it was once unconsciously doing. (1991: 272)

As with almost any definition, Bauman's formulation is not without its problems. It poses as many questions as it tries to answer: 'What is modernity?', 'Have we all gone through the modern era?' and so on. Nevertheless, it constitutes a good starting point in terms of considering the implications of postmodernism for the study of nationalism.

Broadly speaking, it is possible to distinguish two themes that recurrently appear in postmodernist analyses. The first of these is the production and reproduction of national identities through popular culture. This not only requires focusing on communication technologies and popular genres hitherto excluded from the academic agenda, but also 'deconstructing' the meanings and values promoted through these technologies – hence, unravelling the power relations that lie behind them. Accordingly, the visual technologies of film, photography, television and video are scrutinized; a wide range of popular cultural products from books and magazines to food, fashion and dress are dissected (Eley and Suny 1996a). In these studies, the texts are 're-read' and the meanings are 'reconstructed' because, the postmodernists contend, each text is a narrative and each narrative can be interpreted in myriads of different ways. The hegemonic discourses, or 'meta-narratives', are nothing but a sham; thus, they should be explicitly rejected.

In this context, a number of scholars problematized the notion of 'identity'. In the words of Stuart Hall,

[i]dentity is not as transparent or unproblematic as we think. Perhaps instead of thinking identity as an accomplished fact, which the new cultural practices then represent, we should think, instead, of identity as a 'production', which is never complete, always in process, and always constituted within, not outside, representation. (1990: 222)

In this perspective, identities are never fixed, essential or immutable. Rather, they are 'the unstable points of identification or suture, which are made within the discourses of history and culture. Not an essence, but a positioning' (*ibid.*: 226). History changes our conception of ourselves. Key to this change, argues Hall, is the concept of 'Other', because identity is also the relationship between us and the Other: 'only when there is an Other can you know who you are'. There is no identity 'without the dialogic relationship to the Other. The Other is not outside, but also inside the Self, the identity' (1996b: 345).

According to Hall, this 'de-centering' of identity is a consequence of the relativization of the Western world – 'of the discovery of other worlds, other peoples, other cultures, and other languages' (*ibid.*: 341). National identities are gradually eroded by the forces of globalization which increase the interdependence of the planet on the one hand and lead to the formation of strong local identities on the other (see also McCrone 1998: 34–5). In such a context, the idea of a 'unified' national identity – or a 'homogeneous' national culture – is no longer tenable.

Another theme explored by postmodernist scholars, notably Homi Bhabha, is the 'forms of contestation inside nationalism's dominant frame' (Eley and Suny 1996a: 29). Drawing on the writings of Derrida, Fanon, Foucault and Lacan, Bhabha emphasizes the role of the people on the national 'margins', that is ethnic minorities, foreign workers and immigrants, in the process of definition of national identities. According to Bhabha, 'hybrid' populations contest the dominant constructions of the nation by producing their own counter-narratives. These counter-narratives, he argues, 'disturb those ideological manoeuvres through which "imagined communities" are given essentialist identities' (1990a: 300). The resulting conflict among competing narratives, on the other hand, increases the porousness of national boundaries and intensifies the ambivalence of the nation as a cultural and political form (Bhabha 1990a; Rutherford 1990; see also Rattansi 1994).

This brings us to the second broad change generated by the developments in social sciences. This manifested itself in the form of a renewed emphasis on the interdisciplinary nature of the study of nationalism. Before elaborating this point, however, one qualification is in order. The term 'interdisciplinary' is usually taken to mean not being constrained by the boundaries of specific academic disciplines and adopting an eclectic approach in the study of a particular problem. In this sense, nationalism has always been an interdisciplinary subject. Scholars have made use of concepts and theories developed in a variety of disciplines, ranging from sociology and political science to international relations and psychology. However, the studies of the last decade differed from their predecessors in two respects. First, scholars no longer confined themselves to traditional disciplines and incorporated insights developed in such areas as women's studies, race relations theory, discourse analysis, postcolonial theories into their analyses. Second, special emphasis was laid on the multi-dimensional character of 'subjectivity' (Essed 1991; Anthias and Yuval-Davis 1989).

As I have briefly explained above, the studies in question challenged the orthodox conceptions which regarded individuals as coherent subjects with a unified sense of identity. They stressed the various dimensions of subjectivity, such as gender, race, ethnicity and class, noting that these dimensions are inextricably intertwined; hence, it makes no sense to treat them separately. What shapes an individual's preferences is an interaction of various dimensions that make up her/his subjectivity and not a particular dimension of that subjectivity. The experiences and reactions of a Black working class woman from an ethnic minority is different from that of a White middle class man from the dominant ethnic group. This point, which looks like a truism today, was largely overlooked by the participants of the classical debate. What the recent studies attempted to do was to bring these differences to the fore and draw our attention to the multi-dimensionality of the constructions of subjectivity. In short, the interaction between research on nationalism and that conducted in other, 'sister', areas increased in the last decade, which in turn made the study of nationalism more complicated, but also more rewarding.

So far I have tried to summarize the fundamental differences between the studies of the last decade and that of the earlier periods. This summary was intended to substantiate the claim that we have entered a new stage in the debate on nationalism since the late 1980s. The argument can be strengthened further by examining in detail a few studies that question orthodox theorizations about nations and nationalism. Thus, I will devote the following sections to Michael Billig's analysis of the daily reproduction of nationhood and Nira Yuval-Davis' survey of the relationship between gender and nationalist projects.

Reproduction of Nationhood: 'Banal Nationalism'

The reproduction of nations and nationalisms has generally been disregarded by mainstream writings on the subject. The issue was first taken up by scholars who attempted to provide a gendered understanding of nationalism. As we shall see in the next section, these scholars explored the contribution of women into several dimensions of nationalist projects, particularly their role in the biological, symbolic and ideological reproduction of nationalism (Jayawardena 1986; Yuval-Davis and Anthias 1989; Yuval-Davis 1997). Another important exception has been the French Marxist scholar Étienne Balibar who treated the nation as a social formation, in the sense of

> a construction whose unity remains problematic, a configuration of antagonistic social classes that is not entirely autonomous, only becoming *relatively* specific in its opposition to others and via the power struggles, the conflicting interest groups and ideologies which are developed over the *longue durée* by this very antagonism. (1990: 334)

According to Balibar, the main problem posed by the existence of social formations was not that of their beginning or their end, but primarily that of their reproduction, that is, 'the conditions under which they can maintain this conflictual unity which creates their autonomy over long historical periods' (*ibid.*: 334–5). It is the British social psychologist Michael Billig who sets out to specify these conditions. Billig's influential *Banal Nationalism* (1995) can be considered as the first study that provides a systematic analysis of the reproduction of nationalism.

Billig's approach is based on a critique of orthodox theorizations that tend to associate nationalism with 'those who struggle to create new states or with extreme right-wing politics' (1995: 5). According to this view, nationalism is the property of 'others', the peripheral states which have yet to complete their nation-building processes, and not 'ours', the established 'nation-states' of the West. Nationalism is a temporary mood in the West, only manifesting itself under certain 'extraordinary' conditions, that is, in times of crises, suddenly disappearing once normal conditions are restored. In that sense, crises are like infections causing fever in a 'healthy body'. When the crisis abates, 'the temperature passes; the flags are rolled up; and, then, it is business as usual' (*ibid.*). Billig rejects this simplistic, even naive, picture. For him, the crises depend upon existing ideological foundations. They do not create nation-states as nation-states: '[i]n between times the United States of America, France, the United Kingdom and so on continue to exist. Daily, they are reproduced as nations and their citizenry as nationals'. However, 'this reminding is so familiar, so continual, that it is not consciously registered as reminding'. Billig introduces the term 'banal nationalism' to cover 'the ideological habits which enable the established nations of the West to be reproduced': 'The metonymic image of banal nationalism is not a flag which is being consciously waved with fervent passion: it is the flag hanging unnoticed on the public building' (*ibid.*: 6–8).

Such a conception casts doubt on standard interpretations which hold that nationalism becomes something surplus to everyday life once the nation-state is established, only to return when the orderly routines are broken down. According to Billig, nationalism does not disappear when the nation acquires a political roof: instead, it becomes absorbed into the environment of the established homeland (*ibid.*: 41). The symbols of nationhood (coins, bank notes, stamps) become a part of our daily lives. These small reminders turn the background space into 'national' space.

Billig maintains that it is not possible to explain all these routine habits or the popular reaction following the moments of crisis in terms of identity. National identity, he argues, is not a psychological accessory which people always carry with them, to be used whenever it is necessary. Like a mobile phone, this psychological equipment lies quiet for most of the time: '[t]hen the crisis occurs; the president calls; bells ring; the citizens answer; and the patriotic identity is connected' (*ibid.*: 7). According to Billig, this approach does not take us very far. For national identity to do its work, people must know what that identity is. In other words, they must have assumptions about what a nation is and, indeed, what patriotism is.

This information comes from different sources. For instance, national histories tell us the story of a people travelling across time – 'our' people, with 'our' ways of life. On the other hand, national community cannot be imagined without also imagining communities of foreigners which make 'our' culture unique: there can be no 'us' without a 'them' (*ibid.*: 78–9). It is at this stage that stereo-typed judgements come in. Stereotypes become means of distin-guishing 'them' from 'us': 'we' represent the standard, the normal, against which 'their' deviations appear notable. This unique com-munity of culture is also associated with a particular territory, a bounded geographical space which is 'our' homeland. Indeed, the whole world is composed of communities of culture like ours, each tied to a specific piece of land. 'If "our" nation is to be imagined in all its particularity, it must be imagined as a nation amongst other nations' (*ibid.*: 83). For Billig, this international conscious-ness is integral to the modern discourse of nationalism.

These observations raise another question: why do we, in estab-lished nations, not forget our national identity? For Billig, the short answer is that '"we" are constantly reminded that "we" live in nations; "our" identity is continually being flagged'. 'Routinely familiar habits of language' play an important role in this process of reminding. 'Small words, rather than grand memorable phrases' make our national identity unforgettable. To explore such matters, we should not only pay attention to words like 'people' (or 'society'), but also become 'linguistically microscopic' since the secret of banal nationalism lies in tiny words such as 'we', 'this' and 'here' (*ibid.*: 93–4). As might be expected, these words are most commonly used by politicians.

Politicians play an important part in the reproduction of nation-alism, but not because they are figures of great influence. On the contrary, many commentators argue that their weight in the key decision-making mechanisms is constantly declining – partly as a result of increasing globalization. 'Politicians are important because, in the electronic age, they are familiar figures'. Their faces appear regularly in the newspapers or on the television screens. In a way, they are the 'stars' of the modern age: their words daily reach millions (*ibid.*: 96). In such a context, what they say (and how they say it) is of utmost importance. The 'patriotic card' is played by almost all politicians. More importantly, however, politicians claim to speak for the nation. Evoking the whole nation as their audience, they rhetorically present themselves as repre-senting the national interest (*ibid.*: 106). By using a complex deixis of homeland, they invoke the national 'we' and place 'us' within 'our' homeland. When the homeland-making phrases are used regularly, '"we" are unmindfully reminded who "we" are and where "we" are. "We" are identified without even being mentioned'. Moreover, '[w]hat is "ours" is presented as if it were the objective world . . . The homeland is made both present and unnoticeable by being presented as *the* context' (*ibid.*: 109).

On the other hand, politicians are not the only actors contributing to the daily reproduction of nationhood. Their rhetorical forms and deixis are taken up by the newspapers. Like politicians, newspapers claim to stand in the eye of the nation. The opinion and editorial columns evoke a national 'we', including both readers and writers (as well as a universal audience). What unites the reader and the writer, what makes them 'we', is the national identity. The newspapers also contribute to the process of imagining a national 'we' by their internal organization and the structure of presentation of the news. 'Home' news is separated from 'foreign' news. And ' "[h]ome" indicates more than the contents of the particular page: it flags the home of the newspaper and of the assumed, addressed readers'. We, the readers, follow the directing signs and find our way around the familiar territory of the newspaper: 'As we do so, we are habitually at home in a textual structure, which uses the homeland's national boundaries, dividing the world into "homeland" and "foreign" ' (*ibid.*: 119).

One of the most original theses of Billig's study relates to social scientists' role in the reproduction of nationalism. According to Billig, scholars contribute to this process by:

- *Projecting nationalism* – these approaches define nationalism in a very restricted way, as an extreme/surplus phenomenon, thereby confining it to nationalist movements induced by irrational emotions. In this way, nationalism is projected on to 'others'; ' "ours" is overlooked, forgotten, even theoretically denied'.
- *Naturalizing nationalism* – some theorists reduce nationalism to a psychological need by arguing that contemporary loyalties to nation-states are instances of something general, or endemic to human condition. As such, ' "banal nationalism" not only ceases to be nationalism, but it ceases to be a problem for investigation' (*ibid.*: 16–17).

Billig notes that some scholars do both simultaneously. This leads to a theoretical (and rhetorical) distinction: 'our' nationalism is not presented as nationalism, something dangerously irrational, surplus and alien. A new label is found for it, 'patriotism', which is beneficial and necessary (*ibid.*: 55). Consequently, 'our patriotism' is presented as natural, therefore invisible, whereas 'nationalism' is seen as the property of 'others' (*ibid.*: 17).

If banal nationalism is so widespread, then, what should social scientists do? First and foremost, they should confess. Billig admits that he feels pleasure if a citizen from the homeland runs quicker or jumps higher than foreigners. Similarly, he confesses that he reads the 'home' news with greater interest. Generally speaking, we are all participants in the discourse of nationalism: 'it is present in the very words which we might try to use for analysis' (*ibid.*: 12). In that sense, it can be argued that all texts on nationalism – even the critical ones – contribute to its reproduction (see also Periwal 1995: 237). Calhoun sums this up succinctly: 'many of the categories and presumptions of this discourse are so deeply ingrained in our everyday language and our academic theories that it is virtually impossible to shed them, and we can only remind ourselves to take them into account' (1993: 214). We should at least do this because

> . . . whatever else is forgotten in a world of information overload, we do not forget our homelands. . . . If we are being routinely primed for the dangers of the future, then this is not a priming which tops up a reservoir of aggressive energy. It is a form of reading and watching, of understanding and of taking for granted. It is a form of life in which 'we' are constantly invited to relax, at home, within the homeland's borders. This form of life is the national identity, which is being renewed continually, with its dangerous potentials appearing so harmlessly homely. (Billig 1995: 127)

Gender and Nation

A key issue in the analysis of nations and nationalism has been the differential participation of various social groups in nationalist projects. It has been generally recognized that nationalist movements draw upon different constituencies, in uneven ways, and there has been a large body of work analysing various aspects of these movements, such as their class compositions, the levels of education of their participants and so on. However, this body of work has not engaged itself with the differential integration of women and men into national projects (Walby 1996: 235). As Yuval-Davis notes, most hegemonic theorizations about nations and nationalism, sometimes even those written by women (for example Greenfeld 1992), have ignored gender relations as irrelevant (1997: 1). Nationalism has been generally regarded as a male phenomenon, springing from masculinized memory, masculinized humiliation and masculinized hope (Enloe 1989: 44).

These assumptions have been increasingly questioned since the mid-1980s. McClintock, for example, argues that nationalism is constituted from the very beginning as a gendered discourse and cannot be understood without a theory of gender power (1996: 261). Our task, she continues, must be to formulate a feminist theory of nationalism, which might be strategically fourfold:

> (1) investigating the gendered formation of sanctioned male theories; (2) bringing into historical visibility women's active cultural and political participation in national formations; (3) bringing nationalist institutions into critical relation with other social structures and institutions; and (4) at the same time paying scrupulous attention to the structures of racial, ethnic and class power that continue to bedevil privileged forms of feminism. (*Ibid.*)

This was in a way what scholars like Kumari Jayawardena (1986), Cynthia Enloe (1989), Sylvia Walby (1996), Nira Yuval-Davis and Floya Anthias (1989; Yuval-Davis 1997) were attempting to do, namely to provide a gendered understanding of nations and nationalism. Among these, the work of Nira Yuval-Davis was particularly important. In an earlier intervention, Yuval-Davis and her co-editor Floya Anthias (1989) explored the various ways in which women affect and are affected by ethnic/national processes and how these relate to the state. Later, Yuval-Davis elaborated some of the theses developed in this book and expanded them to book length as *Gender and Nation* (1997).

The starting point of Anthias and Yuval-Davis, in the introduction to their seminal *Woman–Nation–State*, is the shortcomings of the feminist critique of the state. For them, the merit of feminists and socialist feminists was to reveal how the state constructs men and women differently. In this way, they were able to shed light on the ways in which the welfare state has constituted the 'state subject' in a gendered way, that is, as essentially male in its capacities and needs (Anthias and Yuval-Davis 1989: 6). However, Anthias and Yuval-Davis contend, it is not enough to criticize the state's understanding of citizenship since this concept only relates to the way the state acts upon the individual and not the way in which the state forms its political project. Therefore, it cannot on its own explain the social forces that are dominant within the state. According to them, the notion of citizenship does not encapsulate adequately the relations of control and negotiation that take place in various areas of social life. What is required, then, is to identify the ways in which women participate in national and ethnic processes within civil society and to explore how these relate to the state. Before doing that, however, Anthias and Yuval-Davis stress that there is no unitary category of women which can be unproblematically conceived as the focus of ethnic, national and state policies: 'Women are divided along class, ethnic and life-cycle lines, and in most societies different strategies are directed at different groups of women' (*ibid.*: 7). In the light of these observations, Anthias and Yuval-Davis suggest five major ways in which women have tended to participate in ethnic and national processes:

(a)   as biological reproducers of members of ethnic collectivities;

(b)   as reproducers of the boundaries of ethnic/national groups;

(c)   as participating centrally in the ideological reproduction of the collectivity and as transmitters of its culture;

(d)   as signifiers of ethnic/national differences – as a focus and symbol in ideological discourses used in the construction, reproduction and transformation of ethnic/national categories; and

(e)   as participants in national, economic, political and military struggles (*ibid.*).

As Biological Reproducers of Members of Ethnic Collectivities

Yuval-Davis notes that most discussions on women's reproductive rights have focused on the effects of the existence or absence of these rights on women as individuals. However, she argues, the pressures on women to have or not to have children often relate to them 'not as individuals, workers and/or wives, but as members of specific national collectivities': '[a]ccording to different national projects, under specific historical circumstances, some or all women of childbearing age groups would be called on, sometimes bribed, and sometimes even forced, to have more, or fewer, children' (1997: 22).

Yuval-Davis identifies three main discourses that tend to dominate nationalist policies of population control. The first is the 'people as power' discourse, in which the future of the nation is seen to depend on its continuous growth (*ibid.*: 29–31). Here, various policies are pursued to encourage women to have more children. In Israel, for example, there were calls for women to bear more children at times of slack immigration or national crisis. This encouragement was usually underpinned by religious discourses about the duty of women to produce more children. Politicians nurtured the fear of a 'demographic holocaust' by drawing attention to popular Palestinian sayings ('The Israelis beat us at the borders but we beat them in the bedrooms'), using it to increase the pressure on women. However, the state does not always rely on ideological mobilization and may adopt less radical measures such as the establishment of child benefit systems or the allocation of loans (maternal benefit schemes) for this purpose (Anthias and Yuval-Davis 1989: 8–9; Yuval-Davis 1989).

The second discourse identified by Yuval-Davis is the Eugenicist. The Eugenics were concerned not with the size of the nation, but with its 'quality' (1997: 31–2). This has given rise to various policies aimed at limiting the physical numbers of members of 'undesirable' groups. These policies may sometimes take the form of immigration controls; at other times, they may include more extreme measures such as the physical expulsion of particular groups or their actual extermination (for example Jews and Gypsies in Nazi Germany). Another strategy is to limit the number of people born in specific ethnic groups by controlling the reproductive capacity of women. Again various policies are pursued here, ranging from forced sterilization to the massive mobilization of birth control campaigns. A corollary of this strategy is the active encouragement of population growth of the 'right kind', that is of the dominant ethnic group (Anthias and Yuval-Davis 1989: 8–9).

Today, eugenistic policies are implemented most vigorously in Singapore, where the Prime Minister Lee Kuan Yew asked the highly educated women to produce more children – as part of their patriotic duty – while poor uneducated mothers were given a cash award of $ 10000 if they agreed to be sterilized (Yuval-Davis 1997: 32).

The final discourse identified by Yuval-Davis is the Malthusian. In stark contrast to the first discourse, the Malthusians see the reduction of the number of children as the way to prevent a future national disaster (1997: 32–5). This discourse is most visible in developing countries, where a number of policies aimed at reducing the overall rate of growth are adopted. 'Women are often the "captive" target population for such policies' (*ibid.*: 33). Yuval-Davis observes that the country which has gone furthest in this respect is China. Here, several measures were taken so that most families would not have more than one baby. Punishments for evading these measures ranged from unemployment for the parents to exclusion from education for the children. According to Yuval-Davis, the effect of Malthusian policies is highly gendered: '[w]here there is strong pressure to limit the number of children, and where male children are more highly valued for social and economic reasons, practices of abortions and infanticide are mainly directed towards baby girls' (*ibid.*: 34).

As Reproducers of the Boundaries of Ethnic/National Groups

Drawing on Armstrong's work, Yuval-Davis argues that the mythical unity of 'national imagined communities' is maintained and ideologically reproduced by a whole system of symbolic 'border guards' which classify people as members and non-members of a specific collectivity. These border guards are closely linked to 'specific cultural codes of style of dress and behaviour as well as to more elaborate bodies of customs, religion, literary and artistic modes of production, and, of course, language' (1997: 23). Gender relations and sexuality play a significant role in all this, as women are generally seen as embodiments and cultural reproducers of ethnic/national collectivities. According to Yuval-Davis, this dimension of women's lives is crucial to understanding their subjectivities as well as their relations with each other, with men and with children.

Given their centrality as symbolic border guards, it is easy to understand why women are controlled not only by being encouraged or discouraged from having children, but also in terms of the 'proper' way in which they should have them – that is, in ways which will reproduce the boundaries of their ethnic group or that of their husbands (Anthias and Yuval-Davis 1989: 9). Hence, in some cases they are not allowed to have sexual relations with men of other groups (as until recently in South Africa). This is particularly the case for women belonging to the dominant ethnic group. Legal marriage is generally a precondition for the child to be recognized as a member of the group. Often, religious and social traditions dictate who can marry whom so that the character and boundaries of the group can be maintained over generations (*ibid.*). In Israel, for example, it is the mother who determines the child's nationality. But if the mother is married to another man, then the child will be an outcast (even if she is divorced by civil, rather than religious law, because civil marriages are not recognized by the religious court) and not allowed to marry another Jew for ten generations (Yuval-Davis 1989: 103).

As Participating Centrally in the Ideological Reproduction of the Collectivity and as the Transmitters of its Culture

As noted above, women are usually seen as the 'cultural carriers' of the ethnic/national group. They are the main socializers of small children, and thus they are often required to transmit the rich heritage of ethnic symbols, traditions and values to the young members of the group (Anthias and Yuval-Davis 1989: 9). Here, Yuval-Davis stresses the need to treat 'culture' not as a reified fixed category, but rather 'as a dynamic process, continuously changing, full of internal contradictions which different social and political agents, differentially positioned, use in different ways' (1997: 67).

As Signifiers of Ethnic/National Differences

Women do not only transmit the cultural heritage of ethnic and national groups, but they also 'symbolize' it. The nation is often imagined as a loved woman in danger or as a mother who lost her sons in battle. It is supposedly for the sake of the 'womenandchildren' (sic) that men go to war (Enloe 1990, cited in Yuval-Davis 1997: 15). Yuval-Davis argues that this 'burden of representation' has brought about the construction of women as the bearers of the collectivity's honour (1997: 45). Hence, specific codes and regulations are usually developed, defining who/what is a 'proper woman' – and a 'proper man'. In the Hitler Youth movement, for example, the motto for girls was 'Be faithful; be pure; be German'. For boys it was 'Live faithfully; fight bravely; die laughing' (*ibid.*). Sometimes, the difference between two ethnic groups is determined by the sexual behaviour of women. For instance, a 'true' Cypriot girl should behave in sexually appropriate ways. If she does not, then neither herself nor her children may belong to the community (Anthias and Yuval-Davis: 10; see also Anthias 1989). In the words of Yuval-Davis,

> [o]ther women in many other societies are also tortured or murdered by their relatives because of adultery, flight from home, and other cultural breaches of conduct which are perceived as bringing dishonour and shame on their male relatives and community. (1997: 46)

As Participants in National, Economic, Political and Military Struggles

The category that is most commonly explored concerns women's role in national and ethnic struggles. Yuval-Davis argues that while women did not always participate directly in the fighting (although it was not uncommon for them to do so), they always had specific roles in the combat, 'whether it was to take care of the dead and wounded or to become the embodied possession of the victorious' (1997: 95). This 'sexual division of labour', however, usually disappears when there is no clear differentiation between the 'battle front' and the 'home front'. At this point, Yuval-Davis refers to the changing nature of warfare and the professionalization of militaries as having a positive impact on the incorporation of women into the military. But, she adds, 'it is only very rarely, if at all, that differential power relations between men and women have been erased, even within the most socially progressively organized national liberation armies or western professional militaries' (*ibid.*: 114).

In *Gender and Nation*, Yuval-Davis also offers a more detailed analysis of the absence of women from mainstream theorizing about nations and nationalism. She mentions two explanations that might be relevant in this respect. The first comes from Carole Pateman who traces the origins of this 'collective scholarly forgetting' back to the classical foundation theories which have shaped the commonsense understanding of Western political and social order. These theories divide the sphere of civil society into two domains, the public and the private, and locate women (and the family) in the private domain, which is not seen as politically relevant (Yuval-Davis 1997: 2). Rebecca Grant, on the other hand, argues that the foundation theories of both Hobbes and Rousseau portray the transition from the state of nature to an orderly society exclusively in terms of what they assume to be male characteristics – the aggressive nature of men (Hobbes) and the capacity for reason in men (Rousseau). Women are not part of this process, hence excluded from the 'social'. Later theories, Grant contends, took these assumptions for granted (*ibid.*).

Yuval-Davis notes that the gender-blindness of the mainstream literature continues unabated, despite a number of rare, thus welcome, exceptions. A recent reader on nationalism provides an excellent illustration of this. The editors of the Oxford Reader *Nationalism* (1994), John Hutchinson and Anthony D. Smith, placed the only extract (among 49) on nationalism and gender relations in the last section called 'Beyond Nationalism' and introduced it with the following words: 'The entry of women into the national arena, as cultural and biological reproducers of the nation and as transmitters of its values, has also redefined the content and boundaries of ethnicity and the nation' (1994: 287). Yuval-Davis' answer is concise: 'But, of course, women did not just "enter" the national arena: they were always there, and central to its constructions and reproductions!' (1997: 3)

Another theme developed in Yuval-Davis' recent study relates to the multi-dimensionality of nationalist projects. Noting that nationalist projects are often multiplex, Yuval-Davis argues that 'different members of the collectivity tend to promote contesting constructions which tend to be more or less exclusionary, more or less linked to other ideologies such as socialism and/or religion' (1997: 21). For her, attempts to classify all these different states and societies according to different types of nationalism would constitute an impossible and ahistorical task. Rather, we should treat these types as different dimensions of nationalist projects which are combined in different ways in specific historical cases.

Drawing on this observation, Yuval-Davis differentiates between three major dimensions of nationalist projects. The first is the 'genealogical' dimension which is constructed around the specific origin of the people or their race (*Volknation*). The second is the 'cultural' dimension in which the symbolic heritage provided by language, religion and/or other customs and traditions is constructed as the 'essence' of the nation (*Kulturnation*). Finally, there is the 'civic' dimension that focuses on citizenship as determining the boundaries of the nation, relating it directly to notions of state sovereignty and specific territoriality (*Staatnation*) (*ibid.*). According to Yuval-Davis, gender relations play an important role in each of these dimensions and are crucial for any valid theorization of them.

Further Reading

The best starting point for anyone interested in recent approaches to nationalism is the excellent overview by Eley and Suny (1996a).

The issue of gender and nation has become the subject of a growing literature since the mid-1980s. The most useful introductions are McClintock (1996) [1991] and Walby (1996) [1992]. Other works which should be consulted are Jayawardena (1986), Yuval-Davis and Anthias (1989) and Yuval-Davis (1997). For an interesting collection of case studies see West (1997).

On postcolonial nationalisms, the works to consult are Chatterjee (1986, 1990). The reproduction of nationalism is analysed in Balibar (1990) and Billig (1995). For a 'deconstructionist' analysis of nationalism see Bhabha (1990b).

Other works of general use are Calhoun (1997) and Brubaker (1996, 1998), both of whom warn us against the dangers of reifying nations and treat nationalism first and foremost as a kind of discourse.

7

By Way of Conclusion

A social formation only reproduces itself as a nation to the extent that, through a network of apparatuses and daily practices, the individual is instituted as homo *nationalis* from cradle to grave, at the same time he/she is instituted as homo *economicus, politicus, religiosus* . . .

Étienne Balibar, 'The Nation Form: History and Ideology'

Summing up the Debate: A Critical Appraisal

In the preceding chapters, I have tried to provide a detailed overview of recent theories of nationalism. While doing this, I confined myself to sketching the main arguments of each theory/approach and the major criticisms levelled against them, and did not engage in a lengthy personal critique. This was, in a way, necessary since my first aim in writing this book was to offer as complete a picture of the theoretical debate as possible, with all viewpoints – more or less – equally represented. In this chapter, however, I will abandon my quest for objectivity (an endless and vain task) and present my own view of the debate. I will first expound my objections to the theories/approaches reviewed so far. For a more systematic presentation, I will divide these objections into two categories, those relating to the 'form' of the debate, that is, the way in which particular approaches are presented, and those relating to the 'content' of the debate, that is the specific arguments propounded by each theorist or group of theorists. I will then propose a framework of analysis that might be used in the study of nationalism on the basis of ideas put

forward by various scholars. I will conclude the book by expressing a few, necessarily speculative, reflections on the future of the
debate.

Criticisms with Regard to the Form of the Debate

As we have already seen, scholars of nationalism are generally
divided into three categories in terms of the particular approach
they espouse: primordialists, modernists and ethno-symbolists. I
have adopted the same classification in this book. My choice,
however, was conditioned by a concern for reflecting the general
tendency in the field, not by a belief in the validity of the classification – although I admit that classifications cannot be empirically
right or wrong (Breuilly 1993a: 9). There are a number of difficulties with this classification. First and foremost, the terms used
to describe various theories/approaches are misleading, that is,
they do not accurately represent the works concerned. This is
mainly caused by the use of ambiguous, ill-defined criteria in the
classification.

   Let us begin with 'primordialism'. I have argued before,
contrary to Eller and Coughlan's (1993) claims, that this term
performs an important function by highlighting the role of perceptions and beliefs in guiding people's reactions. On the other
hand, the concept is of limited use as a term describing a particular approach to nationalism and leads to serious confusions. Mostly
employed to denote the nationalist standpoint, the term is wrongly
stretched to cover the position of scholars like Geertz and Shils
who focus on the ways in which ethnic identities are 'perceived' by
individuals. As I have explained earlier, it makes more sense to call
their approach 'constructivist' since both writers treat culture on
the basis of meanings attached to it. In this view, culture is never
'given' or fixed: it is shaped by the perceptions and beliefs of those
living in a particular community.

   The concept of 'modernism' is even more problematic as it
became a kind of catch-all term under which a number of quite
divergent approaches are subsumed. The only 'apparent' point of
intersection among these diverse interpretations is their belief in
the modernity (in the sense of recent) of nations and nationalism;
hence the term 'modernist', coined by Smith (1986; 1991b; 1994;

1998). However, apart from this shared conviction, there is little in common among the so-called modernists. Being stern critics of each other's work, they stress different, at times sharply conflicting, factors in their explanations. This point is overlooked by ethno-symbolist writers who tend to expand the common denominator joining these scholars. According to them, the modernists regard nations not only as a necessary concomitant of modernization processes, but also as 'invented', thus 'false' or 'artificial', constructions which become instruments of elites and leaders in their universal struggles for power. Moreover, they contend, the modernists believe that nationalism is an historically specific and transitory phenomenon (see for example Smith 1995: 35–7). Presenting these as the shared assumptions of the 'modernists', they then address their criticisms to all these scholars, treating them as a unitary, homogeneous category. This, however, constitutes an oversimplification of the theories concerned.

First, not all 'modernists' accept the 'falsity' of nations. We have already seen how this view, mostly associated with Gellner and Hobsbawm, is rejected by Anderson. His words are worth repeating here: 'Gellner is so anxious to show that nationalism masquerades under false pretences that he assimilates "invention" to "fabrication" and "falsity", rather than to "imagining" and "creation"' (1991: 6). In short, for Anderson, the fact that nations are 'imagined' does not imply that they are 'false' or 'artificial'. On the other hand, the role of elites in nurturing nationalism is explored by scholars like Brass who subscribe to some form of 'instrumentalism'. Gellner, Anderson or neo-Marxist writers do not dwell too much on this issue. Finally, the claim that nationalism is a transitory phenomenon which will disappear (or lose its virulence) once the nation is firmly established and achieves a high level of affluence is only made by Gellner and Hobsbawm. Clearly, these are not minor squabbles. How, then, could ethno-symbolists fail to notice these differences? Part of the answer might lie in ethno-symbolists' steadfast quest for an alternative interpretation. In an attempt to differentiate their position from available approaches, ethno-symbolists overlook the differences between various 'modernist' explanations and treat them as a coherent whole, thereby presenting us with a sharply dichotomized picture of the debate. This enables them to formulate an alternative interpretation by distancing themselves from both the primordialists and the modernists, and present it as a sensible 'middle way' between these polarized accounts. It needs to be noted, however, that any answer to this question, including this one, would be necessarily speculative.

As for ethno-symbolists, I concur with the view, prevalent among the modernists, that they should not be treated as a separate category (Breuilly 1996; Gellner 1996b; *cf.* Lieven 1997). However, it is not easy to decide where to place them given the rigidity of available categories. Ethno-symbolists make two different, in their view compatible, claims. On the one hand, they concede the modernity of nationalism as an ideology and a movement, incorporating many of the factors identified by the 'modernists' into their analyses. On the other hand, they hold that modern nations are built around pre-existing ethnic cores and that earlier ethnic cultures provide the material out of which today's national identities are forged. These claims point to the need to develop a new classification based on a redefinition of the existing categories.

In the light of these considerations, I will opt for a binary classification consisting of 'essentialist' and 'constructivist' approaches. Any attempt to defend this classification should begin by providing a working definition of these terms. Calhoun's definition of 'essentialism' seems to be a good starting point:

> 'Essentialism' refers to a reduction of the diversity in a population to some single criterion held to constitute its defining 'essence' and most crucial character. This is often coupled with the claim that the 'essence' is unavoidable and given by nature. It is common to assume that these cultural categories address really existing and discretely identifiable collections of people. More surprisingly, many also assume that it is possible to understand each category – Germans, say, or women, Blacks, or gays – by focusing solely on its primary identifier rather than on the way it overlaps with, contests and/or reinforces others (1997: 18)

According to this viewpoint, an individual belongs to one and only one nation, as s/he belongs to one and only one race and one gender. Each of these sharply demarcated (and indivisible) categories describes a particular aspect of the individual's being (Calhoun 1997: 18). This implies that the individual can have different self-definitions on the basis of different categories. In that sense, there is no interaction among the categories in question. Such a definition enables us to treat the primordialists and ethno-symbolists together. We have already seen that primordialists consider nationality as a 'natural' part of all human beings. In some cases, ethnic and national identities lay dormant for centuries because of treachery or oppression. But the national 'essence', unchanging and persistent, is always there to be 'reawakened'. Ethno-symbolist claims are not worlds apart. What unites Armstrong and Smith is their belief in the 'persistence' and 'durability' of ethnic ties. Both writers argue that the myths, symbols and values which form the basis of many modern national cultures 'tend to be *exceptionally* durable under "normal" vicissitudes and to persist over *many generations*, even *centuries*', setting limits to elite attempts at manipulation (Smith 1986: 16, emphasis added). In that sense, Smith's acceptance of the modernity of nationalism does not affect his essentialism. Nationalism is modern, but never 'contingent': every nationalism is constructed around 'particular' ethnic traditions. To put it in another way, there is a ethnic/ national 'essence' (a 'myth–symbol complex') underlying many, if not all, contemporary nationalisms. And what impels so many people around the world to lay down their lives for their nation is precisely this 'essence'.

Some scholars have indeed recognized the essentialism inherent in Smith's analysis. According to Norval, for example, Smith's insistence on retaining a pre-existing, pre-modern form of ethnicity leads him to subject the theorization of nations (as imagined communities) to an objectivist reduction, 'a "ground" outside all forms of discursive construction':

> Imagined communities, on these readings, can be nothing other than ideological forms which cover over deeper, underlying objectivities, objectivities which may be revealed by drawing away the veil of manipulation which they seem to construct. (1996: 62)

Patrik Hall raises a similar point, arguing that cultural naturalism (the term he uses for ethno-symbolism) is of the same kind as the 'discovery' of culture during Romanticism:

> Herder's subjectivist notion of *Volkgeist* is of the same type as Smith's notion of the symbolical *Mythomoteur*. In both cases it is

imaginations, myths and symbols which are emphasised, not any 'objective' cultural markers. Both notions stress cultural unity instead of social and political contradictions. (1998: 40)

For both writers, the implications of such an approach can be quite dangerous. As Norval rightly argues,

> [a] rejection of the symbolically constituted nature of certain forms of identification in favor of an uncovering of objective reality falls into a form of theorization which has been decisively problematized for its rationalism, its claims to a realm of truth not accessible to the consciousness of those engaged in the construction of their own identities, and, finally, its possible authoritarian consequences. (1996: 62)

Hall, on the other hand, claims that 'by making it dependent upon a cultural categorisation, nationalism becomes reified or conceived of as a natural expression of ethnicity or culture' (1998: 40). In that sense, 'it matters little that ethnicity or culture are constructions'. The argument, Hall concludes, runs the risk of being used as an apologetic political rhetoric.

These criticisms bring us to the second category, which consists of 'constructivists' who stress the intersubjective character of the process of ethnic/national identity-formation. The term 'socially constructed' is a recent contribution to the literature on nationalism. Tilley argues that this term permits recognition of two crucial points: first, that 'the logics, values and meanings which accrue to customs are interrelated and mutually informative'; and second, that 'such knowledge/value systems are continually reshaped as groups react to changing environmental and social conditions' (1997: 511). The second insight is more important for the purposes of our discussion. It implies that the meanings (and values) attributed to various constituents of the national culture, that is myths, symbols and traditions, are interminably negotiated, revised and redefined. In other words, ethnic membership is neither externally given, nor fixed: it is determined, consciously or unconsciously, by the group itself and varies according to changing circumstances.

This insight allows us to discover another commonality of the so-called 'modernists'. All scholars included in this category argue that it became possible and necessary to 'imagine' or 'invent' nations as a result of changing economic, political or social conditions. The transformation emphasized by each scholar and the underlying factors they identified display a great diversity: for Nairn, the key to understanding nationalism is 'uneven development'; for Hechter, it is 'internal colonialism'; for Breuilly, the rise of the modern state; for Gellner, industrialization; for Anderson, a series of interlinked factors, ranging from a revolution in the conceptions of time to 'print capitalism'. Moreover, they disagree on the degree of 'genuineness' of nations. What joins them, or what remains constant in their theories, is the belief that all human collectivities were subject to some fundamental changes at some point in history which disrupted the existing order, thereby forcing them to find new ways of organizing social/political life. The thread of their argument runs as follows: the older forms of organization become redundant under the impact of changes in economic, political and social life, which also create the conditions necessary to 'imagine' new forms (Anderson, Gellner, Hobsbawm, Breuilly, Nairn and Hechter); with the invention of new forms of collective organization, the concept of political legitimacy is redefined and the older principles of legitimacy, the dynastic and the religious, are abandoned (Anderson, Breuilly, Brass); the emerging elites 'invite the masses into history' in an attempt to get their support for the subsequent process of 'nation-building' (Brass, Breuilly, Nairn, Hroch); the improvements in communication technologies and corresponding increases in schooling and literacy rates help them to get their messages to ever-widening sections of the population (Anderson, Gellner, Hobsbawm, Breuilly, Brass); consequently, small-scale loyalties generated by face-to-face contact are gradually eroded and replaced by large-scale attachments felt for an 'impersonal' and 'anonymous' society the members of which will never meet, nor even hear of most of their fellow-members (Anderson, Gellner, Breuilly, Brass).

For the purposes of classification, it does not matter who 'creates' or 'imagines' the nation in the first place, nor how nationalism spreads among wider strata. Scholars opt for different scenarios to answer these questions. What matters for the classification is to determine the common denominator linking these different scenarios. The process I have sketched above catches this commonality. This process might not be as visible, or conspicuous, as the other criterion – the date of emergence of nations – used in classifying constructivist/modernist approaches; but it is more comprehensive and representative. Actually, the usefulness of the alternative principle of classification is quite debatable. We have already seen that constructivist/modernist scholars propose different dates for the emergence of nations. More importantly, this criterion leads to serious confusions in the case of scholars who are generally considered to be 'modernists', but who take the origins of nations as far back as the Middle Ages.

Liah Greenfeld is a good case in point. For Greenfeld, the modern idea of the nation emerged in sixteenth-century England, which was the first nation in the world and the only one for about two hundred years (1992: 14). On the other hand, Greenfeld, too, locates the origins of nationalism in a process of change (increasing upward or downward social mobility, the appearance of new roles) and people's reaction to it. Nationalism, she holds, was a response of individuals in elite sectors of society, who were personally affected by the contradictions of the society-of-orders. Upwardly-mobile commoners, who reached the top of the social ladder, found inacceptable the traditional image of society in which social mobility was an anomaly, and replaced it with that of a 'nation', making it synonymous with the 'people' of England. As a result of this redefinition, 'every member of the people was elevated to the dignity of the elite, becoming, in principle, equal to any other member' (1993: 49). The remarkable quality of national identity, for Greenfeld, is that 'it guarantees status with dignity to every member of whatever is defined as a polity or society' (*ibid.*). Again, the idea of 'constructivism' seems to be more useful than the alternative criterion of 'modernity' as a principle of classification since it enables us to place Greenfeld neatly within a particular category, that is, that of the 'constructivists'.

Criticisms with Regard to the Content of the Debate

Which of the theories/approaches we have reviewed enhances our understanding of nationalism? In other words, what is the most fruitful approach in terms of 'cracking the nut of nationalism' (Gellner 1995a: 61)? Let us consider each of these approaches in turn, following again the commonly adopted three-legged classification.

There is no need to dwell too much on the primordialist approach. As Brubaker observes, very few scholars today continue to subscribe to the view that nations are primordial, unchanging entities (1996: 15). Almost everybody admits that nations are born at a particular period in history, notwithstanding disagreements on the precise date of their emergence or the relative weight of pre-modern traditions and modern transformations in their formation. The pseudo-scientific, ideologically motivated belief that nations exist since time immemorial has little support in the academia.

This is largely to the credit of modernist studies which have been trying to show for the last four decades that the picture drawn by primordialists is far from representing the reality about nations and nationalism. The general assumptions of modernism seem to be fundamentally correct. Most of the nations that make up the world map today, including the old, 'historic' nations of Western Europe, are the products of the developments of the last two centuries. To substantiate this claim, it suffices to consider the case of 'language', the quintessential symbol of nationhood for many nationalists. Modernist scholars have revealed that in France, for example, 50 per cent of the people did not speak French at all and only 12–13 per cent spoke it correctly in 1789, the year of the Great Revolution. In the case of Italy, on the other hand, only 2.5 per cent of the population used Italian for everyday purposes at the moment of unification (Hobsbawm 1990: 60–1). Despite all efforts to the contrary, Norwegian never established itself as more than a minority language in Norway, which has been a bilingual country since 1947 with Norwegian confined to 20 per cent of the population (*ibid.*: 55). It is possible to multiply these examples. What is important for our purposes, however, is that in most cases nationalism becomes paramount after the state is established. As Pilsudski, the eventual liberator of Poland, recognized: 'It is the state which makes the nation and not the nation the state'. But perhaps the most forthright statement of this view comes from Massimo d'Azeglio who once said: 'We have made Italy, now we have to make Italians' (cited in *ibid.*: 44–5).

In my view, the general thrust of these arguments remains compelling despite the works of Armstrong and Smith. Nations are an outgrowth of the age of nationalism. Obviously, there is nothing modern about the attachments individuals feel for the communities of which they are a member. Throughout history, people felt attached to a great variety of groups or institutions such as city-states, empires, families or guilds. Given this, however, the crucial question is: why these attachments have disappeared or transformed into 'national' loyalties? And what is the degree of similarity between pre-modern attachments and contemporary collective ties felt for the abstract community of the nation which consists of millions of 'strangers'? It is indeed true that ethnic groups were salient and widespread in much of antiquity and the medieval era: but, to what extent do these groups resemble today's nations? Arguably, much less than ethno-symbolists would have us believe if we consider that myriads of 'unfavourable' events, for example migrations, conquests, genocides and intermarriages, have taken place in the course of history, altering the ethnic/cultural composition of any particular group.

Moreover, as Calhoun notes, ethnic identities are constituted, maintained and invoked in social processes involving diverse intentions, constructions of meaning and conflicts: 'not only are there claims from competing possible collective allegiances, there are competing claims as to just what any particular ethnic or other identity means' (1997: 36). In other words, dominant constructions of nationhood are continually challenged by alternative, often conflicting, definitions. The individual, then, has to make two choices: s/he has to decide not only to which community to belong, but also which particular communal definition to endorse. Some of these points are recognized by ethno-symbolist writers. For example, Smith admits that the traditions, customs and institutions of the past are 'reconstructed' and 'reinterpreted' (1991b: 358–9). However, he insists that ethnic cultures tend to persist over many generations, 'forming "moulds" within which all kinds of social and cultural processes can unfold and upon which all kinds of circumstances and pressures can exert an impact' (1986: 16). Then the question that awaits an answer is: to what extent a 'reconstructed' and 'reinterpreted' culture is the same culture? Smith does not address this question directly. The answer lies in the 'discourse' of nationalism. What reconstructs and reinterprets pre-modern cultures is the nationalist discourse. In the age of nationalism, the myths, symbols and traditions of the past are put to different and sometimes conflicting uses. Political concerns play a crucial role in this process since any particular definition will legitimate some claims and delegitimate others (Calhoun 1993: 215). All these attempts are guided by the 'exigencies' of state-building, which is a peculiarly modern phenomenon.

This brings us to another criticism raised against modernist explanations, generally expressed in the form of a question: why do so many people sacrifice their lives for their nations? Would they willingly lay down their lives for the products of the 'collective imagination' (Smith 1991b; 1998: 140)? This criticism, however, misses a crucial point. The fact that nations are 'invented' or 'imagined' does not make them 'less real' in the eyes of those who believe in them. As Halliday observes, the revelation of the falsity of a given myth does not affect its effectiveness because

> . . . once generated and expressed, [myths] can acquire a considerable life of their own. Myths of racist hatred, for example, may begin as lies invented by idle xenophobes, but once conveyed into the political realm and diffused in tense inter-ethnic contexts, they acquire a force and a reality they previously lacked. (1995: 7)

This point is also recognized by scholars who are sympathetic to nationalism. Thus, in his recent defense of nationality, Miller argues that national identities contain a considerable element of myth. Some of these myths are outright inventions; others place a particular interpretation on events whose occurrence is not in dispute (1995: 37–42). Miller continues with a quotation from Orwell: 'Myths which are believed tend to become true, because they set up a type or "persona", which the average person will do his best to resemble' (*ibid.*: 37).

Archard concurs with Miller and notes that national myths, which are deeply rooted within popular culture, will continue to be accepted as true insofar as they do serve important practical purposes: 'Their acceptance will probably depend less on evidence for their truth being compelling than on their meeting a populace's need to feel that they should be true' (1995: 478). This is precisely what ethno-symbolists overlook. The criticism may be valid in the case of Gellner and Hobsbawm who maintain that nations and the myths which go in their making are outright fabrications. However, neither Anderson, nor Breuilly, nor Brass claim that nations are 'false'. What matters is the perceptions and beliefs of the individuals that compose the nation. When believed in, myths become 'real' and nations are reified. In that sense, '*imagination* is not merely a "mental" or "intellectual" exercise; it is *material*, lived, tangible' (Sofos 1996: 251). And it is this reification process that needs to be explored, not the truth or falsity of national (or any other kind of) myths. As Ernst Cassirer observes,

> [t]o inquire into the 'truth' of the political myths is . . . as meaningless and as ridiculous as to ask for the truth of a machine gun or a fighter plane. Both are weapons; and weapons prove their truth by their efficiency. If the political myths could stand this test they needed no other and no better proof. . . . (Cited in Kapferer 1988: 27)

There is a second problem with this criticism. The view that individuals will not lay down their lives for the inventions of their imaginations (which impels Smith to look elsewhere, that is ethnic pasts, to account for the colossal sacrifices generated by nationalism) is based on the implicit assumption that every single member of the nation is completely aware of this process of imagination, in other words, that everybody has unrestricted and equal access to the truths about national myths. This is a highly dubious assumption, to say the least. How would an ordinary 'citizen', who is constantly faced with the 'reality' of the nation, discover that the community to which s/he belongs is in fact an 'imagined community'? By reading Benedict Anderson? Are we to assume that everybody reads Anderson or Hobsbawm? What would happen even if they do so? Would they all of a sudden realize that everything they have learned so far about their nation is nothing but a series of chimerical tales, reflecting the interests of a small number of elites? In my view, such a view will not take us too far. Calhoun summarizes this succinctly:

> What gives tradition (or culture generally) its force is not its antiquity but its immediacy and givenness. Some nationalist self-understandings may be historically dubious yet very real as aspects of lived experience and bases for action . . . People may even join in public rituals that affirm narratives they know to be problematic, but gain an identification with these as 'our stories', a sense of collusion in the production of these fictions,

and a recognition of them as background conditions of everyday life . . . It is thus not the antiquity of Eritrean nationalism
that mattered in mobilizing people against Ethiopian rule, for
example, but the *felt reality of Eritreanness*. (1997: 34–5, emphasis
added)

Another factor that explains the powerful emotions generated by
nationalism is concealed in the familiar terrain of everyday life
(Tilly 1994). The individuals that make up the nation engage in
myriads of 'non-national' social relations throughout their lives.
While doing this, they invest trust, resources and hopes for the
future. All these networks and resources depend directly or indirectly on the state's backing, or at least its existence. Thus, every
threat to the nation's survival reflects on the daily lives of millions
of 'nationals', imperilling everything they value. In other words,
'[t]o the extent that nationally and locally defined solidarities
actually coincide, threats and opportunities for national identities
therefore ramify into local affairs and impinge on the fates of many
people' (Tilly 1994: 18). In that sense, there is a strong connection
between the nation's existence and that of its individual members.
If the nation faces the threat of extinction, so too its citizens.

   Otto Bauer was probably the first scholar to emphasize this point
when he defined the nation as a 'community of destiny'. For him,
'[c]ommunity of destiny does not mean just subjection to a
common fate, but rather common experience of the same fate in
constant communication and ongoing interaction with one
another' (1996: 51). Yuval-Davis argues that this factor can explain
the attachments people feel for their nations in settler societies or
postcolonial states in which there are no shared myths of common
origin (1997: 19). In short, making sacrifices for the nation often
means protecting one's own life – and the things one values –
which explains partly why nationalism is able to command such
powerful emotions (see also Smith 1998: 140).

   The real problem with modernist explanations is their tendency
to explain nationalism in terms of a 'master variable'. Some of
these scholars, notably Nairn and Hechter, have been occasionally
subject to the charge of 'reductionism', but until quite recently
(Calhoun 1997: 20–3) this was not regarded as a problem common
to all modernist accounts. Nationalisms are too varied to be

explained by a single factor: chameleon-like, they take their colour from their context (Smith 1991a: 79). Theories and approaches which attempt to make sense of a phenomenon as protean as nationalism on the basis of a single process fall prey to reductionism, no matter how comprehensive this process is. I will explore this point further when presenting my own framework of analysis.

Here, one further point needs to be stressed, namely that scholars who try to avoid reductionism, or 'causal parsimony' to use Calhoun's term, commit the opposite error, incorporating as many variables as possible into their theory, thereby making it too general to be helpful. Anthony D. Smith's analysis of nationalism is a good case in point. The factors identified by Smith include state centralization, taxation, conscription, bureaucratization, extension of citizenship rights, improvements in communication networks, movement to a market economy, accumulation of capital, decline of ecclesiastical authority, development of secular education and of university learning, increase in the number of popular modes of communication such as novels, journals and plays, the entry of intellectuals and professionals into state apparatuses, rediscovery of ethnic cultures and so on – note that most of these factors are those identified by the modernists (Smith 1991a: 54–68). No wonder that nationalism is 'explained' when so many factors are invoked! It is indeed true that all these factors have contributed to the rise of nationalist movements in one way or the other. But herein lies the problem: 'at the level of practical activity, there are many diverse nationalisms' (Calhoun 1997: 21). It follows that when we are analysing 'nationalism', we are actually dealing with heterogeneous objects of analysis, not with a single, unitary phenomenon: hence the impossibility of 'macro' explanations or a general theory of nationalism.

As for recent studies, most of the criticisms they raised against the mainstream literature seem to be well-grounded. It is true that orthodox theories/approaches, with their Eurocentric and gender-blind outlook, presented us with a biased and incomplete picture of national phenomena. Given the general trends in social sciences, it was inevitable that the neglected issues (or the groups whose 'voices' have been suppressed) would be integrated into the study of nationalism. This task was largely accomplished by the studies of the last decade. In that sense, they filled an important gap in a field hitherto dominated by 'conventional' approaches. It should be stressed that the framework of analysis I will propose below is inspired to a great extent by the ideas developed in these works.

How to Study Nationalism? Towards an Analytical Framework

In the light of the criticisms articulated in the previous section, I will suggest a general framework of analysis for the study of nationalism. Before proceeding, however, two qualifications are in order. To start with, I am not advancing a 'theory of nationalism'. On the contrary, the first proposition of my 'analytical framework' is that there can be no such theory. Secondly, the five propositions that make up the framework are not born in a vacuum: they are a synthesis of the ideas put forward by various scholars. The originality of the framework lies in combining these ideas, distilled from a series of otherwise unrelated (sometimes even defending contradictory positions) works, into a coherent whole.

Proposition 1: There can be no 'General' Theory of Nationalism

This point, made two decades ago by Sami Zubaida (1978), may look like a 'truism' today. It can be asserted that a single, universal theory is not available in the case of most social phenomena, not only nationalism. Strikingly enough, however, the explicit recognition of this point by eminent scholars of nationalism dates only from the 1990s (Hall 1993; Smith 1996b, 1996c). I have already noted that nationalism is a protean phenomenon, capable of taking on a multiplicity of forms depending on the – historical, social and political – context over which it reigns. This diversity precludes the possibility of formulating an 'overarching theory' (Jenkins and Sofos 1996: 11). As Zubaida observes, a sociological theory of nationalism cannot content itself with the ideological homogeneity of nationalisms, but would also entail a sociological homogeneity, that is common social structures and processes which underlie the ideological/political phenomena. This is, for him, precisely what theories of nationalism assume and set out to demonstrate (1978: 56). But such assumptions are misleading and, in fact, ahistorical since nationalisms are born in different historical periods and in a variety of dissimilar settings:

> Why nationalism comes to dominate in those settings where it does – or for some people and not others within an ostensible national population – are questions that by and large can be answered only within specific contexts, with knowledge of local history, of the nature of the state (and other elite) power, and of what other potential and actual movements competed for allegiance. (Calhoun 1997: 25)

Moreover, historical contingencies play an important role in the formation of particular nationalisms. This point is articulated most cogently by Halliday (1997a, 1997b) and Brubaker (1996, 1998). Halliday, for example, observes that many of the ethnic groups who had claimed the status of 'nationhood' failed to obtain it and disappeared in the mists of history. He claims that the actual division of the world into 193 nations is not 'given', as the perennialists would argue, but a product of a series of contingent factors – wars, conflicts, treaties – that could have had very different outcomes. It follows that the world map, as we know it today, could have been very different (1997c).

What should we do then? Should we abandon all attempts at analysing or theorizing nationalisms? James, for instance, accuses Zubaida for falling prey to an 'overly exuberant' poststructuralism that is suspicious of any form of 'grand theory' (1996: 113). In my view, Zubaida does not deserve this criticism. Noting the 'impossibility' of a universal theory of nationalisms does not imply that nationalisms should not (or cannot) be theorized at all. Rather, we might formulate partial theories that account for different aspects of nationalisms. As Calhoun argues, 'grasping nationalism in its multiplicity of forms requires multiple theories' (1997: 8). To address the issue of the reproduction of nationhood will require a different theory from the question of the differential participation of women and men in nationalist projects. Yuval-Davis' (1997) attempt to analyse women's role in the reproduction of ethnic/national collectivities is a good case in point. These 'partial theories' that concentrate on particular aspects of nationalisms are more helpful than ambitious 'grand theories' which purport to explain all nationalisms (for a recent defense of 'grand theories' see Smith 1998: 219–20, 225).

Proposition 2: There is no 'One' Nationalism

The project of formulating an Euclidean theory is further impeded by the internal variations (and shifting contents) of particular nationalisms. Not only are there different types of nationalism, but different members of the nation promote different, often conflicting, constructions of nationhood (McClintock 1996: 264). A number of, at times quite divergent, ideologies and movements compete to capture the allegiance of the 'nationals'. In that sense, 'nationalism is rarely the nationalism of the nation, but rather represents the site where very different views of the nation contest and negotiate with each other' (Duara 1993: 2). Thus, it is not meaningful to speak of a single, unitary French nationalism or Turkish nationalism.

In Turkey, for example, Islamists, secular Kemalists, ultra-nationalists and liberals have different conceptions of nationhood. While Kemalists opt for (at least on the surface) a 'civic-territorial' national identity, ultra-nationalists deny any form of cultural pluralism, promoting instead the ethnic and cultural unity, even 'identity', of all those living in Turkey. Liberals subscribe to Western models of nationhood, whereas leftists espouse anti-imperialist Third World nationalisms which are largely inimical to the West. In short, there is no 'one' Turkish nationalism; rather, there are Turkish nationalisms. This shows clearly that we are faced with 'heterogeneous objects of analysis' (Calhoun 1997: 21). The differences among and within nationalisms cannot be embraced by a single Euclidean theory, however comprehensive and sophisticated its premises are. Therein lies the dilemma of conventional studies which take great pains to explain why there are so many exceptions to the particular approach they promote. The major source of this dilemma is their tendency to treat any particular nationalism as a coherent, homogeneous whole.

What, then, unites all these different nationalisms? In other words, how are we able to identify an enormous range of movements, policies and ideologies as 'nationalist'?

*Proposition 3: What Unites these Diverse Forms of Nationalism is the
'Discourse of Nationalism'*

The answer to these questions lies in the nationalist discourse: 'The
common denominator among Japanese economic protectionism,
Serbian ethnic cleansing and Americans singing the "Star-
Spangled Banner" before baseball games . . . is a discursive form
that shapes and links all of them' (Calhoun 1997: 21–2). A variety
of movements, ideologies and policies, arising in different contexts
and following different historical trajectories, are joined by the use
of a common rhetoric. Nationalism is first and foremost 'a form of
reading and watching, of understanding and of taking for granted'
that shapes our consciousness (Billig 1995: 127), or briefly, a way
of constructing the social reality we live (Calhoun 1997: 12; see
also Brubaker 1998: 291–2). Both the Japanese government and
the Serbian soldier would explain their deeds by resorting to a
common rhetoric, that is, the rhetoric of 'national interest'. In that
sense, the discourse of nationalism is the ultimate explanatory, and
legitimating, framework in today's world.

This also captures the 'modernity' of nationalisms. What defines
cultural collectivities as 'nations' and the members of these collectivities as 'citizens' is the discourse of nationalism. Nations can
only exist in the context of nationalism. And this is precisely what
separates earlier ethnic communities from contemporary nations.

On the other hand, the use of a common rhetoric enables us to
formulate an 'umbrella definition' of nationalism, that is 'a particular way of constructing the social reality we experience', which
is, in my view, more helpful than alternative objective or subjective
definitions of national phenomena. It is, of course, possible to
make a list of the objective characteristics which a collectivity
should possess to become a nation, such as common religion,
ethnicity, language, a specific territory and so on. However, formulating the 'perfect list' is a difficult, if not impossible, task – in
fact, as Yuval-Davis notes, some of these lists sound like a shopping
list (1997: 19). Most of today's nations lack one or more of the
characteristics commonly cited by scholars of nationalism. Furthermore, we will never be in a position to ascertain how many of
these characteristics a collectivity should possess – and which ones
– to become a nation. As for subjective characteristics like loyalty

or solidarity, they are necessary but not sufficient conditions to be a nation. Individuals feel attached to many other collectivities and institutions, including their families, kinsmen or regions. Thus, attachments *per se* cannot account for the existence of a nation or of nationalism. The key element of an 'umbrella definition', then, is the discourse of nationalism, which is shared by all movements, policies or ideologies we call 'nationalist' (Calhoun 1997: 21–2). All nations make use of this discourse to define, justify and reproduce themselves.

If the discourse of nationalism is the common denominator of all nationalisms, thus the most important element of an umbrella definition, then, we should be more specific about it. The nationalist discourse has three main characteristics:

- It claims that the interests and values of the nation override all other interests and values (Breuilly 1993a: 2; Smith 1991a: 74).
- It regards the nation as the only source of legitimacy. Here, I do not only mean 'political legitimacy'. The nation (or nationalism) can be used to justify all kinds of actions that would not otherwise be condoned or tolerated. As Löfgren observes, '[t]here is an empowering magic in the national prefix . . . This simple addition transforms its subject, makes it more official, more sacred, more emotional' (1993: 161).
- It operates through binary divisions – between 'us' and 'them', 'friends' and 'foes'. These categories are sharply separated from each other by 'mutually exclusive sets of assigned rights and duties, moral significance and behavioural principles' (Bauman 1992: 678; see also McCrone 1998: 116–19). It defines 'us' in terms of the Other: 'it is only through the relation to the Other, the relation to what it is not, to precisely what it lacks, to what has been called its *constitutive outside* that the "positive" meaning of [identity] can be constructed'. (Hall 1996a: 4–5)

Proposition 4: The Nationalist Discourse can Only be Effective if it is Reproduced on a Daily Basis

As Brubaker convincingly argues, 'nationalism is not a "force" to be measured as resurgent or receding. It is a heterogeneous set of "nation"-oriented idioms, practices, and possibilities that are continuously available or "endemic" in modern cultural and political life' (1996: 10). Why, then, is nationalism so essential to modern politics and culture? Or in Billig's words, 'why do "we", in established, democratic nations, not forget "our" national identity' (1995: 93)? The answers to these questions lie in the reproduction of nationhood on a daily basis. We cannot fully comprehend nationalism without taking its everyday manifestations into account since 'macro' structures, for example ideologies, are created and reproduced at a 'micro' level, that is through the social relations and routine practices of everyday life (Billig 1995; *cf.* Essed 1991; van Dijk 1993, 1998). In that sense, it would be misleading to confine nationalism to blatant racism, more subtle discourses of racial and ethnic domination or to aggressive ethnocentrism. Nationalism also involves the everyday, mundane opinions, attitudes and the seemingly naive acts of discrimination (van Dijk 1993: 5). The traces of nationalism can be found in all structures, institutions, processes and policies that perpetrate the hegemony of one (ethnic/national) group over another.

As Essed (1991) remarks, without a minimum knowledge of how to cope in everyday life, for example knowledge of language, norms, customs and rules, one cannot handle living in society. This knowledge is provided by a range of institutions, from family and school to media and workplace. Together, these institutions form the socialization process and transmit the stock of knowledge necessary to cope in everyday life from one generation to the next – thereby ensuring that the existing system is internalized. Inspired by Essed's notion of 'everyday racism', I will introduce the term 'everyday nationalism' and define it (paraphrasing Essed's concise definition) as 'the integration of nationalism into everyday situations through practices that activate underlying power relations' (1991: 50). When the nationalist discourse seeps into everyday life, its reproduction becomes inevitable. As long as the system reproduces itself, it reproduces 'everyday nationalism' (*ibid.*).

The implication of these observations is not hard to guess: the language we use in our everyday life and the attitudes that guide our social relations are not as innocent as they seem. Ostensibly naive statements such as 'Muslims have different cultural norms than ours' transform easily into stereotyping statements like 'Muslims are terrorists' under crisis situations. It is worth noting that this transformation is not generally registered consciously. We tend (or prefer) to forget that naive descriptions form the basis of many stereotypes and prejudices.

Proposition 5: As there are Different Constructions of Nationhood, any Study of Nationalism should Acknowledge the Differences of Ethnicity, Gender, Class or Place in the Life-cycle that Affect the Definition and Redefinition of National Identities

I have already argued that the nationalist discourse promotes categorical identities over relational ones. For Calhoun, this is not surprising because nationalism addresses 'large-scale collectivities in which most people could not conceivably enter into face-to-face relationships with most others' (1997: 46). However, identity is not a fixed and 'given' category: on the contrary, it is 'always mobile and processual, partly self-construction, partly categorization by others, partly a condition, a status, a label, a weapon, a shield, a fund of memories, et cetera' (Malkki 1996: 447–8). Individual self-definitions change according to one's differential positioning along the dimensions of gender, race, ethnicity, class or place in the life-cycle. The most important contribution of the studies of the last decade was to incorporate these dimensions into the study of nationalisms, hence presenting us with a more complete picture of the formation of national identities (Yuval-Davis and Anthias 1989; Yuval-Davis 1997).

Obviously, these are tentative propositions. New ones can be added to this list or the existing propositions can be elaborated further. In that sense, my 'embryonic' framework of analysis can be considered as a first step in the formulation of a more comprehensive approach to the study of nationalisms. But at least, I believe, it is a step in the right direction.

The Future?

It is clear that we have not yet reached 'the end of history' in a world torn apart by nationalist conflicts, cruel acts of ethnic cleansing and all kinds of fundamentalisms (for the thesis of the end of history see Fukuyama 1989). In fact, the revolutions of 1989 were not much of a watershed in terms of the incidence of conflict on the world political scene. In the meantime, we are 'inundated' by the discourse of the 'return of the repressed', which claims that the collapse of communism has unleashed a new wave of nationalist hatred, dashing hopes for a more peaceful new world order (see for example Ignatieff 1993: 2). The popular commentaries we encounter daily in the newspapers or on the television screens reproduce this discourse, maintaining that the ideological skirmish between communism and capitalism has been replaced by nationalist and religious wars, or by a 'clash of civilisations' (Huntington 1993). The value of these interpretations is open to question. Nationalism has never been absent from the inter*national* arena in the last two hundred years, forming the mould within which all kinds of political claims have been cast. Moreover, it is too early to proclaim the end of ideological conflicts in a world where thousands of people are living in hardship as a result of (ideologically motivated) embargoes. In short, the world we live in is as chaotic as ever.

Given that nationalism is one of the most important forces in this world, the need to understand it is all the more urgent. There are, I think, two fruitful ways of doing this. Both of them require us to reject the fundamental assumptions of the classical debate on nationalism. The first strategy is to address the issues neglected or ignored by the mainstream literature – without, however, ignoring the analytical gains of the past, particularly the insights provided by modernism. This would allow us to formulate a series of 'partial theories', each illuminating a particular aspect of national phenomena such as the reproduction of nationalisms, the differential participation of various groups into nationalist projects and so on. The second strategy, on the other hand, is inspired by another shortcoming of the classical debate, which is most cogently exposed by Halliday (1997b). For him, the debate on nationalism has already reached an impasse with an array of general theories offset against a mass of individual accounts, with relatively little interaction between the two. The way out of this impasse, argues Halliday, lies in producing 'theoretically informed' comparative histories, which will at the same time test the theories concerned against historical evidence. Whichever way we choose, there is still much to be done. Yet as Greenfeld notes, 'as long as history goes on, there is hope' (1993: 61).

Bibliography

Acton, Lord (1996) [1862] 'On Nationality', in Gopal Balakrishnan (ed.), *Mapping the Nation*, London: Verso, 17–38.

Agger, B. (1991) 'Critical Theory, Poststructuralism, Postmodernism', *Annual Review of Sociology*, 17, 105–31.

Agnew, J. (1989) 'Nationalism: Autonomous Force or Practical Politics? Place and Nationalism in Scotland', in C. H. Williams and E. Kofman (eds), *Community, Conflict, Partition and Nationalism*, London and New York: Routledge, 167–93.

Alp, T. [Moise Cohen] (1971) [1937] 'The Restoration of Turkish History', in E. Kedourie (ed.), *Nationalism in Asia and Africa*, London: Weidenfeld & Nicolson, 207–24.

Alter, P. (1989) *Nationalism*, London: Edward Arnold.

Anderson, B. (1991) [1983] *Imagined Communities: Reflections on the Origins and Spread of Nationalism*, London: Verso, 2nd edn.

Anderson, B. (1995) 'Ice Empire and Ice Hockey: Two *Fin de Siècle* Dreams', *New Left Review*, 214, 146–50.

Anderson, B. (1996) 'Introduction', in G. Balakrishnan (ed.), *Mapping the Nation*, London: Verso, 1–16.

Anderson, B. (1998) *Spectres of Comparison: Nationalism, Southeast Asia and the World*, London and New York: Verso.

Anderson, P. (1992) *A Zone of Engagement*, London: Verso.

Anthias, F. (1989) 'Women and Nationalism in Cyprus', in N. Yuval-Davis and F. Anthias (eds), *Woman–Nation–State*, London: Macmillan, 150–67.

Anthias, F. and N. Yuval-Davis (1989) 'Introduction', in N. Yuval-Davis and F. Anthias (eds), *Woman–Nation–State*, London: Macmillan, 1–15.

Archard, D. (1995) 'Myths, Lies and Historical Truth: A Defence of Nationalism', *Political Studies*, 43, 472–81.

Armstrong, J. (1982) *Nations before Nationalism*, Chapel Hill: University of North Carolina Press.

Armstrong, J. (1990) 'Contemporary Ethnicity: The Moral Dimension in Comparative Perspective', *The Review of Politics*, 52(2), 163–89.

Armstrong, J. (1992) 'The Autonomy of Ethnic Identity: Historic Cleavages and Nationality Relations in the USSR', in A. J. Motyl (ed.), *Thinking Theoretically about Soviet Nationalities: History and Comparison in the Study of the USSR*, New York: Columbia University Press, 23–44.

Armstrong, J. (1995) 'Towards a Theory of Nationalism: Consensus and Dissensus', in S. Periwal (ed.), *Notions of Nationalism*, Budapest: Central European University Press, 34–43.

Balakrishnan, G. (1996a) 'The National Imagination', in G. Balakrishnan (ed.), *Mapping the Nation*, London: Verso, 198–213.

Balakrishnan, G. (ed.) (1996b) *Mapping the Nation*, London: Verso.

Balibar, É. (1990) 'The Nation Form: History and Ideology', *New Left Review*, XIII(3), 329–61.

Barnard, F. M. (1983) 'National Culture and Political Legitimacy: Herder and Rousseau', *Journal of the History of Ideas*, XLIV(2), 231–53.

Barnard, F. M. (1984) 'Patriotism and Citizenship in Rousseau: A Dual Theory of Public Willing?', *The Review of Politics*, 46(2), 244–65.

Barth, F. (ed.) (1969) *Ethnic Groups and Boundaries*, Boston: Little, Brown & Co.

Bauer, O. (1996) [1924] 'The Nation', in G. Balakrishnan (ed.), *Mapping the Nation*, London: Verso, 39–77.

Bauman, Z. (1991) *Modernity and Ambivalence*, Cambridge: Polity Press.

Bauman, Z. (1992) 'Soil, Blood and Identity', *The Sociological Review*, 40, 675–701.

Baycroft, T. (1998) *Nationalism in Europe 1789–1945*, Cambridge: Cambridge University Press.

Bhabha, H. (1990a) 'DissemiNation: Time, Narrative and the Margins of the Modern Nation', in H. Bhabha (ed.), *Nation and Narration*, London: Routledge, 291–322.

Bhabha, H. (ed.) (1990b) *Nation and Narration*, London: Routledge.

Billig, M. (1995) *Banal Nationalism*, London: Sage.

Bloom, W. (1990) *Personal Identity, National Identity and International Relations*, Cambridge: Cambridge University Press.

Bourdieu, P. and J.-C. Passeron (1977) *Reproduction in Education, Society and Culture*, London and Beverly Hills, Cal.: Sage.

Brand, J. A. (1985) 'Nationalism and the Noncolonial Periphery: A Discussion of Scotland and Catalonia', in E. A. Tiryakian and R. Rogowski (eds), *New Nationalisms of the Developed West*, Boston: Allen & Unwin, 277–93.

Brass, P. R. (1977) 'A Reply to Francis Robinson', *Journal of Commonwealth and Comparative Politics*, 15(3), 230–4.

Brass, P. R. (1979) 'Elite Groups, Symbol Manipulation and Ethnic Identity among the Muslims of South Asia', in D. Taylor and M. Yapp (eds), *Political Identity in South Asia*, London: Curzon Press, 35–68.

Brass, P. R. (ed.) (1985) *Ethnic Groups and the State*, London: Croom Helm.

Brass, P. R. (1991) *Ethnicity and Nationalism: Theory and Comparison*, New Delhi and Newbury Park: Sage.

Breuilly, J. (1985) 'Reflections on Nationalism', *Philosophy of the Social Sciences*, 15, 65–75.

Breuilly, J. (1993a) [1982] *Nationalism and the State*, Manchester: Manchester University Press, 2nd edn.

Breuilly, J. (1993b) 'Nationalism and the State', in R. Michener (ed.),

Nationality, Patriotism and Nationalism in Liberal Democratic Societies, Minnesota: Professors World Peace Academy, 19–48.

Breuilly, J. (1996) [1994] 'Approaches to Nationalism', in G. Balakrishnan (ed.), *Mapping the Nation,* London: Verso, 146–74.

Brubaker, R. (1996) *Nationalism Reframed: Nationhood and the National Question in the New Europe,* Cambridge: Cambridge University Press.

Brubaker, R. (1998) 'Myths and Misconceptions in the Study of Nationalism', in J. A. Hall (ed.), *The State of the Nation: Ernest Gellner and the Theory of Nationalism,* Cambridge: Cambridge University Press.

Calhoun, C. (1991) 'Indirect Relationships and Imagined Communities: Large-Scale Social Integration and the Transformation of Everyday Life', in P. Bourdieu and J. S. Coleman (eds), *Social Theory for a Changing Society,* Boulder, Col.: Westview Press, 95–121.

Calhoun, C. (1993) 'Nationalism and Ethnicity', *Annual Review of Sociology,* 19, 211–39.

Calhoun, C. (1995) *Critical Social Theory: Culture, History, and the Challenge of Difference,* Oxford: Blackwell.

Calhoun, C. (1997) *Nationalism,* Buckingham: Open University Press.

Carr, E. H. (1945) *Nationalism and After,* London: Macmillan.

Chatterjee, P. (1986) *Nationalist Thought and the Colonial World: A Derivative Discourse?,* New Jersey: Zed Books.

Chatterjee, P. (1990) 'The Nationalist Resolution of the Women's Question', in K. Sanghari and S. Vaid (eds), *Recasting Women: Essays in Colonial History,* New Brunswick, N.J.: Rutgers University Press, 233–53.

Chatterjee, P. (1996) [1993] 'Whose Imagined Community?', in G. Balakrishnan (ed.), *Mapping the Nation,* London: Verso, 214–25.

Connor, W. (1984) *The National Question in Marxist–Leninist Theory and Strategy,* Princeton: Princeton University Press.

Connor, W. (1994) *Ethnonationalism: The Quest for Understanding,* Princeton: Princeton University Press.

Conversi, D. (1995) 'Reassessing Current Theories of Nationalism: Nationalism as Boundary Maintenance and Creation', *Nationalism and Ethnic Politics,* 1(1), 73–85.

Cordellier, S. (ed.) (1995) *Nations et Nationalismes,* Paris: La Découverte.

Dahbour, O. and M. R. Ishay (eds) (1995) *The Nationalism Reader,* New Jersey: Humanities Press International.

Delannoi, G. and P.-A. Taguieff (eds) (1991) *Théories du Nationalisme: Nation, Nationalité, Ethnicité,* Paris: Kimé.

Deutsch, K. W. (1966) [1953] *Nationalism and Social Communication: An Inquiry into the Foundations of Nationality,* Cambridge, Mass.: MIT Press, 2nd edn.

Duara, P. (1993) 'De-constructing the Chinese Nation', *The Australian Journal of Chinese Affairs,* 30, 1–26.

Eley, G. (1996) 'Is All the World a Text? From Social History to the History of Society Two Decades Later', in T. J. McDonald (ed.), *The Historic Turn in the Human Sciences*, Ann Arbor: The University of Michigan Press, 193–245.

Eley, G. and R. G. Suny (1996a) 'Introduction: From the Moment of Social History to the Work of Cultural Representation', in G. Eley and R. G. Suny (eds), *Becoming National: A Reader*, New York and Oxford: Oxford University Press, 3–38.

Eley, G. and R. G. Suny (eds) (1996b) *Becoming National: A Reader*, New York and Oxford: Oxford University Press.

Eller, J. D. and R. M. Coughlan (1993) 'The Poverty of Primordialism: The Demystification of Ethnic Attachments', *Ethnic and Racial Studies*, 16(2), 183–201.

Elshtain, J. B. (1991) 'Sovereignty, Identity, Sacrifice', *Millennium: Journal of International Studies*, 20(3), 395–406.

Enloe, C. (1989) *Bananas, Beaches, Bases: Making Feminist Sense of International Politics*, London: Pandora.

Enloe, C. (1995) 'Feminism, Nationalism and Militarism: Wariness Without Paralysis?', in C. R. Sutton (ed.), *Feminism, Nationalism and Militarism*, US: The Association for Feminist Anthropology/ American Anthropological Association, 13–32.

Eriksen, T. H. (1993a) 'Formal and Informal Nationalism', *Ethnic and Racial Studies*, 16(1), 1–25.

Eriksen, T. H. (1993b) *Ethnicity and Nationalism: Anthropological Perspectives*, London: Pluto Press.

Essed, P. (1991) *Understanding Everyday Racism*, Newbury Park and London: Sage.

Fine, R. (1994) 'The "New Nationalism" and Democracy: A Critique of *Pro Patria*', *Democratization*, 1(3), 423–43.

Finlayson, A. (1998) 'Ideology, Discourse and Nationalism', *Journal of Political Ideologies*, 3(1), 99–119.

Forgacs, D. (1989) 'Gramsci and Marxism in Britain', *New Left Review*, 176, 70–88.

Fukuyama, F. (1989) 'The End of History', *The National Interest*, 16(1), 3–18.

Geertz, C. (1993) [1973] *The Interpretation of Cultures: Selected Essays*, London: Fontana, 2nd edn.

Gellner, D. N. (1997) 'Preface', in E. Gellner, *Nationalism*, London: Weidenfeld & Nicolson.

Gellner, E. (1964) *Thought and Change*, London: Weidenfeld & Nicolson.

Gellner, E. (1979) *Spectacles and Predicaments: Essays in Social Theory*, Cambridge: Cambridge University Press.

Gellner, E. (1983) *Nations and Nationalism*, Oxford: Blackwell.

Gellner, E. (1987) *Culture, Identity and Politics*, Cambridge: Cambridge University Press.

Gellner, E. (1995a) *Encounters with Nationalism*, Oxford: Blackwell.

Gellner, E. (1995b) 'Introduction', in S. Periwal (ed.), *Notions of Nationalism*, Budapest: Central European University Press, 1–7.
Gellner, E. (1996a) [1993] 'The Coming of Nationalism and its Interpretation: The Myths of Nation and Class', in G. Balakrishnan (ed.), *Mapping the Nation*, London: Verso, 98–145.
Gellner, E. (1996b) 'Reply: Do Nations Have Navels?', *Nations and Nationalism*, 2(3), 366–71.
Gellner, E. (1996c) 'Reply to Critics', in J. A. Hall and I. Jarvie (eds), *The Social Philosophy of Ernest Gellner*, Atlanta and Amsterdam: Rodopi, 623–86.
Gellner, E. (1997) *Nationalism*, London: Weidenfeld & Nicolson.
Giddens, A. (1984) *The Constitution of Society*, Cambridge: Polity Press.
Giddens, A. (1985) *The Nation State and Violence*, Cambridge: Polity Press.
Greenfeld, L. (1992) *Nationalism: Five Roads to Modernity*, Cambridge, Mass.: Harvard University Press.
Greenfeld, L. (1993) 'Transcending the Nation's Worth', *Daedalus*, 122(3), 47–62.
Grewal, I. and C. Kaplan (eds) (1994) *Scattered Hegemonies: Postmodernity and Transnational Feminist Practices*, Minneapolis: University of Minnesota Press.
Grosby, S. (1994) 'The Verdict of History: The Inexpungeable Tie of Primordiality – a Response to Eller and Coughlan', *Ethnic and Racial Studies*, 17(1), 164–71.
Guibernau, M. (1996) *Nationalisms: The Nation-State and Nationalism in the Twentieth Century*, Cambridge: Polity Press.
Hall, J. A. (1993) 'Nationalisms: Classified and Explained', *Daedalus*, 122(3), 1–28.
Hall, J. A. (1998) 'Introduction', in J. A. Hall (ed.), *The State of the Nation: Ernest Gellner and the Theory of Nationalism*, Cambridge: Cambridge University Press, 1–20.
Hall, J. A. and I. Jarvie (1996a) 'The Life and Times of Ernest Gellner', in J. A. Hall and I. Jarvie (eds), *The Social Philosophy of Ernest Gellner*, Atlanta and Amsterdam: Rodopi, 11–21.
Hall, J. A. and I. Jarvie (eds) (1996b) *The Social Philosophy of Ernest Gellner*, Atlanta and Amsterdam: Rodopi.
Hall, P. (1998) *The Social Construction of Nationalism: Sweden as an Example*, Lund: Lund University Press.
Hall, S. (1990) 'Cultural Identity and Diaspora', in J. Rutherford (ed.), *Identity: Community, Culture and Difference*, London: Lawrence & Wishart, 222–37.
Hall, S. (1996a) 'Introduction: Who Needs "Identity"?', in S. Hall and P. du Gay (eds), *Questions of Cultural Identity*, London: Sage, 1–17.
Hall, S. (1996b) [1989] 'Ethnicity: Identity and Difference', in G. Eley and R. G. Suny (eds), *Becoming National: A Reader*, New York and Oxford: Oxford University Press, 339–51.

Halliday, F. (1992) 'Bringing the "Economic" Back in: The Case of Nationalism', *Economy and Society*, 21(4), 483–90.

Halliday, F. (1995) *Islam and the Myth of Confrontation: Religion and Politics in the Middle East*, London: I.B. Tauris.

Halliday, F. (1997a) 'The Nationalism Debate and the Middle East', *Kaller Public Lecture*, Dayan Centre for Middle Eastern and African Studies, Tel Aviv, 5 May.

Halliday, F. (1997b) 'The Formation of Yemeni Nationalism: Initial Reflections', in J. Jankowski and I. Gershoni (eds), *Rethinking Nationalism in the Middle East*, New York: Columbia University Press, 26–42.

Halliday, F. (1997c) 'Irish Nationalisms in Perspective', *Torkel Opsahl Lecture* (under the auspices of Democratic Dialogue), Belfast, 10 December.

Halliday, F. (1997d) 'Nationalism', in J. Baylis and S. Smith (eds), *The Globalization of World Politics*, Oxford: Oxford University Press, 359–73.

Handler, R. (1994) 'Is "Identity" a Useful Concept?', in J. R. Gillis (ed.), *Commemorations: The Politics of National Identity*, Princeton: Princeton University Press, 27–40.

Hastings, A. (1997) *The Construction of Nationhood: Ethnicity, Religion and Nationalism*, Cambridge: Cambridge University Press.

Hayes, C. (1926) *Essays on Nationalism*, New York: Macmillan.

Hayes, C. (1955) [1931] *The Historical Evolution of Modern Nationalism*, New York: Macmillan, 5th edn.

Hechter, M. (1975) *Internal Colonialism: The Celtic Fringe in British National Development, 1536–1966*, London and Henley: Routledge & Kegan Paul.

Hechter, M. (1985) 'Internal Colonialism Revisited', in E. A. Tiryakian and R. Rogowski (eds), *New Nationalisms of the Developed West*, Boston: Allen & Unwin, 17–26.

Hechter, M. and M. Levi (1979) 'The Comparative Analysis of Ethnoregional Movements', *Ethnic and Racial Studies*, 2(3), 260–74.

Herzfeld, M. (1997) *Cultural Intimacy: Social Poetics in the Nation-State*, New York and London: Routledge.

Hobsbawm, E. J. (1972) 'Some Reflections on Nationalism', in T. J. Nossiter, A. H. Hanson and S. Rokkan (eds), *Imagination and Precision in Social Sciences*, London: Faber & Faber, 385–406.

Hobsbawm, E. J. (1990) *Nations and Nationalism since 1780: Programme, Myth, Reality*, Cambridge: Cambridge University Press.

Hobsbawm, E. J. (1996) [1992] 'Ethnicity and Nationalism in Europe Today', in G. Balakrishnan (ed.), *Mapping the Nation*, London: Verso, 255–66.

Hobsbawm, E. J. and T. Ranger (eds) (1983) *The Invention of Tradition*, Cambridge: Cambridge University Press.

Hroch, M. (1985) *Social Preconditions of National Revival in Europe: A Comparative Analysis of the Social Composition of Patriotic Groups among the Smaller European Nations*, Cambridge: Cambridge University Press.

Hroch, M. (1993) 'From National Movement to the Fully-Formed Nation: The Nation-Building Process in Europe', *New Left Review*, 198, 3–20.

Hroch, M. (1995) 'National Self-Determination from a Historical Perspective', in S. Periwal (ed.), *Notions of Nationalism*, Budapest: Central European University Press, 65–82.

Hroch, M. (1996) 'Nationalism and National Movements: Comparing the Past and the Present of Central and Eastern Europe', *Nations and Nationalism*, 2(1), 35–44.

Hroch, M. (1998) 'Real and Constructed: The Nature of the Nation', in J. A. Hall (ed.), *The State of the Nation: Ernest Gellner and the Theory of Nationalism*, Cambridge: Cambridge University Press, 91–106.

Huntington, S. P. (1993) 'The Clash of Civilizations', *Foreign Affairs*, 72(3), 22–49.

Hutchinson, J. (1994) *Modern Nationalism*, London: Fontana.

Hutchinson, J. and A. D. Smith (1994) 'Introduction', in J. Hutchinson and A. D. Smith (eds), *Nationalism*, Oxford: Oxford University Press, 3–13.

Ignatieff, M. (1993) *Blood and Belonging*, London: Vintage.

Ishay, M. (1995) 'Introduction', in O. Dahbour and M. R. Ishay (eds), *The Nationalism Reader*, New Jersey: Humanities Press International, 1–21.

James, P. (1996) *Nation Formation: Towards a Theory of Abstract Community*, London: Sage.

Janowitz, M. (1983) *The Reconstruction of Patriotism: Education for Civic Consciousness*, Chicago and London: University of Chicago Press.

Jayawardena, K. (1986) *Feminism and Nationalism in the Third World*, London: Zed Books.

Jenkins, B. and S. A. Sofos (1996) 'Nation and Nationalism in Contemporary Europe: A Theoretical Perspective', in B. Jenkins and S. A. Sofos (eds), *Nation and Identity in Contemporary Europe*, London: Routledge, 9–32.

Jenkins, R. (1995) 'Nations and Nationalisms: Towards More Open Models', *Nations and Nationalism*, 1(3), 369–90.

Jordan, G. and C. Weedon (1995) *Cultural Politics: Class, Gender, Race and the Postmodern World*, Oxford: Blackwell.

Kamenka, E. (1976) 'Political Nationalism – The Evolution of an Idea', in E. Kamenka (ed.), *Nationalism: The Nature and Evolution of an Idea*, London: Edward Arnold, 2–36.

Kapferer, B. (1988) *Legends of People, Myths of State: Violence, Intolerance, and Political Culture in Sri Lanka and Australia*, Washington D.C. and London: Smithsonian Institution Press.

Kedourie, E. (ed.) (1971) *Nationalism in Asia and Africa*, London: Weidenfeld & Nicolson.

Kedourie, E. (1994) [1960] *Nationalism*, Oxford: Blackwell, 4th edn.

Kellas, J. G. (1991) *The Politics of Nationalism and Ethnicity*, London: Macmillan.

Kellner, D. (1988) 'Postmodernism as Social Theory: Some Challenges and Problems', *Theory, Culture and Society*, 5(2–3), 239–70.

Kemiläinen, A. (1964) *Nationalism: Problems Concerning the Word, the Concept and Classification*, Yvaskyla: Kustantajat Publishers.

Kitching, G. (1985) 'Nationalism: The Instrumental Passion', *Capital & Class*, 25, 98–116.

Kitromilides, P. M. (1989) ' "Imagined Communities" and the Origins of the National Question in the Balkans', *European History Quarterly*, 19, 149–94.

Koelble, T. A. (1995) 'Towards a Theory of Nationalism: Culture, Structure and Choice Analyses Revisited', *Nationalism and Ethnic Politics*, 1(4), 73–89.

Kohn, H. (1949) 'The Paradox of Fichte's Nationalism', *Journal of the History of Ideas*, x(3), 319–43.

Kohn, H. (1950) 'Romanticism and the Rise of German Nationalism', *The Review of Politics*, 12(4), 443–72.

Kohn, H. (1957) [1946] *Prophets and Peoples: Studies in Nineteenth Century Nationalism*, New York: Macmillan, 4th edn.

Kohn, H. (1967) [1944] *The Idea of Nationalism*, New York: Collier, 2nd edn.

Lerner, D. (1958) *The Passing of Traditional Society*, New York: Free Press.

Lieven, A. (1997) 'Qu'est-ce qu'une Nation?', *The National Interest*, 49, 10–22.

Lincoln, B. (1989) *Discourse and the Construction of Society: Comparative Studies of Myth, Ritual, and Classification*, New York: Oxford University Press.

Llobera, J. R. (1994) *The God of Modernity: The Development of Nationalism in Western Europe*, Oxford and Providence: Berg Publishers.

Llobera, J. R. (1998) 'The Concept of the Nation in French Social Theory: The Work of Dominique Schnapper', *Nations and Nationalism*, 4(1), 113–21.

Löfgren, O. (1993) 'Materializing the Nation in Sweden and America', *Ethnos*, 58(iii–iv), 161–96.

Lutz, H., A. Phoenix and N. Yuval-Davis (eds) (1995) *Crossfires: Nationalism, Racism and Gender in Europe*, London: Pluto Press.

MacLaughlin, J. (1987) 'Nationalism as an Autonomous Social Force: A Critique of Recent Scholarship on Ethnonationalism', *Canadian Review of Studies in Nationalism*, xiv(1), 1–18.

Malkki, L. (1996) [1992] 'National Geographic: The Rooting of Peoples and the Territorialization of National Identity among Scholars and Refugees', in G. Eley and R. G. Suny (eds), *Becoming National: A Reader*, New York and Oxford: Oxford University Press, 434–55.

Mann, M. (1995) [1994] 'A Political Theory of Nationalism and its

Excesses', in S. Periwal (ed.), *Notions of Nationalism,* Budapest: Central European University Press, 44–64.

Mann, M. (1996) 'The Emergence of Modern European Nationalism', in J. A. Hall and I. Jarvie (eds), *The Social Philosophy of Ernest Gellner,* Atlanta and Amsterdam: Rodopi, 147–70.

Marx, K. and F. Engels (1976) *Collected Works,* vol. 6, London: Lawrence & Wishart.

Mayall, J. (1990) *Nationalism and International Society,* Cambridge: Cambridge University Press.

McClintock, A. (1996) [1991] ' "No Longer in a Future Heaven": Nationalism, Gender, and Race', in G. Eley and R. G. Suny (eds), *Becoming National: A Reader,* New York and Oxford: Oxford University Press, 260–85.

McCrone, D. (1998) *The Sociology of Nationalism,* London: Routledge.

McDonald, T. J. (ed.) (1996) *The Historic Turn in the Human Sciences,* Ann Arbor: The University of Michigan Press.

Mill, J. S. (1996) [1861] 'Nationality', in S. Woolf (ed.), *Nationalism in Europe, 1815 to the Present: A Reader,* London and New York: Routledge, 40–7.

Miller, D. (1995) *On Nationality,* Oxford: Oxford University Press.

Minogue, K. (1996) 'Ernest Gellner and the Dangers of Theorising Nationalism', in J. A. Hall and I. Jarvie (eds), *The Social Philosophy of Ernest Gellner,* Atlanta and Amsterdam: Rodopi, 113–28.

Montaigne, M. de (1982) *Denemeler.* İstanbul: Cem.

Mosse, G. L. (1985) *Nationalism and Sexuality: Middle Class Morality and Sexual Norms in Modern Europe,* Madison, Wisc.: University of Wisconsin Press.

Mouzelis, N. (1998) 'Ernest Gellner's Theory of Nationalism: Some Definitional and Methodological Issues', in J. A. Hall (ed.), *The State of the Nation: Ernest Gellner and the Theory of Nationalism,* Cambridge: Cambridge University Press, 158–65.

Munck, R. (1986) *The Difficult Dialogue: Marxism and Nationalism,* London: Zed Books.

Nairn, T. (1974) 'Scotland and Europe', *New Left Review,* 83, 92–125.

Nairn, T. (1981) [1977] *The Break-up of Britain: Crisis and Neo-Nationalism,* London: Verso, 2nd edn.

Nairn, T. (1993) 'Internationalism and the Second Coming', *Daedalus,* 122(3), 155–70.

Nairn, T. (1997) *Faces of Nationalism: Janus Revisited,* London: Verso.

Nairn, T. (1998) 'The Curse of Rurality: Limits of Modernisation Theory', in J. A. Hall (ed.), *The State of the Nation: Ernest Gellner and the Theory of Nationalism,* Cambridge: Cambridge University Press, 107–34.

The New International Webster's Comprehensive Dictionary of the English Language (1996 edn), Florida: Trident Press International.

Nimni, E. (1991) *Marxism and Nationalism: Theoretical Origins of a Political Crisis,* London: Pluto.

Norval, A. J. (1996) 'Thinking Identities: Against a Theory of Ethnicity', in E. N. Wilmsen and P. McAllister (eds), *The Politics of Difference: Ethnic Premises in a World of Power*, Chicago: The University of Chicago Press, 59–70.

O'Leary, B. (1996) 'On the Nature of Nationalism: An Appraisal of Ernest Gellner's Writings on Nationalism', in J. A. Hall and I. Jarvie (eds), *The Social Philosophy of Ernest Gellner*, Atlanta and Amsterdam: Rodopi, 71–112.

O'Leary, B. (1998) 'Ernest Gellner's Diagnoses of Nationalism: A Critical Overview, or, What is Living and What is Dead in Ernest Gellner's Philosophy of Nationalism', in J. A. Hall (ed.), *The State of the Nation: Ernest Gellner and the Theory of Nationalism*, Cambridge: Cambridge University Press, 40–88.

Orridge, A. W. (1981a) 'Uneven Development and Nationalism – 1', *Political Studies*, xxix(1), 1–15.

Orridge, A. W. (1981b) 'Uneven Development and Nationalism – 2', *Political Studies*, xxix(2), 181–90.

Page, E. (1978) 'Michael Hechter's Internal Colonial Thesis: Some Theoretical and Methodological Problems', *European Journal of Political Research*, 6, 295–317.

Parker, A., M. Russo, D. Sommer and P. Yaeger (eds) (1992) *Nationalisms and Sexualities*, London: Routledge.

Periwal, S. (1995) 'Conclusion' in S. Periwal (ed.), *Notions of Nationalism*, Budapest: Central European University Press, 228–40.

Rattansi A. (1994) ' "Western" Racisms, Ethnicities and Identities in a "Postmodern" Frame', in A. Rattansi and S. Westwood (eds), *Racism, Modernity and Identity: on the Western Front*, Cambridge: Polity Press, 15–86.

Renan, E. (1990) [1882] 'What is a Nation?', in H. Bhabha (ed.), *Nation and Narration*, London: Routledge, 8–22.

Reynolds, V., V. S. E. Falger and I. Vine (eds) (1987) *The Sociobiology of Ethnocentrism: Evolutionary Dimensions of Xenophobia, Discrimination, Racism and Nationalism*, London: Croom Helm.

Rizman, R. R. (1996) 'Book Review: *Notions of Nationalism*', *Nations and Nationalism*, 2(2), 338–40.

Robinson, F. (1977) 'Nation Formation: The Brass Thesis and Muslim Separatism', *Journal of Commonwealth and Comparative Politics*, 15(3), 215–30.

Robinson, F. (1979) 'Islam and Muslim Separatism', in D. Taylor and M. Yapp (eds), *Political Identity in South Asia*, London: Curzon Press, 78–107.

Rutherford, J. (1990) 'The Third Space: Interview with Homi Bhabha', in J. Rutherford (ed.), *Identity: Community, Culture and Difference*, London: Lawrence & Wishart, 207–21.

Safran, W. (1995) 'Nations, Ethnic Groups, States and Politics', *Nationalism and Ethnic Politics*, 1(1), 1–10.

Said, E. (1978) *Orientalism*, London: Routledge.

Samuel, R. and P. Thompson (eds) (1990) *The Myths We Live by*, London: Routledge.
Schnapper, D. (1994) *La Communauté des Citoyens*, Paris: Gallimard.
Scott, G. M., Jr. (1990) 'A Resynthesis of the Primordial and Circumstantial Approaches to Ethnic Group Solidarity: Towards an Explanatory Model', *Ethnic and Racial Studies*, 13(2), 147–71.
Shils, E. (1957) 'Primordial, Personal, Sacred and Civil Ties', *British Journal of Sociology*, 8(2), 130–45.
Shotter, J. (1993) *Cultural Politics of Everyday Life: Social Constructionism, Rhetoric and Knowing of the Third Kind*, Buckingham: Open University Press.
Smith, A. D. (1973) 'Nationalism: A Trend Report and Annotated Bibliography', *Current Sociology*, 21(3), 7–180.
Smith, A. D. (1983) [1971] *Theories of Nationalism*, London: Duckworth, 2nd edn.
Smith, A. D. (1984) 'Review Article: Ethnic Persistence and National Transformation', *British Journal of Sociology*, xxxv(3), 452–61.
Smith, A. D. (1986) *The Ethnic Origins of Nations*, Oxford: Blackwell.
Smith, A. D. (1991a) *National Identity*, London. Penguin.
Smith, A. D. (1991b) 'The Nation: Invented, Imagined, Reconstructed?', *Millennium: Journal of International Studies*, 20(3), 353–68.
Smith, A. D. (1992) 'Chosen Peoples: Why Ethnic Groups Survive?', *Ethnic and Racial Studies*, 15(3), 436–56.
Smith, A. D. (1993) 'The Ethnic Sources of Nationalism', in M. E. Brown (ed.), *Ethnic Conflict and International Security*, Princeton: Princeton University Press, 27–42.
Smith, A. D. (1994) 'The Problem of National Identity: Ancient, Medieval and Modern?', *Ethnic and Racial Studies*, 17(3), 375–99.
Smith, A. D. (1995) *Nations and Nationalism in a Global Era*, Cambridge: Polity Press.
Smith, A. D. (1996a) [1992] 'Nationalism and the Historians', in G. Balakrishnan (ed.), *Mapping the Nation*, London: Verso, 175–97.
Smith, A. D. (1996b) 'Memory and Modernity: Reflections on Ernest Gellner's Theory of Nationalism', *Nations and Nationalism*, 2(3), 371–88.
Smith, A. D. (1996c) 'Opening Statement: Nations and their Pasts', *Nations and Nationalism*, 2(3), 358–65.
Smith, A. D. (1996d) 'History and Modernity: Reflections on the Theory of Nationalism', in J. A. Hall and I. Jarvie (eds), *The Social Philosophy of Ernest Gellner*, Atlanta and Amsterdam: Rodopi, 129–46.
Smith, A. D. (1998) *Nationalism and Modernism*, London: Routledge.
Snyder, L. (1954) *The Meaning of Nationalism*, New Brunswick: Rutgers University Press.
Snyder, L. (1968) *The New Nationalism*, Ithaca, New York: Cornell University Press.
Snyder, T. (1997) 'Kazimierz Kelles-Krauz (1872–1905): A Pioneering Scholar of Modern Nationalism', *Nations and Nationalism*, 3(2), 231–50.

Sofos, S. A. (1996) 'Culture, Politics and Identity in Former Yugoslavia', in B. Jenkins and S. A. Sofos (eds), *Nation and Identity in Contemporary Europe*, London: Routledge, 251–82.

Somers, M. (1992) 'Narrativity, Narrative Identity, and Social Action: Rethinking English Working-Class Formation', *Social Science History*, 16(4), 591–630.

Stalin, J. (1994) [1973] 'The Nation', in J. Hutchinson and A. D. Smith (eds), *Nationalism*, Oxford: Oxford University Press, 18–21.

Stargardt, N. (1995) 'Origins of the Constructivist Theory of the Nation', in S. Periwal (ed.), *Notions of Nationalism*, Budapest: Central European University Press, 83–105.

Stern, P. C. (1995) 'Why do People Sacrifice for Their Nations?', in J. L. Comaroff and P. C. Stern (eds), *Perspectives on Nationalism and War*, Amsterdam: Gordon & Breach, 99–121.

Sugar, P. F. (1969) 'External and Domestic Roots of Eastern European Nationalism', in P. F. Sugar and I. J. Lederer (eds), *Nationalism in Eastern Europe*, Seattle: University of Washington Press.

Symmons-Symonolewicz, K. (1981) 'National Consciousness in Medieval Europe: Some Theoretical Problems', *Canadian Review of Studies in Nationalism*, VIII(1), 151–65.

Symmons-Symonolewicz, K. (1985a) 'The Concept of Nationhood: Toward a Theoretical Clarification', *Canadian Review of Studies in Nationalism*, XII(2), 215–22.

Symmons-Symonolewicz, K. (1985b) 'Book Review: *Nationalism and the State*', *Canadian Review of Studies in Nationalism*, XII(2), 359–60.

Tilley, V. (1997) 'The Terms of the Debate: Untangling Language about Ethnicity and Ethnic Movements', *Ethnic and Racial Studies*, 20(3), 497–522.

Tilly, C. (ed.) (1975) *The Formation of National States in Western Europe*, Princeton: Princeton University Press.

Tilly, C. (1990) *Coercion, Capital and European States, AD 990–1990*, Cambridge, Mass.: Oxford: Blackwell.

Tilly, C. (1993) 'National Self-Determination as a Problem for All of Us', *Daedalus*, 122(3), 29–36.

Tilly, C. (1994) 'A Bridge Halfway: Responding to Brubaker', *Contention*, 4(1), 15–19.

Tilly, C. (1995) 'States and Nationalism in Europe 1492–1992', in J. L. Comaroff and P. C. Stern (eds), *Perspectives on Nationalism and War*, Amsterdam: Gordon & Breach, 187–204.

Tiryakian, E. A. (1985) 'Introduction', in E. A. Tiryakian and R. Rogowski (eds), *New Nationalisms of the Developed West*, Boston: Allen & Unwin, 1–13.

Tiryakian, E. A. (1995) 'Nationalism and Modernity', in J. L. Comaroff and P. C. Stern (eds), *Perspectives on Nationalism and War*, Amsterdam: Gordon & Breach, 205–35.

van den Berghe, P. (1978) 'Race and Ethnicity: A Sociobiological Perspective', *Ethnic and Racial Studies*, 1(4), 401–11.

van den Berghe, P. (1979) *The Ethnic Phenomenon*, New York: Elsevier.

van Dijk, T. A. (1993) *Elite Discourse and Racism*, Newbury Park and London: Sage.
van Dijk, T. A. (1998) *Ideology*, London: Sage.
Verdery, K. (1993) 'Whither "Nation" and "Nationalism"?', *Daedalus*, 122(3), 37–46.
Walby, S. (1994) 'Is Citizenship Gendered?', *Sociology*, 28(2), 379–95.
Walby, S. (1996) [1992] 'Woman and Nation', in G. Balakrishnan (ed.), *Mapping the Nation*, London: Verso, 235–54.
West, L. A. (ed.) (1997) *Feminist Nationalism*, New York and London: Routledge.
Woolf, S. (ed.), *Nationalism in Europe, 1815 to the Present: A Reader*, London: Routledge
Yumul, A. and U. Özkırımlı (1997) 'Milliyetçiliğin Farkedilmeyen Yüzü' [The Hidden Face of Nationalism], *Varlık*, 1076, 6–11.
Yun, M. S. (1990) 'Ethnonationalism, Ethnic Nationalism, and Mini-Nationalism: A Comparison of Connor, Smith and Snyder', *Ethnic and Racial Studies*, 13(4), 527–41.
Yuval-Davis, N. (1989) 'National Reproduction and "the Demographic Race" in Israel', in N. Yuval-Davis and F. Anthias (eds), *Woman–Nation–State*, London: Macmillan, 92–108.
Yuval-Davis, N. (1997) *Gender and Nation*, London: Sage.
Yuval-Davis, N. and F. Anthias (1989) *Woman–Nation–State*, London: Macmillan.
Žižek, S. (1990) 'Eastern Europe's Republics of Gilead', *New Left Review*, 183, 50–63.
Zubaida, S. (1978) 'Theories of Nationalism', in G. Littlejohn, B. Smart, J. Wakefield and N. Yuval-Davis (eds), *Power and the State*, London: Croom Helm, 52–71.
Zubaida, S. (1989) 'Nations: Old and New. Comments on Anthony D. Smith's "The Myth of the Modern Nation and the Myths of Nations"', *Ethnic and Racial Studies*, 12(3), 329–39.

Index